AF147729

The English Utilitarians
Vol. 2

by

Leslie Stephen

The English Utilitarians
Vol. 2
by Leslie Stephen

Copyright © 2023

All Rights reserved.

No part of this publication may be reproduced,
stored in a retrieval system, or transmitted in any
form or by any means, electronic, mechanical,
photocopying or Otherwise, without the written
permission of the publisher.
The author/editor asserts the moral right to
be identified as the author/editor of this work.

ISBN: 978-93-59324-54-8

Published by

DOUBLE 9 BOOKS

2/13-B, Ansari Road
Daryaganj, New Delhi – 110002
info@double9books.com
www.double9books.com
Tel. 011-40042856

This book is under public domain

ABOUT THE AUTHOR

Sir Leslie Stephen KCB FBA (November 28, 1832 – February 22, 1904) was an English novelist, critic, historian, biographer, climber, and early humanist campaigner. He was also Virginia Woolf's and Vanessa Bell's father. Sir Leslie Stephen was the son of Sir James Stephen and (Lady) Jane Catherine (née Venn) Stephen, and was born at 14 (later renumbered 42) Hyde Park Gate, Kensington in London. His father was a prominent abolitionist and Colonial Undersecretary of State. His siblings included James Fitzjames Stephen (1829-1894) and Caroline Emelia Stephen (1834-1909), the fourth of five children. His ancestors belonged to the Clapham Sect, an early-nineteenth-century group of primarily evangelical Christian social reformers. He saw a lot of the Macaulays, James Spedding, Sir Henry Taylor, and Nassau Senior at his father's residence. Leslie Stephen attended Eton College, King's College London, and Trinity Hall, Cambridge, where he earned his B.A. (20th wrangler) in 1854 and his M.A. in 1857. In 1854, he was elected a fellow of Trinity Hall, and in 1856, he was appointed a junior tutor. He was ordained in 1859, but his study of philosophy, along with the religious disputes surrounding Charles Darwin's publication of On the Origin of Species (1859), caused him to lose his faith in 1862, and he resigned from his positions at Cambridge and relocated to London in 1864.

CONTENTS

CHAPTER I
JAMES MILL

I. EARLY LIFE

Bentham's mantle fell upon James Mill. [1] Mill expounded in the tersest form the doctrines which in Bentham's hands spread into endless ramifications and lost themselves in minute details. Mill became the leader of Bentham's bodyguard; or, rather, the mediator between the prophet in his 'hermitage' and the missionaries who were actively engaged on the hustings and in committee-rooms. The special characteristics of English Utilitarianism in the period of its greatest activity were thus more affected by Mill than by any other leader of opinion.

James Mill was one of the countless Scots who, having been trained at home in strict frugality and stern Puritanic principles, have fought their way to success in England. He was born 6th April 1773 in the parish of Logie Pert, Forfarshire. His father, also named James Mill, was a village shoemaker, employing two or three journeymen when at the height of his prosperity. His mother, Isabel Fenton, daughter of a farmer, had been a servant in Edinburgh. Her family had some claims to superior gentility; she was fastidious, delicate in frame, and accused of pride by her neighbours. She resolved to bring up James, her eldest son, to be a gentleman, which practically meant to be a minister. He probably showed early promise of intellectual superiority. He received the usual training at the parish school, and was then sent to the Montrose Academy, where he was the school-fellow and friend of a younger lad, Joseph Hume (1777-1855), afterwards his political ally. He boarded with a Montrose shopkeeper for 2s. 6d. a week, and remained at the Academy till he was seventeen. He was never put to work in his father's shop, and devoted himself entirely to study. The usual age for beginning to attend a Scottish university was thirteen or fourteen; and it would have been the normal course for a lad in Mill's position to be sent at that age to Aberdeen. Mill's education was prolonged by a connection which was of great service to him. Sir John Stuart (previously Belches), of Fettercairn House, in Mill's neighbourhood, had married Lady Jane Leslie, and was by her father of an only child, Wilhelmina. Lady Jane was given to charity, and had set up a fund to educate promising lads for the ministry. Mill was probably recommended to her by the parish minister, as likely to do credit to her patronage. He also acted as tutor to Wilhelmina, who afterwards became the object of Scott's early passion. Mill spent much time at Fettercairn House, and appears to have won the warm regards both of the Stuarts and of their daughter, who spoke of him affectionately 'with almost her last breath.' [2] The Stuarts passed their winters at Edinburgh, whither Mill accompanied them. He entered the university in 1790, and seems to have applied himself chiefly to Greek and to philosophy. He became so good a Greek scholar that long afterwards (1818) he had some thoughts of standing for the Greek chair at Glasgow. [3] He was always a keen student of Plato. He read the ordinary Scottish authorities, and attended the lectures of Dugald Stewart. Besides reading Rousseau, he studied Massillon, probably with a view to his future performances in the pulpit. Massillon might be suggested to him by quotations in Adam Smith's *Moral Sentiments*. There are few records of acquaintanceship with any of his distinguished contemporaries, except the chemist Thomas Thomson, who became a lifelong friend. He probably made acquaintance with Brougham, and may have known Jeffrey; but he was not a member of the Speculative Society, joined by most young men of promise.

In 1794 he began his course of divinity, and on 4th October 1798 was licensed to preach. He lived in his father's house, where part of the family room was screened off to form a study for him. He delivered some sermons, apparently with little success. He failed to obtain a call from any parish; and there are vague reports of his acting as tutor in some families, and of a rebuff received at the table of the marquis of Tweeddale, father of one of his pupils, which made him resolve to seek for independence by a different career.

In 1802 Mill went to London in company with Sir John Stuart, who was about to take his seat in parliament. Stuart procured admission for him to the gallery of the House of Commons, where he attended many debates, and acquired an interest in politics. His ambition, however, depended upon his pen; and at first, it would seem, he was not more particular than other journalists as to the politics of the papers to which he contributed. He had obtained a testimonial from Thomson, on the strength of which he introduced himself to John Gifford, editor of the *Anti-Jacobin Review*.[4] This was a monthly magazine, which had adopted the name and politics of the deceased *Anti-Jacobin*, edited by William Gifford. Mill obtained employment, and wrote articles implying an interest in the philosophy, and especially in the political economy, of the time. It is noteworthy, considering his later principles, that he should at this time have taken part in a strong

Tory organ. He wrote a pamphlet in 1804 (the first publication under his name) to prove the impolicy of a bounty upon the exportation of grain; and in 1807 replied in *Commerce Defended* to William Spence's *Britain independent of Commerce*. Meanwhile he had found employment of a more regular kind. He had formed a connection with a bookseller named Baldwin, for whom he undertook to help in rewriting a book called *Nature Delineated*. This scheme was changed for a periodical called the *Literary Journal*, which started at the beginning of 1803, and lived through four years with Mill as editor. At the same time apparently he edited the *St. James's Chronicle*, also belonging to Baldwin, which had no very definite political colour. The *Journal* professed to give a systematic survey of literary, scientific, and philosophical publications. For the scientific part Mill was helped by Thomson. His own contributions show that, although clearly a rationalist, he was still opposed to open infidelity. A translation of Villers' *History of the Reformation* implies similar tendencies. Other literary hack-work during this and the next few years is vaguely indicated. Mill was making about £500 a year or something more during his editorships, and thought himself justified in marrying. On 5th June 1805 he became the husband of Harriett Burrow, daughter of a widow who kept a private lunatic asylum originally started by her husband. The Mills settled in a house in Pentonville belonging to Mrs. Burrow, for which they paid £50 a year.

The money question soon became pressing. The editorships vanished, and to make an income by periodical writing was no easy task. His son observes that nothing could be more opposed to his father's later principles than marrying and producing a large family under these circumstances. Nine children were ultimately born, all of whom survived their father. The family in his old home were an additional burthen. His mother died before his departure from Scotland. His father was paralysed, and having incautiously given security for a friend, became bankrupt. His only brother, William, died soon afterwards, and his only sister, Mary, married one of her father's journeymen named Greig, and tried to carry on the business. The father died about 1808, and the Greigs had a hard struggle, though two of the sons ultimately set up a business in Montrose. James Mill appears to have helped to support his father, whose debts he undertook to pay, and to have afterwards helped the Greigs. They thought, it seems, that he ought to have done more, but were not unlikely to exaggerate the resources of a man who was making his way in England. Mill was resolute in doing his duty, but hardly likely to do it graciously. At any rate, in the early years, it must have been a severe strain to do anything.

In spite of all difficulties Mill, by strict frugality and unremitting energy, managed to keep out of debt. In the end of 1806 he undertook the history of British India. This was to be the great work which should give him a name, and enable him to rise above the herd of contemporary journalists. He calculated the time necessary for its completion at three years, but the years were to be more than trebled before the book was actually finished. At that period there were fewer facilities than there could now be for making the necessary researches: and we do not know what were the reasons which prompted the selection of a subject of which he could have no first-hand knowledge. The book necessarily impeded other labours; and to the toil of writing Mill added the toil of superintending the education of his children. His struggle for some years was such as to require an extraordinary strain upon all his faculties. Mill, however, possessed great physical and mental vigour. He was muscular, well-made, and handsome; he had marked powers of conversation, and made a strong impression upon all with whom he came in contact. He gradually formed connections which effectually determined his future career.

II. BENTHAM'S LIEUTENANT

The most important influence in Mill's life was the friendship with Bentham. This appears to have begun in 1808. Mill speedily became a valued disciple. He used to walk from Pentonville to dine with Bentham in Queen's Square Place. Soon the elder man desired to have his new friend nearer at hand. In 1810 Mill moved to the house in Bentham's garden, which had once belonged to Milton; when this proved unsuitable, he was obliged to move to a more distant abode at Stoke Newington; but finally, in 1814, he settled in another house belonging to Bentham, 1 Queen's Square, close under the old gentleman's wing. Here for some years they lived in the closest intimacy. The Mills also stayed with Bentham in his country-houses at Barrow Green, and afterwards at Ford Abbey. The association was not without its troubles. Bentham was fanciful, and Mill stern and rigid. No one, however, could be a more devoted disciple. The most curious illustration of their relations is a letter written to Bentham by Mill, 19th September 1814, while they were both at Ford Abbey. Mill in this declares himself to be a 'most faithful and fervent disciple' of the truths which Bentham had the 'immortal honour' of propounding. He had fancied himself to be his master's favourite disciple. No one is so completely of Bentham's way of thinking, or so qualified by position for carrying on the propaganda. Now, however, Bentham showed that he had taken umbrage at some part of Mill's behaviour. An open quarrel would bring discredit upon both sides, and upon their common beliefs. The great dangers to friendship are pecuniary obligation and too close intimacy. Mill has made it a great purpose of his life to avoid pecuniary obligation, though he took pride in receiving obligations from Bentham.

He has confined himself to accepting Bentham's house at a low rent, and allowing his family to live for part of the year at Bentham's expense. He now proposes so to arrange his future life that they shall avoid an excessively close intimacy, from which, he thinks, had arisen the 'umbrage.' The letter, which is manly and straightforward, led to a reconciliation, and for some years the intercourse was as close as ever.[5]

Mill's unreserved adoption of Bentham's principles, and his resolution to devote his life to their propagation, implies a development of opinion. He had entirely dropped his theology. In the early years of his London life, Mill had been only a rationalist. He had by this time become what would now be called an agnostic. He thought 'dogmatic atheism' absurd, says J. S. Mill;[6] 'but he held that we can know nothing whatever as to the origin of the world.' The occasion of the change, according to his family, was his intercourse with General Miranda, who was sitting at Bentham's feet about this time. J. S. Mill states that the turning-point in his father's mind was the study of Butler's *Analogy*. That book, he thought, as others have thought, was conclusive against the optimistic deism which it assails; but he thought also that the argument really destroyed Butler's own standing-ground. The evils of the world are incompatible with the theory of Almighty benevolence. The purely logical objection was combined with an intense moral sentiment. Theological doctrines, he thought, were not only false, but brutal. His son had heard him say 'a hundred times' that men have attributed to their gods every trait of wickedness till the conception culminated in the Christian doctrine of hell. Mill still attended church services for some time after his marriage, and the children were christened. But the eldest son did not remember the period of even partial conformity, and considered himself to have been brought up from the first without any religious belief. James Mill had already taken up the uncompromising position congenial to his character, although the reticence which the whole party observed prevented any open expression of his sentiments.

Mill's propaganda of Benthamism was for some time obscure. He helped to put together some of Bentham's writings, especially the book upon evidence. He was consulted in regard to all proposed publications, such as the pamphlet upon jury-packing, which Mill desired to publish in spite of Romilly's warning. Mill endeavoured also to disseminate the true faith through various periodicals. He obtained admission to the *Edinburgh Review*, probably through its chief contributor, Brougham. Neither Brougham nor Jeffrey was likely to commit the great Whig review to the support of a creed still militant and regarded with distrust by the respectable. Mill contributed various articles from 1808 to 1813, but chiefly upon topics outside of the political sphere. The *Edinburgh Review*, as I have said, had taken a condescending notice of Bentham in 1804. Mill tried to introduce a better tone into an article upon Bexon's *Code de la Législation pénale*, which he was permitted to publish in the number for October 1809. Knowing Jeffrey's 'dislike of praise,' he tried to be on his guard, and to insinuate his master's doctrine without openly expressing his enthusiasm. Jeffrey, however, sadly mangled the review, struck out every mention but one of Bentham, and there substituted words of his own for Mill's. Even as it was, Brougham pronounced the praise of Bentham to be excessive. [7] Mill continued to write for a time, partly, no doubt, with a view to Jeffrey's cheques. Almost his last article (in January 1813) was devoted to the Lancasterian controversy, in which Mill, as we shall directly see, was in alliance with the Whigs. But the Edinburgh Reviewers were too distinctly of the Whig persuasion to be congenial company for a determined Radical. They would give him no more than a secondary position, and would then take good care to avoid the insertion of any suspicious doctrine. Mill wrote no more after the summer of 1813.

Meanwhile he was finding more sympathetic allies. First among them was William Allen (1770-1843), chemist, of Plough Court. Allen was a Quaker; a man of considerable scientific tastes; successful in business, and ardently devoted throughout his life to many philanthropic schemes. He took, in particular, an active part in the agitation against slavery. He was, as we have seen, one of the partners who bought Owen's establishment at New Lanark; and his religious scruples were afterwards the cause of Owen's retirement. These, however, were only a part of his multifarious schemes. He was perhaps something of a busybody; his head may have been a little turned by the attentions which he received on all hands; he managed the affairs of the duke of Kent; was visited by the Emperor Alexander in 1814; and interviewed royal personages on the Continent, in order to obtain their support in attacking the slave-trade, and introducing good schools and prisons. But, though he may have shared some of the weaknesses of popular philanthropists, he is mentioned with respect even by observers such as Owen and Place, who had many prejudices against his principles. He undoubtedly deserves a place among the active and useful social reformers of his time.

I have already noticed the importance of the Quaker share in the various philanthropic movements of the time. The Quaker shared many of the views upon practical questions which were favoured by the freethinker. Both were hostile to slavery, in favour of spreading education, opposed to all religious tests and restrictions, and advocates of reform in prisons, and in the harsh criminal law. The fundamental differences of theological belief were not so productive of discord in dealing with the Quakers as with other sects; for it was the very essence of the old Quaker spirit to look rather to the spirit than to the letter. Allen, therefore, was only acting in the spirit of his society when he could be on equally good terms with the Emperor Alexander or the duke of Kent, and, on the other hand, with James Mill, the denouncer of kings and autocrats. He could join hands with Mill in assailing slavery, insisting upon prison reform, preaching toleration and advancing civilisation, although he heartily disapproved of the doctrines with which Mill's practical principles were associated. Mill, too, practised—even to a questionable degree—the method of reticence, and took good care not to offend his coadjutor.

Their co-operation was manifested in a quarterly journal called the *Philanthropist*, which appeared during the seven years, 1811-1817, and was published at Allen's expense. Mill found in it the opportunity of advocating many of his cherished opinions. He defended toleration in the name of Penn, whose life had been published by Clarkson. He attacked the slave-owners, and so came into alliance with Wilberforce, Zachary Macaulay, and others of the evangelical persuasion. He found, at the same time, opportunities for propagating the creed of Bentham in connection with questions of prison reform and the penal code. His most important article, published in 1812, was another contribution to the Lancasterian controversy. In this Mill had allies of a very different school; and his activity brings him into close connection with one of the most remarkable men of the time.[8]

This was Francis Place, the famous Radical tailor. Place, born 3rd November 1771, had raised himself from the position of a working-man to be occupant of a shop at Charing Cross, which became the centre of important political movements. Between Place and Mill there was much affinity of character. Place, like Mill, was a man of rigid and vigorous intellect. Dogmatic, self-confident, and decidedly censorious, not attractive by any sweetness or grace of character, but thoroughly sincere and independent, he extorts rather than commands our respect by his hearty devotion to what he at least believed to be the cause of truth and progress. Place was what is now called a thorough 'individualist.' He believed in self-reliance and energy, and held that the class to which he belonged was to be raised, as he had raised himself, by the exercise of those qualities, not by invoking the direct interference of the central power, which, indeed, as he knew it, was only likely to interfere on the wrong side. He had the misfortune to be born in London instead of Scotland, and had therefore not Mill's educational advantages. He tried energetically, and not unsuccessfully, to improve his mind, but he never quite surmounted the weakness of the self-educated man, and had no special literary talent. His writing, in fact, is dull and long-winded, though he has the merit of judging for himself, and of saying what he thinks.

Place had been a member of the Corresponding Society, and was at one time chairman of the weekly committee. He had, however, disapproved of their proceedings, and retired in time to escape the imprisonment which finally crushed the committee. He was now occupied in building up his own fortunes at Charing Cross. When, during the second war, the native English Radicalism began again to raise its head, Place took a highly important share in the political agitation. Westminster, the constituency in which he had a vote, had long been one of the most important boroughs. It was one of the few large popular constituencies, and was affected by the influences naturally strongest in the metropolis. After being long under the influence of the court and the dean and chapter, it had been carried by Fox during the discontents of 1780, when the reform movement took a start and the county associations were symptoms of a growing agitation. The great Whig leader, though not sound upon the question of reform, represented the constituency till his death, and reform dropped out of notice for the time. Upon Fox's death (13th September 1806) Lord Percy was elected without opposition as his successor by an arrangement among the ruling families. Place was disgusted at the distribution of 'bread and cheese and beer,' and resolved to find a truly popular candidate. In the general election which soon followed at the end of 1806 he supported Paull, an impecunious adventurer, who made a good fight, but was beaten by Sir J. Hood and Sheridan. Place now proposed a more thorough organisation of the constituency, and formed a committee intended to carry an independent candidate. Sir Francis Burdett, a typical country gentleman of no great brains and of much aristocratic pride, but a man of honour, and of as much liberal feeling as was compatible with wealth and station, had sat at the feet of the old Radical, Home Tooke. He had sympathised with the French revolution; but was mainly, like his mentor, Tooke, a reformer of the English type, and a believer in Magna Charta and the Bill of Rights. He had sat in parliament, and in 1802 had been elected for Middlesex. After a prolonged litigation, costing enormous sums, the election had been finally annulled in 1806. He had subscribed £1000 towards Paull's expenses; but was so disgusted with his own election experiences that he refused to come forward as a candidate. Place's committee resolved therefore to elect him and Paull free of expense. Disputes between Paull and Burdett led to a duel, in which both were wounded. The committee threw over Paull, and at the election on the dissolution of parliament in the spring of 1807, Burdett and Cochrane—afterwards Lord Dundonald—were triumphantly elected, defeating the Whig candidates, Sheridan and Elliot. The election was the first triumph of the reformers, and was due to Place more than any one. Burdett retained his seat for Westminster until 1837, and, in spite of many quarrels with his party, was a leading representative of the movement, which henceforward slowly gathered strength. Place, indeed, had apparently but scanty respect for the candidate whose success he had secured. Burdett and his like aimed at popularity, while he was content to be ignored so long as he could by any means carry the measures which he approved. Place, therefore, acted as a most efficient wire-puller, but had no ambition to leave his shop to make speeches on the hustings.

The scandals about the duke of York and the Walcheren expedition gave a chance to the Radicals and to their leader in the House of Commons. Events in 1810 led to a popular explosion, of which Burdett was the hero. John Gale Jones, an old member of the Corresponding Societies, had put out a placard denouncing the House of Commons for closing its doors during a debate upon the Walcheren expedition. The House proceeded against Jones, who was more or less advised by Place in his proceedings. Burdett took the part of Jones, by a paper published in Cobbett's *Register*, and was ultimately committed to the Tower in consequence. The whole of London was for a time in a state of excitement, and upon the verge of an outbreak. Burdett refused to submit to the arrest. Mobs collected; soldiers filled the streets and were pelted. Burdett, when at last he was forced to admit the officers, appeared in his drawing-room in the act of expounding Magna Charta to his son. That, it was to be supposed, was his usual occupation of an afternoon. Meetings were held, and resolutions passed, in support of the martyr to liberty; and when his imprisonment terminated on the prorogation of parliament, vast crowds collected, and a procession was arranged to convoy him to his home. Place had been active in arranging all the details of what was to be a great popular manifestation. To his infinite disgust, Burdett shrank from the performance, and went home by water. The crowd was left to expend its remaining enthusiasm upon the hackney carriage which contained his fellow-sufferer Jones. Jones, in the following December, was sentenced to twelve months' imprisonment for a libel. Cobbett, Burdett's special supporter at this time, was also imprisoned in June 1810. For a time the popular agitation collapsed. Place seems to have thought that the failure was due to Burdett's want of courage, and dropped all communication with him till a later contest at Westminster.

Place was thus at the centre of the political agitation which, for the time, represented the most energetic reforming movement. It was in 1811 or 1812 that he became acquainted with Mill.[9] In Mill he recognised a congenial spirit, and a man able to defend and develop principles. He perhaps, as Professor Bain thinks, made advances to Mill upon the strength of the history of India; and in 1814 he was certainly endeavouring to raise money to put Mill above the need of precarious hack-work.[10] The anticipated difficulty of persuading Mill so far to sacrifice his independence was apparently fatal to the scheme. Place was in occasional communication with Bentham, and visited him at Ford Abbey in 1817. He became intimate with the great man; helped him in business affairs; and was one of the disciples employed to prepare his books for publication.[11] Bentham was the source of philosophy, and Mill only his prophet. But Mill, who was capable of activity in practical affairs, was more useful to a man of the world. The first business which brought them into close connection was the Lancasterian controversy. The strong interest roused by this agitation was significant of many difficulties to come. The average mind had been gradually coming to the conclusion that the poor should be taught to read and write. Sunday schools and Hannah More's schools in Somersetshire had drawn the attention of the religious world to the subject. During the early years of the century the education question had steadily become more prominent, and the growing interest was shown by a singularly bitter and complicated controversy. The opposite parties fought under the banners of Bell and Lancaster. Andrew Bell, born at St. Andrews, 27th March 1753, was both a canny Scot and an Anglican clergyman. He combined philanthropy with business faculties. He sailed to India in 1787 with £128, 10s. in his pocket to be an army chaplain; he returned in 1796 with £25,000 and a new system of education which he had devised as superintendent of an orphan asylum. He settled in England, published an account of his plan, and did something to bring it into operation. Meanwhile Joseph Lancaster (1770-1838), a young Quaker, had set up a school in London; he devised a plan similar to that of Bell, and in 1803 published an account of his improvements in education with acknowledgments to Bell. For a time the two were on friendly terms. Lancaster set about propagating his new system with more enthusiasm than discretion. His fame rapidly spread till it reached the throne. In 1805 George iii. sent for him; the royal family subscribed to his schools; and the king declared his wish that every child in his dominions should be taught to read the Bible. The king's gracious wish unconsciously indicated a difficulty. Was it safe to teach the Bible without the safeguard of authorised interpretation? Orthodox opponents feared the alliance with a man whose first principle was toleration, and first among them was the excellent Mrs. Trimmer, who had been already engaged in the Sunday-school movement. She pointed out in a pamphlet that the schismatic Lancaster was weakening the Established Church. The *Edinburgh Review* came to his support in 1806 and 1807; for the Whig, especially if he was also a Scot, was prejudiced against the Church of England. Lancaster went on his way, but soon got into difficulties, for he was impetuous, careless of money, and autocratic. William Allen, with another

Quaker, came to his support in 1808, and founded the Royal Lancasterian Society to maintain his school in the Borough Road, and propagate its like elsewhere. Lancaster travelled through the country, and the agitation prospered, and spread even to America. The church, however, was now fairly aroused. Bishop Marsh preached a sermon in St. Paul's, and followed it up by pamphlets; the cause was taken up by the *Quarterly Review* in 1811, and in the same year the National Society was founded to 'educate the poor in the principles of the Established Church.' Bell had suggested a national system, but the times were not ripe. Meanwhile the controversy became furious. The *Edinburgh* and the *Quarterly* thundered on opposite sides. Immense importance was attached by both parties to the scheme devised by Bell, and partly adopted by Lancaster. The war involved a personal element and the charges of plagiarism which give spice to a popular controversy. All parties, and certainly the Utilitarians, strangely exaggerated the value of the new method. They regarded the proposal that children should be partly taught by other children instead of being wholly taught by adults as a kind of scientific discovery which would enormously simplify and cheapen education. Believers in the 'Panopticon' saw in it another patent method of raising the general level of intelligence. But the real question was between church and dissent. Was the church catechism to be imposed or not? This, as we have seen, was the occasion of Bentham's assault upon church and catechism. On the other side, Bell's claims were supported with enthusiasm by all the Tories, and by such men as Southey and Coleridge. Southey, who had defended Bell in the *Quarterly*,[12] undertook to be Bell's biographer[13] and literary executor. Coleridge was so vehement in the cause that when lecturing upon 'Romeo and Juliet' in 1811, he plunged by way of exordium into an assault upon Lancaster's modes of punishment.[14] De Quincey testifies that he became a positive bore upon Bell's virtues. In 1812 Lancaster had got deeply into debt to the trustees of the Society, who included besides Allen, Joseph Fox—a 'shallow, gloomy bigot' according to Place—and some other Quakers. Lancaster resented their control, and in 1812 made over his Borough Road school to them, and set up one of his own at Tooting. They continued, however, to employ him, and in 1813 formed themselves into the 'British and Foreign' School Society. Place had known Lancaster from 1804, and Mill had supported him in the press. They both became members of the committee, though Place took the most active part. He makes many grave charges against Lancaster, whom he regarded as hopelessly flighty and impracticable, if not worse. Ultimately in 1814 Lancaster resigned his position, and naturally retorted that Place was an infidel. Place, meanwhile, was ill at ease with the 'gloomy bigot,' as he calls Fox. After many quarrels, Fox succeeded in getting the upper hand, and Place finally withdrew from the committee in 1815.

Two other schemes arose out of this, in which Mill was specially interested, but which both proved abortive. Mill and Place resolved in 1813 to start a 'West London Lancasterian Institution,' which was to educate the whole population west of Temple Bar. They were joined by Edward Wakefield, father of the Edward Gibbon Wakefield who in later years was known as an economist, and himself author of a work of considerable reputation, *An Account of Ireland, Statistical and Political* (1812). The three joined Joseph Fox, and ultimately a meeting was held in August 1813. Sir James Mackintosh was in the chair. Mill wrote the address, and motions were proposed by his friend Joseph Hume and by William Allen. Papers were circulated, headed 'Schools for all,'[15] and the institution was launched with a sufficiency of applause. But the 'gloomy bigot' was secretary. He declared that he would rather see the institution destroyed than permit it to be used for infidel purposes. The Bible was, of course, to be read in the schools, but Fox wished that the Bible alone should be read. As the committee, according to Place, included four infidels, three Unitarians, six Methodists, two Baptists, two Roman Catholics, and several members of the Established Church, it was hardly a happy family. To add to the confusion, Sir Francis Burdett, who had contributed a thousand pounds, had taken it into his head that Place was a government spy.[16] The Association, as is hardly surprising, ceased to exist in 1816, after keeping up a school of less than three hundred children, and ended in hopeless failure. The Utilitarians had higher hopes from a scheme of their own. This was the Chrestomathic school which occasioned Bentham's writing. An association was formed in February 1814. Mackintosh, Brougham, Mill, Allen, Fox, and Wakefield were to be trustees. The school was to apply Lancasterian principles to the education of the middle classes, and Bentham was to supply them with a philosophy and with a site in his garden. There the old gentleman was to see a small version of the Panopticon building, and, for a time, he took great delight in the prospect. Gradually, however, it seems to have dawned upon him that there might be inconveniences in being overlooked by a set of even model schoolboys. There were difficulties as to funds. Ricardo offered £200 and collected subscriptions for £900, but Place thought that he might have been more liberal. About 1817 they counted upon subscriptions for £2310. Allen was treasurer, Place secretary, and the dukes of Kent and York were on the committee. Romilly was persuaded to join, and they had hopes of the £1000 given by Burdett to the West London Institution. But the thing could never be got into working order, in spite of Place's efforts and Mill's counsels; and, after painful haulings and tuggings, it finally collapsed in 1820.[17]

The efforts of the Utilitarians to effect anything directly in the way of education thus fell completely flat. One moral is sufficiently obvious. They were, after all, but a small clique, regarded with suspicion by all outsiders; and such a system as could seriously affect education could only be carried out either by government, which was thinking of very different things, or by societies already connected with the great religious bodies. The only function which could be adequately discharged by the little band of Utilitarians was to act upon public opinion; and this, no doubt, they could do to some purpose. I have gone so far into these matters in order to illustrate their position; but, as will be seen, Mill, though consulted at every stage by Place, and doing what he could to advocate the cause, was, after all, in the background. He was still wrestling with the Indian History, which was, as he hoped, to win for him an independent position. The effort was enormous. In 1814 he told Place that he was working at the History from 5 a.m. till 11 p.m. When at Ford Abbey his regular day's work began at 6 a.m. and lasted till 11 p.m., during which time three hours were given to teaching his children, and a couple of short walks supplied him with recreation. How, with all his energy, he managed to pay his way is a mystery, which his biographer is unable fully to solve.[18]

The History at last appeared in 3 vols. 4to, at the end of 1817. Dry and stern as its author, and embodying some of his political prejudices, it was at least a solid piece of work, which succeeded at once, and soon became the standard book upon the subject. Mill argues in the preface with characteristic courage that his want of personal knowledge of India was rather an advantage. It made him impartial. A later editor[19] has shown that it led to some serious misconceptions. It is characteristic of the Utilitarian attitude to assume that a sufficient knowledge of fact can always be obtained from blue-books and statistics. Some facts require imagination and sympathy to be appreciated, and there Mill was deficient. He could not give an adequate picture of Hindoo beliefs and customs, though he fully appreciated the importance of such questions. Whatever its shortcomings, the book produced a remarkable change in Mill's position. He applied for a vacant office in the India House. His friends, Joseph Hume and Ricardo, made interest for him in the city. Place co-operated energetically.[20] Canning, then president of the Board of Control, is said to have supported him; and the general impression of his ability appears to have caused his election, in spite of some Tory opposition. He became Assistant to the Examiner of India Correspondence, with a salary of £800 on 12th May 1819. On 10th April 1821 he became Second Assistant, with £1000 a year; on 9th April 1823 he was made Assistant Examiner, with £1200 a year; and on 1st December 1830 Examiner, with £1900, which on 17th February 1836 was raised to £2000. The official work came in later years to absorb the greatest part of Mill's energy, and his position excluded him from any active participation in politics, had he ever been inclined for it. Mill, however, set free from bondage, was able to exert himself very effectually with his pen; and his writings became in a great degree the text-books of his sect.

During 1818 he had again co-operated with Place in a political matter. The dissolution of parliament in 1818 produced another contest at Westminster. Place and Mill were leaders in the Radical committee, which called a public meeting, where Burdett and Kinnaird were chosen as candidates. They were opposed to Romilly, the old friend of Bentham and of Mill himself. Both Mill and Bentham regarded him as not sufficiently orthodox. Romilly, however, was throughout at the head of the poll, and the Radical committee were obliged to withdraw their second candidate, Kinnaird, in order to secure the election of Burdett against the government candidate Maxwell. Romilly soon afterwards dined at Bentham's house, and met Mill, with Dumont, Brougham, and Rush, on friendly terms. On Romilly's sad death on 2nd November following, Mill went to Worthing to offer his sympathy to the family, and declared that the 'gloom' had 'affected his health.' He took no part in the consequent election, in which Hobhouse stood unsuccessfully as the Radical candidate.

III. LEADER OF THE UTILITARIANS

Politics were beginning to enter upon a new phase. The period was marked by the 'Six Acts' and the 'Peterloo massacre.' The Radical leaders who upheld the cause in those dark days were not altogether to the taste of the Utilitarians. After Burdett, John Cartwright (1740-1824) and Henry (or 'Orator') Hunt (1773-1835), hero of the 'Peterloo massacre,' were the most conspicuous. They were supported by Cobbett, the greatest journalist of the time, and various more obscure writers. The Utilitarians held them in considerable contempt. Burdett was flashy, melodramatic, and vain; Hunt an 'unprincipled demagogue'; and Cartwright, the Nestor of reform, who had begun his labours in 1780, was, according to Place, wearisome, impracticable, and a mere nuisance in matters of business. The Utilitarians tried to use such men, but shared the Tory opinion of their value. They had some relations with other obscure writers who were martyrs to the liberty of the press. Place helped William Hone in the *Reformer's Register*, which was brought out in 1817. The famous trial in which Hone triumphed over Ellenborough occurred at the end of that year. Richard Carlile (1790-1843), who reprinted Hone's pamphlets, and in 1818 published Paine's works, was sentenced in 1819 to three years' imprisonment; and while in confinement began the *Republican*, which appeared from 1819 to 1826. Ultimately he passed nine years in jail, and showed unflinching courage in maintaining the liberty of speech. The Utilitarians, as Professor Bain believes, helped him during his imprisonments, and John Mill's first publication was a protest against his prosecution.[21] A 'republican, an atheist, and Malthusian,' he was specially hated by the respectable, and had in all these capacities claims upon the sympathy of the Utilitarians. One of Carlile's first employments was to circulate the *Black Dwarf*, edited by Thomas Jonathan Wooler from 1817 to 1824.[22] This paper represented Cartwright, but it also published Bentham's reform *Catechism*, besides direct contributions and various selections from his works.

The Utilitarians were opposed on principle to Cobbett, a reformer of a type very different from their own; and still more vitally opposed to Owen, who was beginning to develop his Socialist schemes. If they had sympathy for Radicalism of the Wooler or Carlile variety, they belonged too distinctly to the ranks of respectability, and were too deeply impressed with the necessity of reticence, to allow their sympathies to appear openly. As, on the other hand, they were too Radical in their genuine creed to be accepted by Edinburgh Reviewers and frequenters of Holland House, there was a wide gap between them and the genuine Whig. Their task therefore was to give a political theory which should be Radical in principle, and yet in such a form as should appeal to the reason of the more cultivated readers without too openly shocking their prejudices.

James Mill achieved this task by the publication of a series of articles in the Supplement to the *Encyclopædia Britannica*, which appeared from 1816 to 1823, of which I shall presently speak at length. It passed for the orthodox profession of faith among the little circle of friends who had now gathered round him. First among them was David Ricardo. He had become known to Mill in 1811. 'I,' said Bentham, 'was the spiritual father of Mill, and Mill the spiritual father of Ricardo.'[23] Mill was really the disciple of Ricardo in economics; but it was Mill who induced him to publish his chief work, and Mill's own treatise upon the subject published in 1820 is substantially an exposition of Ricardo's doctrine. Mill, too, encouraged Ricardo to take a seat in parliament in 1818, and there for the short remainder of his life, Ricardo defended the characteristic Utilitarian principles with the authority derived from his reputation as an economist.[24] The two were now especially intimate. During Mill's first years in the India House, his only recreation was an annual visit to Ricardo at Gatcombe. Meetings at Ricardo's house in London led to the foundation of the 'Political Economy Club' in 1821. Mill drafted the rules of the club, emphasising the duty of members to propagate sound economic opinions through the press. The club took root and helped to make Mill known to politicians and men of commercial influence. One of the members was Malthus, who is said, and the assertion is credible enough, to have been generally worsted by Mill in the discussions at the club. Mill was an awkward antagonist, and Malthus certainly not conspicuous for closeness of logic. The circle of Mill's friends naturally extended as his position in the India House enabled him to live more at his ease and brought him into contact with men of political position. His old school-fellow Joseph Hume had made a fortune in India, and returned to take a seat in parliament and become the persistent and tiresome advocate of many of the Utilitarian doctrines. A younger generation was growing up, enthusiastic in the cause of reform, and glad to sit at the feet of men who claimed at least to be philosophical leaders. John Black (1783-1855), another sturdy Scot, who came from Duns in Berwickshire, had, in 1817, succeeded Perry as editor of the *Morning Chronicle*. The *Chronicle* was an opposition paper, and day by day Black walked with Mill from the India House, discussing the topics of the time and discharging himself through the *Chronicle*. The *Chronicle* declined after 1821, owing to a change in the proprietorship.[25] Albany Fonblanque (1793-1872) took to journalism at an early age, succeeded Leigh Hunt as leader-writer for the *Examiner* in 1826, became another exponent of Utilitarian principles, and for some time in alliance with John Stuart Mill was among the most effective representatives of the new school in the press. John Ramsay M'Culloch (1789-1864) upheld the economic battle in the *Scotsman* at Edinburgh from 1817-1827, and edited it from 1818-1820. He afterwards devoted himself to lecturing in London, and was for many years the most ardent apostle of the 'dismal science.' He was a genial, whisky-loving Scot; the favourite object of everybody's mimicry; and was especially intimate with James Mill. Many other brilliant young men contributed their help in various ways. Henry Bickersteth (1783-1851), afterwards Lord Langdale and Master of the Rolls, had brought Bentham and Burdett into political alliance; and his rising reputation at the bar led to his being placed in 1824 upon a commission for reforming the procedure of the Court of Chancery, one of the most cherished objects of the Utilitarian creed. Besides these there were the group of young men, who were soon to be known as the 'philosophical Radicals.' John Stuart Mill, upon whom the mantle of his father was to descend, was conspicuous by his extraordinary precocity, and having been carefully educated in the orthodox faith, was employed in 1825 upon editing Bentham's great work upon evidence. George Grote (1794-1871), the future historian, had been introduced to Mill by Ricardo; and was in 1821 defending Mill's theory of government against Mackintosh, and in 1822 published the *Analysis of Revealed Religion*, founded upon Bentham's manuscripts and expressing most unequivocally the Utilitarian theory of religion. With them were associated the two Austins, John (1790-1859) who, in 1821, lived close to Bentham and Mill in Queen's Square, and who was regarded as the coming teacher of the Utilitarian system of jurisprudence; and Charles (1799-1874), who upheld the true faith among the young gentlemen at Cambridge with a vigour and ability which at least rivalled the powers of his contemporary, Macaulay. Meanwhile, Mill himself was disqualified by his office from taking any direct part in political agitations. Place continued an active connection with the various Radical committees and associations; but the younger disciples had comparatively little concern in such matters. They were more interested in discussing the applications of Utilitarianism in various directions, or, so far as they had parliamentary aspirations, were aspiring to found a separate body of 'philosophical Radicals,' which looked down upon Place and his allies from the heights of superior enlightenment.

Mill could now look forward to a successful propaganda of the creed which had passed so slowly through its period of incubation. The death of Ricardo in 1823 affected him to a degree which astonished his friends, accustomed only to his stern exterior. A plentiful crop of young proselytes, however, was arising to carry on the work; and the party now became possessed of the indispensable organ. The *Westminster Review* was launched at the beginning of 1824. Bentham provided the funds; Mill's official position prevented him from undertaking the editorship, which was accordingly given to Bentham's young disciple, Bowring, helped for a time by Henry Southern. The *Westminster* was to represent the Radicals as the two older reviews represented the Whigs and the Tories; and to show that the new party had its philosophers and its men of literary cultivation as well as its popular agitators and journalists. It therefore naturally put forth its claims by opening fire in the first numbers against the *Edinburgh* and the *Quarterly Reviews*. The assault upon the *Edinburgh Review*, of which I shall speak presently, made an impression, and, as J. S. Mill tells us, brought success to the first number of the new venture. The gauntlet was thrown down with plenty of vigour, and reformers were expected to rally round so thoroughgoing a champion. In later numbers Mill afterwards (Jan. 9, 1826) fell upon Southey's *Book of the Church*, and (April 1826) assailed church establishments in general. He defended toleration during the same year in a review of Samuel Bailey's *Formation of Opinions*, and gave a general account of his political creed in an article (October) on the 'State of the Nation.' This was his last contribution to the *Westminster*; but in 1827 he contributed to the *Parliamentary History and Review*, started by James Marshall of Leeds, an article upon recent debates on reform, which ended for a time his political writings.

The Utilitarians had no great talent for cohesion. Their very principles were indeed in favour of individual independence, and they were perhaps more ready to diverge than to tolerate divergence. The *Westminster Review* had made a good start, and drew attention to the rising 'group'—J. S. Mill declares that it never formed a 'school.'[26] From the very first the Mills distrusted Bowring and disapproved of some articles; the elder Mill failed to carry his disciples with him, partly because they were already in favour of giving votes to women; and as the *Review* soon showed itself unable to pay its way, some new arrangement became necessary. It was finally bought by Perronet Thompson, and ceased for a time to be the official organ of Benthamism.

Another undertaking occupied much of Mill's attention in the following years. The educational schemes of the Utilitarians had so far proved abortive. In 1824, however, it had occurred to the poet, Thomas Campbell, then editing the *New Monthly Magazine*, that London ought to possess a university comparable to that of Berlin, and more on a level with modern thought than the old universities of Oxford and Cambridge, which were still in the closest connection with the church. Campbell addressed a letter to Brougham, and the scheme was taken up energetically on several sides. Place[27] wrote an article, which he offered to Campbell for the *New Monthly*, who declined out of modesty to publish it in his own organ. It was then offered to Bowring for the *Westminster*, and ultimately suppressed by him, which may have been one of the causes of his differences with the Mills. Brougham took a leading part in the agitation; Joseph Hume promised to raise £100,000. George Birkbeck, founder of the Mechanics' Institution, and Zachary Macaulay, who saw in it a place of education for dissenting ministers, joined the movement, and among the most active members of the new body were James Mill and Grote. A council was formed at the end of 1825, and after various difficulties a sum of £160,000 was raised, and the university started in Gower Street in 1828. Among the first body of professors were John Austin and M'Culloch, both of them sound Utilitarians. The old difficulty, however, made itself felt. In order to secure the unsectarian character of the university, religious teaching was omitted. The college was accused of infidelity. King's College was started in opposition; and violent antipathies were aroused. A special controversy raged within the council itself. Two philosophical chairs were to be founded; and philosophy cannot be kept clear of religion. After long discussions, one chair was filled by the appointment of the Reverend John Hoppus, an independent minister. Grote, declaring that no man, pledged by his position to the support of any tenets, should be appointed, resigned his place on the council.[28] The university in 1836 became a college combined with its rival King's College under the newly formed examining body called the University of London. It has, I suppose, been of service to education, and may be regarded as the one practical achievement of the Utilitarians in that direction, so far as its foundation was due to them. It must, however, be admitted that the actual body still falls very far short of the ideal present to the minds of its founders.

From 1822 James Mill spent his vacations at Dorking, and afterwards at Mickleham. He had devoted them to a task which was necessary to fill a gap in the Utilitarian scheme. Hitherto the school had assumed, rather than attempted to establish, a philosophical basis of its teaching. Bentham's fragmentary writings about the Chrestomathic school supplied all that could by courtesy be called a philosophy. Mill, however, had been from the first interested in philosophical questions. His reading was not wide; he knew something of the doctrines taught by Stewart and Stewart's successor, Brown. He had been especially impressed by Hobbes, to some degree by Locke and Hume, but above all by Hartley. He knew something, too, of Condillac and the French Ideologists. Of recent German speculation he was probably quite ignorant. I find indeed that Place had called his attention to the account of Kant, published by Wirgman in the *Encyclopædia Londinensis* 1817. Mill about the same time tells Place that he has begun to read *The Critic of Pure Reason*. 'I see clearly enough,' he says, 'what poor Kant would be about, but it would require some time to give an account of him.' He wishes (December 6, 1817) that he had time to write a book which would 'make the human mind as plain as the road from Charing Cross to St. Paul's.'[29] This was apparently the task to which he applied himself in his vacations. The *Analysis* appeared in 1829, and, whatever its defects of incompleteness and one-sidedness from a philosophical point of view, shows in the highest degree Mill's powers of close, vigorous statement; and lays down with singular clearness the psychological doctrine, which from his point of view supplied the fundamental theorems of knowledge in general. It does not appear, however, to have made an impression proportionate to the intellectual power displayed, and had to wait a long time before reaching the second edition due to the filial zeal of J. S. Mill.

James Mill, after his articles in the *Westminster*, could take little part in political agitation. He was still consulted by Place in regard to the Reform movement. Place himself took an important part at the final crisis, especially by his circulation in the week of agony of the famous placard, 'Go for Gold.' But the Utilitarians were now lost in the crowd. The demand for reform had spread through all classes. The attack upon the ruling class carried on by the Radicals of all shades in the dark days of Sidmouth and the six Acts was now supported by the nation at large. The old Toryism could no longer support itself by appealing to the necessities of a struggle for national existence. The prestige due to the victorious end of the war had faded away. The Reform Bill of 1832 was passed, and the Utilitarians hoped that the millennium would at least begin to dawn.

Mill in 1830 removed from Queen's Square to Vicarage Place, Kensington. He kept his house at Mickleham, and there took long Sunday walks with a few of his disciples. His strength was more and more absorbed in his official duties. He was especially called upon to give evidence before the committees which from 1830 to 1833 considered the policy to be adopted in renewing the charter of the East India Company. Mill appeared as the advocate of the company, defended their policy, and argued against the demands of the commercial body which demanded the final suppression of the old trading monopoly of the Company. The abolition, indeed, was a foregone conclusion; but Mill's view was not in accordance with the doctrines of the thoroughgoing freetraders. His official experience, it seems, upon this and other matters deterred him from the *a priori* dogmatism too characteristic of his political speculations. Mill also suggested the formation of a legislative council, which was to contain one man 'versed in the philosophy of men and government.' This was represented by the appointment of the legal member of council in the Act of 1833. Mill approved of Macaulay as the first holder of the post. It was 'very handsome' of him, as Macaulay remarks, inasmuch as the famous articles written by Macaulay himself, in which the *Edinburgh* had at last retorted upon the Utilitarians, must still have been fresh in his memory. The 'Penal Code' drawn by Macaulay as holder of the office was the first actual attempt to carry out Bentham's favourite schemes under British rule, and the influence of the chief of Bentham's disciples at the India House may have had something to do with its initiation. Macaulay's chief subordinate, it may be remarked, Charles Hay Cameron, was one of the Benthamites, and had been proposed by Grote for the chair at the London University ultimately filled by Hoppus.

After 1830 Mill wrote the severe fragment on Mackintosh, which, after a delay caused by Mackintosh's death, appeared in 1835. He contributed some articles to the *London Review*, founded by Sir W. Molesworth, as an organ of the 'philosophical Radicals,' and superintended, though not directly edited, by J. S. Mill. These, his last performances, repeat the old doctrines. It does not appear, indeed, that Mill ever altered one of his opinions. He accepted Bentham's doctrine to the end, as unreservedly as a mathematician might accept Newton's *Principia*.

Mill's lungs had begun to be affected. It was supposed that they were injured by the dust imbibed on coach journeys to Mickleham. He had a bad attack of hæmorrhage in August 1835, and died peacefully on 23rd June 1836.

What remains to be said of Mill personally may be suggested by a noticeable parallel. S. T. Coleridge, born about six months before Mill, died two years before him. The two lives thus coincided for more than sixty years, and each man was the leader of a school. In all else the contrast could hardly be greater. If we were to apply the rules of ordinary morality, it would be entirely in Mill's favour. Mill discharged all his duties as strenuously as a man could, while Coleridge's life was a prolonged illustration of the remark that when an action presented itself to him as a duty he became physically incapable of doing it. Whatever Mill undertook he accomplished, often in the face of enormous difficulties. Coleridge never finished anything, and his works are a heap of fragments of the prolegomena to ambitious schemes. Mill worked his hardest from youth to age, never sparing labour or shirking difficulties or turning aside from his path. Coleridge dawdled through life, solacing himself with opium, and could only be coaxed into occasional activity by skilful diplomacy. Mill preserved his independence by rigid self-denial, temperance, and punctuality. Coleridge was always dependent upon the generosity of his friends. Mill brought up a large family, and in the midst of severe labours found time to educate them even to excess. Coleridge left his wife and children to be cared for by others. And Coleridge died in the odour of sanctity, revered by his disciples, and idolised by his children; while Mill went to the grave amidst the shrugs of respectable shoulders, and respected rather than beloved by the son who succeeded to his intellectual leadership.

The answer to the riddle is indeed plain enough; or rather there are many superabundantly obvious answers. Had Mill defended orthodox views and Coleridge been avowedly heterodox, we should no doubt have heard more of Coleridge's opium and of Mill's blameless and energetic life. But this explains little. That Coleridge was a man of genius and, moreover, of exquisitely poetical genius, and that Mill was at most a man of remarkable talent and the driest and sternest of logicians is also obvious. It is even more to the purpose that Coleridge was overflowing with kindliness, though little able to turn goodwill to much effect; whereas Mill's morality took the form chiefly of attacking the wicked. This is indicated by the saying attributed by Bowring to Bentham that Mill's sympathy for the many sprang out of his hatred of the oppressing few.[30] J. S. Mill very properly protested against this statement when it was quoted in the *Edinburgh Review*. It would obviously imply a gross misunderstanding, whether Bentham, not a good observer of men, said so or not. But it indicates the side of Mill's character which made him unattractive to contemporaries and also to posterity. He partook, says his son,[31] of the Stoic, the Epicurean, and the Cynic character. He was a Stoic in his personal qualities; an Epicurean so far as his theory of morals was concerned; and a Cynic in that he cared little for pleasure. He thought life a 'poor thing' after the freshness of youth had passed; and said that he had never known an old man happy unless he could live over again in the pleasures of the young. Temperance and self-restraint were therefore his favourite virtues. He despised all 'passionate emotions'; he held with Bentham that feelings by themselves deserved neither praise nor blame; he condemned a man who did harm whether the harm came from malevolence or from intellectual error. Therefore all sentiment was objectionable, for sentiment means neglect of rules and calculations. He shrank from showing feeling with more than the usual English reserve; and showed his devotion to his children by drilling them into knowledge with uncompromising strictness. He had no feeling for the poetical or literary side of things; and regarded life, it would seem, as a series of arguments, in which people were to be constrained by logic, not persuaded by sympathy. He seems to have despised poor Mrs. Mill, and to have been unsuccessful in concealing his contempt, though in his letters he refers to her respectfully. Mill therefore was a man little likely to win the hearts of his followers, though his remarkable vigour of mind dominated their understandings.

The amiable and kindly, whose sympathies are quickly moved, gain an unfair share of our regard both in life and afterwards. We are more pleased by an ineffectual attempt to be kindly, than by real kindness bestowed ungraciously. Mill's great qualities should not be overlooked because they were hidden by a manner which seems almost deliberately repellent. He devoted himself through life to promote the truth as he saw it; to increase the scanty amounts of pleasures enjoyed by mankind; and to discharge all the duties which he owed to his neighbours. He succeeded beyond all dispute in forcibly presenting one set of views which profoundly influenced his countrymen; and the very narrowness of his intellect enabled him to plant his blows more effectively.

FOOTNOTES:

[1] The chief authority for James Mill is *James Mill: a Biography*, by Alexander Bain, Emeritus Professor of Logic in the University of Aberdeen, London, 1882. The book contains very full materials; and, if rather dry, deals with a dry subject.

[2] Wallas's *Francis Place*, p. 70 *n*.

[3] Bain's *James Mill*, p. 166.

[4] Gifford's real name was John Richards Green. The identity of his assumed name with that of the more famous

William Gifford has led to a common confusion between the two periodicals. 'Peter Pindar' assaulted William Gifford under the erroneous impression that he was editor of the second.

[5] Letter in Bain's *James Mill*, pp. 136-40.

[6] *Autobiography*, p. 39.

[7] Bain's *James Mill*, pp. 97-106. Mill appears to have said something 'extravagant' about Bentham in an article upon Miranda in the *Edinburgh Review* for January 1809. He also got some praises of Bentham into the *Annual Review* of 1809 (Bain, 92-96).

[8] See the very interesting Life of Francis Place, by Mr. Graham Wallas, 1898.

[9] Bain's *James Mill*, p. 78, and Wallas's *Francis Place*, p. 66.

[10] Wallas's *Francis Place*, p. 68.

[11] He 'put together' the *Not Paul but Jesus* at Ford Abbey in 1817, and helped to preface the Reform *Catechism*. Wallas's *Francis Place*, p. 84.

[12] The article of 1811 was also published separately.

[13] He wrote only the first volume. Two others were added by Cuthbert Southey.

[14] *Lectures* (Ashe, 1885), pp. 32, 61.

[15] James Mill, according to Place, wrote a 'memorable and admirable essay, "Schools for all, not schools for Churchmen only."' —Wallas's *Francis Place*, 99 *n*.

[16] This absurd suspicion was aroused by the quarrel about Burdett's arrest. See Wallas's *Place*, p. 56.

[17] Mr. Wallas gives an account of these schemes in chap. iv. of his Life of Place. I have also consulted Place's collections in Additional mss., 27,823.

[18] Bain's *James Mill*, p. 162.

[19] H. H. Wilson in his preface to the edition of 1840.

[20] Wallas's *Francis Place*, p. 78.

[21] Bain's *James Mill*, p. 435.

[22] *Ibid.*

[23] Bentham's *Works*, p. 498.

[24] See Carman in *Economic Review*, 1894.

[25] See under Black in *Dictionary of National Biography*.

[26] *Autobiography*, p. 101.

[27] See Place's account in Additional mss. 27,823.

[28] G. C. Robertson, *Philosophical Remains*, p. 166; and under George Grote in *Dictionary of National Biography*.

[29] Letters communicated by Mr. Graham Wallas. See Mr. Wallas's *Francis Place*, p. 91.

[30] So Place observed that Mill 'could help the mass, but could not help the individual, not even himself or his own.' —Wallas's *Francis Place*, p. 79.

[31] *Autobiography*, p. 48.

CHAPTER II
REFORM MOVEMENTS

I. POLITICAL CHANGE

The last years of Mill's life correspond to the period in which Utilitarianism reached, in certain respects, its highest pitch of influence. The little band who acknowledged him as their chief leader, and as the authorised lieutenant of Bentham, considered themselves to be in the van of progress. Though differing on many points from each other, and regarded with aversion or distrust by the recognised party leaders, they were in their most militant and confident state of mind. They were systematically reticent as to their religious views: they left to popular orators the public advocacy of their favourite political measures; and the credit of finally passing such of those measures as were adopted fell chiefly to the hands of the great political leaders. The Utilitarians are ignored in the orthodox Whig legend. In the preface to his collected works, Sydney Smith runs over the usual list of changes which had followed, and, as he seems to think, had in great part resulted from, the establishment of the *Edinburgh Review*. Smith himself, and Jeffrey and Horner and, above all, 'the gigantic Brougham,' had blown the blast which brought down the towers of Jericho. Sir G. O. Trevelyan, in his *Life of Macaulay*, describes the advent of the Whigs to office in a similar sense. 'Agitators and incendiaries,' he says, 'retired into the background, as will always be the case when the country is in earnest: and statesmen who had much to lose, and were not afraid to risk it, stepped quietly and firmly to the front. The men and the sons of the men who had so long endured exclusion from office, embittered by unpopularity, at length reaped their reward.' [32] The Radical version of the history is different. The great men, it said, who had left the cause to be supported by agitators so long as the defence was dangerous and profitless, stepped forward now that it was clearly winning, and received both the reward and the credit. Mill and Place could not find words to express their contempt for the trimming, shuffling Whigs. They were probably unjust enough in detail; but they had a strong case in some respects. The Utilitarians represented that part of the reforming party which had a definite and a reasoned creed. They tried to give logic where the popular agitators were content with declamation, and represented absolute convictions when the Whig reformers were content with tentative and hesitating compromises. They had some grounds for considering themselves to be the 'steel of the lance'; the men who formulated and deliberately defended the principles which were beginning to conquer the world.

The Utilitarians, I have said, became a political force in the concluding years of the great war struggle. The catastrophe of the revolution had unchained a whole whirlwind of antagonisms. The original issues had passed out of sight; and great social, industrial, and political changes were in progress which made the nation that emerged from the war a very different body from the nation that had entered it nearly a generation before. It is not surprising that at first very erroneous estimates were made of the new position when peace at last returned.

The Radicals, who had watched on one side the growth of debt and pauperism, and, on the other hand, the profits made by stockjobbers, landlords, and manufacturers, ascribed all the terrible sufferings to the selfish designs of the upper classes. When the war ended they hoped that the evils would diminish, while the pretext for misgovernment would be removed. A bitter disappointment followed. The war was followed by widespread misery. Plenty meant ruin to agriculturists, and commercial 'gluts' resulting in manufacturers' warehouses crammed with unsaleable goods. The discontent caused by misery had been encountered during the war by patriotic fervour. It was not a time for redressing evils, when the existence of the nation was at stake. Now that the misery continued, and the excuse for delaying redress had been removed, a demand arose for parliamentary reform. Unfortunately discontent led also to sporadic riotings, to breaking of machinery and burning of ricks. The Tory government saw in these disturbances a renewal of the old Jacobin spirit, and had visions—apparently quite groundless—of widespread conspiracies and secret societies ready to produce a ruin of all social order. It had recourse to the old repressive measures, the suspension of the Habeas Corpus Act, the passage of the 'Six Acts,' and the prosecution of popular agitators. Many observers fancied that the choice lay between a servile insurrection and the establishment of arbitrary power.

By degrees, however, peace brought back prosperity. Things settled down; commerce revived; and the acute distress passed away. The whole nation went mad over the wrongs of Queen Caroline; and the demand for political reform became for the time less intense. But it soon appeared that, although this crisis had been surmounted, the temper of the nation had profoundly changed. The supreme power still belonged constitutionally to the landed interest. But it had a profoundly modified social order behind it.

The war had at least made it necessary to take into account the opinions of larger classes. An appeal to patriotism means that some regard must be paid to the prejudices and passions of people at large. When enormous sums were to be raised, the moneyed classes would have their say as to modes of taxation. Commerce and manufactures went through crises of terrible difficulty due to the various changes of the war; but, on the whole, the industrial classes were steadily and rapidly developing in wealth, and becoming relatively more important. The war itself was, in one aspect at least, a war for the maintenance of the British supremacy in trade. The struggle marked by the policy of the 'Orders in Council' on one side, and Napoleon's decrees on the other, involved a constant reference to Manchester and Liverpool and the rapidly growing manufacturing and commercial interests. The growth, again, of the press, at a time when every one who could read was keenly interested in news of most exciting and important events, implied the rapid development of a great organ of public opinion.

The effects of these changes soon became palpable. The political atmosphere was altogether different; and an entirely new set of influences was governing the policy of statesmen. The change affected the Tory as much as the Whig. However strongly he might believe that he was carrying on the old methods, he was affected by the new ideas which had been almost unconsciously incorporated in his creed. How great was the change, and how much it took the shape of accepting Utilitarian theories, may be briefly shown by considering a few characteristic facts.

The ablest men who held office at the time were Canning, Huskisson, and Peel. They represented the conservatism which sought to distinguish itself from mere obstructiveness. Their influence was felt in many directions. The Holy Alliance had the sympathy of men who could believe that the war had brought back the pre-revolutionary order, and that its main result had been to put the Jacobin spirit in chains. Canning's accession to office in 1822 meant that the foreign policy of England was to be definitely opposed to the policy of the 'Holy Alliance.' A pithy statement of his view is given in a remarkable letter, dated 1st February 1823, to the prince who was soon to become Charles x. [33] The French government had declared that a people could only receive a free constitution as a gift from their legitimate kings. Should the English ministry, says Canning, after this declaration, support the French in their attack upon the constitutional government of Spain, it would be driven from office amid 'the execration of Tories and Whigs alike.' He thought that the doctrine of the sovereignty of the people was less alien to the spirit of the British Constitution than the opposite doctrine of the legitimists. In the early days, when Canning sat at the feet of Pitt, the war, if not in their eyes an Anti-Jacobin crusade, had to be supported by stimulating the Anti-Jacobin sentiment. In later days, the war had come to be a struggle against the oppression of nations by foreign despots. Canning could now accept the version of Pitt's policy which corresponded to the later phase. Englishmen in general had no more sympathy for despots who claimed a divine right than for despots who acted in the name of democracy— especially when the despots threatened to interfere with British trade. When Canning called 'the new world into existence to redress the balance of the old,' [34] he declared that English policy should resist threats from the Holy Alliance directed against some of our best customers. The general approval had special force among the Utilitarians. In the South American States Bentham had found eager proselytes, and had hoped to become a Solon. He had been consulted by the constitutionalists in Spain and Portugal; and he and his disciples, Joseph Hume in particular, had joined the Greek Committee, and tried to regenerate Athens by sound Utilitarian tracts. All English Liberals sympathised with the various movements which were more or less favoured by Canning's policy; but the Utilitarians could also see in them the opening of new fields already white for the harvest.

The foreign policy was significant. It proved that the war, whatever else it had done, had not brought back the old order; and the old British traditions in favour of liberty of speech and action would revive now that they were no longer trammelled by the fears of a destructive revolution. The days of July in 1830 gave fresh importance to the reaction of foreign upon English politics.

II. LAW REFORM

Meanwhile, however, the Utilitarians had a far stronger interest in domestic problems. In the first place, in Bentham's especial province a complete change of feeling had taken place. Romilly was Bentham's earliest disciple (so Bentham said), and looked up to him with 'filial reverence.' Every 'reformatiuncle' introduced by Romilly in parliament had been first brought to Bentham, to be conned over by the two. [35] With great difficulty Romilly had got two or three measures through the House of Commons, generally to be thrown out by Eldon's influence in the Lords. [36] After Romilly's death in 1818, the cause was taken up by the Whig philosopher, Sir James Mackintosh, and made a distinct step in advance. Though there were still obstacles in the upper regions, a committee was obtained to consider the frequency of capital punishment, and measures were passed to abolish it in particular cases. Finally, in 1823, the reform was adopted by Peel. Peel was destined to represent in the most striking way the process by which new ideas were gradually infiltrating the upper sphere. Though still a strong Tory and a representative of the university of Oxford, he was closely connected with the manufacturing classes, and had become aware, as he wrote to Croker (23rd March 1820), that public opinion had grown to be too large for its accustomed channels. As Home Secretary, he took up the whole subject of the criminal law, and passed in the next years a series of acts consolidating and mitigating the law, and repealing many old statutes. A measure of equal importance was his establishment in 1829 of the metropolitan police force, which at last put an end to the old chaotic muddle described by Colquhoun of parish officers and constables. Other significant legal changes marked the opening of a new era. Eldon was the very incarnation of the spirit of obstruction; and the Court of Chancery, over which he presided for a quarter of a century, was thought to be the typical stronghold of the evil principles denounced by Bentham. An attack in 1823 upon Eldon was made in the House of Commons by John Williams (1777-1846), afterwards a judge. Eldon, though profoundly irritated by the personal imputations involved, consented to the appointment of a commission, which reported in 1825, and recommended measures of reform. In 1828, Brougham made a great display upon which he had consulted Bentham. [37] In a speech of six hours' length he gave a summary of existing abuses, which may still be read with interest. [38] Commissions were appointed to investigate the procedure of the Common Law Court and the law of real property. Another commission, intended to codify the criminal law, was appointed in 1833. Brougham says that of 'sixty capital defects' described in his speech, fifty-five had been removed, or were in course of removal, when his speeches were collected (*i.e.* 1838). Another speech of Brougham's in 1828 dealt with the carrying into execution of a favourite plan of Bentham's—the formation of local courts, which ultimately became the modern county courts. [39] The facts are significant of a startling change—no less than an abrupt transition from the reign of entire apathy to a reign of continuous reform extending over the whole range of law. The Reform Bill accelerated the movement, but it had been started before Bentham's death. The great stone, so long immovable, was fairly set rolling.

Bentham's influence, again, in bringing about the change is undeniable. He was greatly dissatisfied with Brougham's speech, and, indeed, would have been dissatisfied with anything short of a complete logical application of his whole system. He held Brougham to be 'insincere,' [40] a trimmer and popularity-hunter, but a useful instrument. Brougham's astonishing vanity and self-seeking prompted and perverted his amazing activity. He represents the process, perhaps necessary, by which a philosopher's ideas have to be modified before they can be applied to practical application. Brougham, however, could speak generously of men no longer in a position to excite his jealousy. He says in the preface to his first speech that 'the age of law reform and the age of Jeremy Bentham' were the same thing, and declares Bentham to be the 'first legal philosopher' who had appeared in the world. As the Chief advocates of Bentham he reckons Romilly, his parliamentary representative; Dumont, his literary interpreter; and James Mill, who, in his article upon 'jurisprudence,' had popularised the essential principles of the doctrine.

The Utilitarians had at last broken up the barriers of obstruction and set the stream flowing. Whigs and Tories were taking up their theories. They naturally exaggerated in some respects the completeness of the triumph. The English law has not yet been codified, and it was characteristic of the Benthamite school to exaggerate the facility of that process. In their hatred of 'judge-made law' they assumed too easily that all things would be arranged into convenient pigeon-holes as soon as 'Judge and Co.' were abolished. It was a characteristic error to exaggerate the simplicity of their problem, and to fail to see that 'judge-made' law corresponds to a necessary inductive process by which the complex and subtle differences have to be gradually ascertained and fitted into a systematic statement. One other remark suggests itself. The Utilitarians saw in the dogged obstructiveness of Eldon and his like the one great obstacle to reform. It did not occur to them that the clumsiness of parliamentary legislation might be another difficulty. They failed to notice distinctly one tendency of their reforms. To make a code you require a sovereign strong enough to dominate the lawyers, not a system in which lawyers are an essential part of a small governing class. Codification, in short, means centralisation in one department. Blindness to similar results elsewhere was a characteristic of the Utilitarian thinkers.

III. ECONOMIC REFORM

In another department the Utilitarians boasted, and also with good reason, of the triumph of their tenets. Political economy was in the ascendant. Professorships were being founded in Oxford, Cambridge, [41] London, and Edinburgh. Mrs. Marcet's *Conversations* (1818) were spreading the doctrine among babes and sucklings. The Utilitarians were the sacred band who defended the strictest orthodoxy against all opponents. They spoke as recognised authorities upon some of the most vital questions of the day, of which I need here only notice Free Trade, the doctrine most closely associated with the teaching of their revered Adam Smith. In 1816 Ricardo remarks with satisfaction that the principle 'is daily obtaining converts' even among the most prejudiced classes; and he refers especially to a petition in which the clothiers of Gloucestershire [42] expressed their willingness to give up all restrictions. There was, indeed, an important set-off against this gain. The landowners were being pledged to protection. They had decided that in spite of the peace, the price of wheat must be kept up to 80s. a quarter. They would no longer be complimented as Adam Smith had complimented them on their superior liberality, and were now creating a barrier only to be stormed after a long struggle. Meanwhile the principle was making rapid way among their rivals. One symptom was the adoption by the London merchants in 1820 of a famous petition on behalf of free trade. [43] It was drawn up by Thomas Tooke (1774-1858), who had long been actively engaged in the Russian trade, and whose *History of Prices* is in some respects the most valuable economic treatise of the time. Tooke gives a curious account of his action on this occasion. [44] He collected a few friends engaged in commerce, who were opposed to the corn laws. He found that several of them had 'crude and confused' notions upon the subject, and that each held that his own special interests should be exempted on some pretext from the general rule. After various dexterous pieces of diplomacy, however, he succeeded in obtaining the signature of Samuel Thornton, a governor of the bank of England, and ultimately procured a sufficient number of signatures by private solicitation. He was favourably received by the Prime Minister Lord Liverpool, and Vansittart (then Chancellor of the Exchequer), and finally got the petition presented to the House of Commons by Alexander Baring (afterwards Lord Ashburton). Tooke remarks that the Liverpool administration was in advance, not only of the public generally, but of the 'mercantile community,' Glasgow and Manchester, however, followed in the same steps, and the petition became a kind of official manifesto of the orthodox doctrine. The Political Economy Club formed next year at Tooke's instigation (April 18, 1821) was intended to hasten the process of dispersing crude and confused ideas. It was essentially an organ of the Utilitarian propaganda.

The influence of the economists upon public policy was shown by the important measures carried through chiefly by Huskisson. Huskisson (1770-1830) was a type of the most intelligent official of his time. Like his more brilliant friend Canning, he had been introduced into office under Pitt, and retained a profound reverence for his early leader. Huskisson was a thorough man of business, capable of wrestling with blue-books, of understanding the sinking-fund, and having theories about the currency; a master of figures and statistics and the whole machinery of commerce. Though eminently useful, he might at any moment be applying some awkward doctrine from Adam Smith.

Huskisson began the series of economic reforms which were brought to their full development by Peel and Gladstone. The collection of his speeches [45] incidentally brings out very clearly his relation to the Utilitarians. The most remarkable is a great speech of April 24, 1826 [46] (upon the state of the silk manufacture), of which Canning declared that he had never heard one abler, or which made a deeper impression upon the House. In this he reviews his policy, going over the most important financial measures of the preceding period. They made a new era, and he dates the beginning of the movement from the London petition, and the 'luminous speech' made by Baring when presenting it. We followed public opinion, he says, and did not create it. [47] Adopting the essential principles of the petition, the government had in the first place set free the great woollen trade. The silk trade had been emancipated by abolishing the Spitalfield Acts passed in the previous century, which enabled magistrates to fix the rates of wages. The principle of prohibition had been abandoned, though protective duties remained. The navigation laws had been materially relaxed, and steps taken towards removing restrictions of different kinds upon trade with France and with India. One symptom of the change was the consolidation of the custom law effected by James Deacon Hume (1774-1842), an official patronised by Huskisson, and an original member of the Political Economy Club. By a law passed in 1825, five hundred statutes dating from the time of Edward i. were repealed, and the essence of the law given in a volume of moderate size. Finally, the removal of prohibitions was undermining the smugglers.

The measures upon which Huskisson justly prided himself might have been dictated by the Political Economy Club itself. So far as they went they were an application of the doctrines of its thoroughgoing members, of Mill, Ricardo, and the orthodox school. They indeed supported him in the press. The *Morning Chronicle*, which expressed their views, declared him to be the most virtuous minister, that is (in true Utilitarian phrase), the most desirous of national welfare who had ever lived. The praise of Radicals would be not altogether welcome. Canning, in supporting his friend, maintained that sound commercial policy belonged no more to the Whigs than to the Tories. Huskisson and he were faithful disciples of Pitt, whose treaty with France in 1786, assailed by Fox and the Whigs, had been the first practical application of the Wealth of Nations. Neither party, perhaps, could claim a special connection with good or bad political economy; and certainly neither was prepared to incur political martyrdom in zeal for scientific truth. A question was beginning to come to the front which would make party lines dependent upon economic theories, and Huskisson's view of this was characteristic.

The speech from which I have quoted begins with an indignant retort upon a member who had applied to him Burke's phrase about a perfect-bred metaphysician exceeding the devil in malignity and contempt for mankind. Huskisson frequently protested even against the milder epithet of theorist. He asserted most emphatically that he appealed to 'experience' and not to 'theory,' a slippery distinction which finds a good exposure in Bentham's *Book of Fallacies*. [48] The doctrine, however, was a convenient one for Huskisson. He could appeal to experience to show that commercial restrictions had injured the woollen trade, and their absence benefited the cotton trade, [49] and when he was not being taunted with theories, he would state with perfect clearness the general free trade argument. [50] But he had to keep an eye to the uncomfortable tricks which theories sometimes play. He argued emphatically in 1825 [51] that analogy between manufactures and agriculture is 'illogical.' He does not wish to depress the price of corn, but to keep it at such a level that our manufactures may not be hampered by dear food. Here he was forced by stress of politics to differ from his economical friends. The country gentleman did not wish to pay duties on his silk or his brandy, but he had a direct and obvious interest in keeping up the price of corn. Huskisson had himself supported the Corn Bill of 1815, but it was becoming more and more obvious that a revision would be necessary. In 1828 he declared that he 'lamented from the bottom of his soul the mass of evil and misery and destruction of capital which that law in the course of twelve years had produced.' [52] Ricardo, meanwhile, and the economists had from the first applied to agriculture the principles which Huskisson applied to manufactures. [53] Huskisson's melancholy death has left us unable to say whether upon this matter he would have been as convertible as Peel. In any case the general principle of free trade was as fully adopted by Huskisson and Canning as by the Utilitarians themselves. The Utilitarians could again claim to be both the inspirers of the first principles, and the most consistent in carrying out the deductions. They, it is true, were not generally biassed by having any interest in rents. They were to be the allies or teachers of the manufacturing class which began to be decidedly opposed to the squires and the old order.

In one very important economic question, the Utilitarians not only approved a change of the law, but were the main agents in bringing it about. Francis Place was the wire-puller, to whose energy was due the abolition of the Conspiracy Laws in 1824. Joseph Hume in the House of Commons, and M'Culloch, then editor of the *Scotsman*, had the most conspicuous part in the agitation, but Place worked the machinery of agitation. The bill passed in 1824 was modified by an act of 1825; but the modification, owing to Place's efforts, was not serious, and the act, as we are told on good authority, 'effected a real emancipation,' and for the first time established the right of 'collective bargaining.' [54] The remarkable thing is that this act, carried on the principles of 'Radical individualism' and by the efforts of Radical individualists, was thus a first step towards the application to practice of socialist doctrine. Place thought that the result of the act would be not the encouragement, but the decline, of trades-unions. The unions had been due to the necessity of combining against oppressive laws, and would cease when those laws were abolished. [55] This marks a very significant stage in the development of economic opinion.

IV. CHURCH REFORM

The movement which at this period was most conspicuous politically was that which resulted in Roman Catholic emancipation, and here, too, the Utilitarians might be anticipating a complete triumph of their principles. The existing disqualifications, indeed, were upheld by little but the purely obstructive sentiment. When the duke of York swore that 'so help him God!' he would oppose the change to the last, he summed up the whole 'argument' against it. Canning and Huskisson here represented the policy not only of Pitt, but of Castlereagh. The Whigs, indeed, might claim to be the natural representatives of toleration. The church of England was thoroughly subjugated by the state, and neither Whig nor Tory wished for a fundamental change. But the most obvious differentia of Whiggism was a dislike to the ecclesiastical spirit. The Whig noble was generally more or less of a freethinker; and upon such topics Holland House differed little from Queen's Square Place, or differed only in a rather stricter reticence. Both Whig and Tory might accept Warburton's doctrine of an 'alliance' between church and state. The Tory inferred that the church should be supported. His prescription for meeting discontent was 'more yeomanry' and a handsome sum for church-building. The Whig thought that the church got a sufficient return in being allowed to keep its revenues. On the Tory view, the relation might be compared to that of man and wife in Christian countries where, though the two are one, the husband is bound to fidelity. On the Whig view it was like a polygamous system, where the wife is in complete subjection, and the husband may take any number of concubines. The Whig noble regarded the church as socially useful, but he was by no means inclined to support its interests when they conflicted with other political considerations. He had been steadily in favour of diminishing the privileges of the establishment, and had taken part in removing the grievances of the old penal laws. He was not prepared to uphold privileges which involved a palpable danger to his order.

This position is illustrated by Sydney Smith, the ideal divine of Holland House. The *Plymley Letters* [56] give his views most pithily. Smith, a man as full of sound sense as of genuine humour, appeals to the principles of toleration, and is keenly alive to the absurdity of a persecution which only irritates without conversion. But he also appeals to the danger of the situation. 'If Bonaparte lives,' [57] he says, 'and something is not done to conciliate the Catholics, it seems to me absolutely impossible but that we must perish.' We are like the captain of a ship attacked by a pirate, who should begin by examining his men in the church catechism, and forbid any one to sponge or ram who had not taken the sacrament according to the forms of the church of England. He confesses frankly that the strength of the Irish is with him a strong motive for listening to their claims. To talk of 'not acting from fear is mere parliamentary cant.' [58] Although the danger which frightened Smith was evaded, this was the argument which really brought conviction even to Tories in 1829. In any case the Whigs, whose great boast was their support of toleration, would not be prompted by any Quixotic love of the church to encounter tremendous perils in defence of its privileges.

Smith's zeal had its limits. He observes humorously in his preface that he had found himself after the Reform Bill engaged in the defence of the National Church against the archbishop of Canterbury and the bishop of London. The letters to Archdeacon Singleton, written when the Whigs were flirting with the Radicals, show how much good an old Whig could find in the establishment. This marks the difference between the true Whig and the Utilitarian. The Whig would not risk the country for the sake of church; he would keep the clerical power strictly subordinate to the power of the state, but then, when considered from the political side, it was part of a government system providing him with patronage, and to be guarded from the rude assaults of the Radical reformer. The Utilitarian, though for the moment he was in alliance with the Whig, regarded the common victory as a step to something far more sweeping. He objected to intolerance as decidedly as the Whig, for absolute freedom of opinion was his most cherished doctrine. He objected still more emphatically to persecution on behalf of the church, because he entirely repudiated its doctrines. The objection to spreading true doctrine by force is a strong one, but hardly so strong as the objection to a forcible spread of false doctrine. But, besides this, the church represented to the Utilitarian precisely the very worst specimen of the corruptions of the time. The Court of Chancery was bad enough, but the whole ecclesiastical system with its vast prizes, [59] its opportunities for corrupt patronage, its pluralism and non-residence was an evil on a larger scale. The Radical, therefore, unlike the Whig, was an internecine enemy of the whole system. The 'church of England system,' as Bentham calmly remarks, is 'ripe for dissolution.' [60] I have already noticed his quaint proposal for giving effect to his views. Mill, in the *Westminster Review*, denounced the church of England as the worst of all churches. [61] To the Utilitarian, in short, the removal of the disqualification of dissenters and Catholics was thus one step to the consummation which their logic demanded — the absolute disestablishment and disendowment of the church. Conservatives in general anticipated the confiscation of church revenues as a necessary result of reform; and so far as the spirit of reformers was represented by the Utilitarians and their Radical allies, they had good grounds for the fear. James Mill's theory is best indicated by a later article published in the *London Review* of July 1835. After pointing out that the church of England retains all the machinery desired for supporting priests and preventing the growth of intellect and morality, he proceeds to ask what the clergy do for their money. They read prayers, which is a palpable absurdity; they preach sermons to spread superstitious notions of the Supreme Being, and perform ceremonies—baptism, and so forth—which are obviously silly. The church is a mere state machine worked in subservience to the sinister interest of the governing classes. The way to reform it would be to equalise the pay: let the clergy be appointed by a 'Minister of Public Instruction' or the county authorities; abolish the articles, and constitute a church 'without dogmas or ceremonies'; and employ the clergy to give lectures on ethics, botany, political economy, and so forth, besides holding Sunday meetings, dances (decent dances are to be specially invented for the purpose), and social meals, which would be a revival of the 'agapai' of the early Christians. For this purpose, however, it might be necessary to substitute tea and coffee for wine. In other words, the church is to be made into a popular London University. The plan illustrates the incapacity of an isolated clique to understand the real tone of public opinion. I need not pronounce upon Mill's scheme, which seems to have some sense in it, but one would like to know whether Newman read his article.

V. SINISTER INTERESTS

In questions of foreign policy, of law reform, of political economy, and of religious tests, the Utilitarians thus saw the gradual approximation to their most characteristic views on the part of the Whigs, and a strong infiltration of the same views among the less obstructive Tories. They held the logical creed, to which others were slowly approximating, either from the force of argument or from the great social changes which were bringing new classes into political power. The movement for parliamentary reform which for a time overshadowed all other questions might be regarded as a corollary from the position already won. Briefly, it was clear that a new social stratum was exercising a vast influence; the doctrines popular with it had to be more or less accepted; and the only problem worth consideration by practical men was whether or not such a change should be made in the political machinery as would enable the influence to be exercised by direct and constitutional means. To the purely obstructive Tory parliamentary reform was a step to the general cataclysm. The proprietor of a borough, like the proprietor of a church patronage or commission in the army, had a right to his votes, and to attack his right was simply confiscation of private property. The next step might be to confiscate his estate. But even the more intelligent Conservative drew the line at such a measure. Canning, Huskisson, and even Peel might accept the views of the Utilitarians in regard to foreign policy, to law reform, to free trade, or the removal of religious tests, declaring only that they were obeying 'experience' instead of logic, and might therefore go just as far as they pleased. But they were all pledged to resist parliamentary reform to the utmost. Men thoroughly steeped in official life, and versed in the actual working of the machinery, were naturally alive to the magnitude of the change to be introduced. They saw with perfect clearness that it would amount to a revolution. The old system in which the ruling classes carried on business by family alliances and bargains between ministers and great men would be impracticable. The fact that so much had been done in the way of concession to the ideas of the new classes was for them an argument against the change. If the governing classes were ready to reform abuses, why should they be made unable to govern? A gradual enfranchisement of the great towns on the old system might be desirable. Such a man as Huskisson, representing great commercial interests, could not be blind to the necessity. But a thorough reconstruction was more alarming. As Canning had urged in a great speech at Liverpool, a House of Commons, thoroughly democratised, would be incompatible with the existence of the monarchy and the House of Lords. So tremendously powerful a body would reduce the other parts of the constitution to mere excrescences, feeble drags upon the new driving-wheel in which the whole real force would be concentrated.

That this expressed, in point of fact, a serious truth, was, I take it, undeniable. The sufficient practical answer was, that change was inevitable. To refuse to adapt the constitutional machinery to the altered political forces was not to hinder their growth, but to make a revolution necessary. When, accordingly, the excluded classes began seriously to demand admission, the only question came to lie between violent and peaceable methods. The alarm with which our fathers watched the progress of the measure may seem to us exaggerated, but they scarcely overestimated the magnitude of the change. The old rulers were taking a new partner of such power, that whatever authority was left to them might seem to be left on sufferance. As soon as he became conscious of his strength, they would be reduced to nonentities. The Utilitarians took some part in the struggle, and welcomed the victory with anticipations destined to be, for the time at least, cruelly disappointed. But they were still a small minority, whose views rather scandalised the leaders of the party with which they were in temporary alliance. The principles upon which they based their demands, as formulated by James Mill, looked, as we shall see, far beyond the concessions of the moment.

One other political change is significant, though I am unable to give an adequate account of it. Bentham's denunciation of 'sinister interests' — one of his leading topics — corresponds to the question of sinecures, which was among the most effective topics of Radical declamation. The necessity of limiting the influence of the crown and excluding 'placemen' from the House of Commons had been one of the traditional Whig commonplaces, and a little had been done by Burke's act of 1782 towards limiting pensions and abolishing obsolete offices. When English Radicalism revived, the assault was renewed in parliament and the press. During the war little was achieved, though a revival of the old complaints about placemen in parliament was among the first symptoms of the rising sentiment. In 1812 an attack was made upon the 'tellers of the Exchequer.' Romilly [62] says that the value of one of these offices had risen to £26,000 or £27,000 a year. The income came chiefly from fees, and the actual work, whatever it was, was done by deputy. The scandal was enormous at a time when the stress upon the nation was almost unbearable. One of the tellerships was held by a member of the great Grenville family, who announced that they regarded the demand for reform as a personal attack upon them. The opposition, therefore, could not muster even its usual strength, and the motion for inquiry was rejected. When the war was over, even the government began to feel that something must be done. In 1817 some acts were passed [63] abolishing a variety of sinecure offices and 'regulating certain offices in the Court of Exchequer.' The Radicals considered this as a mere delusion, because it was provided at the same time that pensions might be given to persons who had held certain great offices. The change, however, was apparently of importance as removing the chief apology for sinecures, and the system with modifications still remains. The marquis of Camden, one of the tellers of the Exchequer, voluntarily resigned the fees and accepted only the regular salary of £2500. His action is commended in the *Black Book*, [64] which expresses a regret that the example had not been followed by other great sinecurists. Public opinion was beginning to be felt. During the subsequent period the cry against sinecures became more emphatic. The *Black Book*, published originally in 1820 and 1823, and afterwards reissued, gave a list, so far as it could be ascertained, of all pensions, and supplied a mass of information for Radical orators. The amount of pensions is stated at over £1,000,000, including sinecure offices with over £350,000 annually; [65] and the list of offices (probably very inaccurate in detail) gives a singular impression of the strange ramifications of the system. Besides the direct pensions, every new department of administration seems to have suggested the foundation of offices which tended to become sinecures. The cry for 'retrenchment' was joined to the cry for reform. [66] Joseph Hume, who first entered parliament in 1818, became a representative of the Utilitarian Radicalism, and began a long career of minute criticism which won for him the reputation of a stupendous bore, but helped to keep a steady pressure upon ministers. [67] Sir James Graham (1792-1861) was at this time of Radical tendencies, and first made himself conspicuous by demanding returns of pensions. [68] The settlements of the civil lists of George iv., William iv., and Victoria, gave opportunities for imposing new restrictions upon the pension system. Although no single sweeping measure was passed, the whole position was changed. By the time of the Reform Bill, a sinecure had become an anachronism. The presumption was that whenever an opportunity offered, it would be suppressed. Some of the sinecure offices in the Court of Chancery, the 'Keeper of the Hanaper,' the 'Chaffwax,' and so forth, were abolished by an act passed by the parliament which had just carried the Reform Bill. [69] In 1833 a reform of the system of naval administration by Sir James Graham got rid of some cumbrous machinery; and Graham again was intrusted in 1834 with an act under which the Court of Exchequer was finally reformed, and the 'Clerk of the Pells' and the 'Tellers of the Exchequer' ceased to exist. [70] Other offices seem to have melted away by degrees, whenever a chance offered.

Many other of the old abuses had ceased to require any special denunciations from political theorists. The general principle was established, and what remained was to apply it in detail. The prison system was no longer in want of a Howard or a Bentham. Abuses remained which occupied the admirable Mrs. Fry; and many serious difficulties had to be solved by a long course of experiment. But it was no longer a question whether anything should be doing, but of the most efficient means of bringing about an admittedly desirable end. The agitation for the suppression of the slave-trade again had been succeeded by the attack upon slavery. The system was evidently doomed, although not finally abolished till after the Reform Bill; and ministers were only considering the question whether the abolition should be summary or gradual, or what compensation might be made to vested interests. The old agitation had been remarkable, as I have said, not only for its end but for the new kind of machinery to which it had applied. Popular agitation [71] had taken a new shape. The county associations formed in the last days of the American war of independence, and the societies due to the French revolution had set a precedent. The revolutionary societies had been suppressed or had died out, as opposed to the general spirit of the nation, although they had done a good deal to arouse political speculation. In the period of distress which followed the war the Radical reformers had again held public meetings, and had again been met by repressive measures. The acts of 1817 and 1819 [72] imposed severe restrictions upon the right of public meeting. The old 'county meeting,' which continued to be common until the reform period, and was summoned by the lord-lieutenant or the sheriff on a requisition from the freeholders, had a kind of constitutional character, though I do not know its history in detail. [73] The extravagantly repressive measures were an anachronism, or could only be enforced during the pressure of an intense excitement. In one way or other, public meetings were soon being held as frequently as ever. The trial of Queen Caroline gave opportunity for numerous gatherings, and statesmen began to find that they must use instead of suppressing them. Canning [74] appears to have been the first minister to make frequent use of speeches addressed to public meetings; and meetings to which such appeals were addressed soon began to use their authority to demand pledges from the speakers. [75] Representation was to be understood more and more as delegation. Meanwhile the effect of public meetings was enormously increased when a general organisation was introduced. The great precedent was the Catholic Association, founded in 1823 by O'Connell and Sheil. The peculiar circumstances of the Irish people and their priests gave a ready-made machinery for the agitation which triumphed in 1829. The Political Union founded by Attwood at Birmingham in the same year adopted the method, and led to the triumph of 1832. Political combination henceforth took a different shape, and in the ordinary phrase, 'public opinion' became definitely the ultimate and supreme authority. This enormous change and the corresponding development of the power of the press, which affected to mould and, at any rate, expressed public opinion, entirely fell in with Utilitarian principles. Their part in bringing about the change was of no special importance except in so far as they more or less inspired the popular orators. They were, however, ready to take advantage of it. They had the *Westminster Review* to take a place beside the *Edinburgh* and *Quarterly Reviews*, which had raised periodical writing to a far higher position than it had ever occupied, and to which leading politicians and leading authors on both sides had become regular contributors. The old contempt for journalism was rapidly vanishing. In 1825 Canning expresses his regret for having given some information to a paper of which an ill use had been made. He had previously abstained from all communication with 'these gentry,' and was now resolved to have done with *hoc genus omne* for good and all. [76] In 1839 we find his former colleague, Lord Lyndhurst, seeking an alliance with Barnes, the editor of the *Times*, as eagerly as though Barnes had been the head of a parliamentary party. [77]

The newspapers had probably done more than the schools to spread habits of reading through the country. Yet the strong interest which was growing up in educational matters was characteristic. Brougham's phrase, 'the schoolmaster is abroad' (29th January 1821), became a popular proverb, and rejoiced the worthy Bentham. [78] I have already described the share taken by the Utilitarians in the great Bell and Lancaster controversy. Parliament had as yet done little. A bill brought in by Whitbread had been passed in 1807 by the House of Commons, enabling parishes to form schools on the Scottish model, but according to Romilly, [79] it was passed in the well-grounded confidence that it would be thrown out by the peers. A committee upon education was obtained by Brougham after the peace, which reported in 1818, and which led to a commission upon school endowments. Brougham introduced an education bill in 1820, but nothing came of it. The beginning of any participation by government in national education was not to take place till after the Reform Bill. Meanwhile, however, the foundation of the London University upon unsectarian principles was encouraging the Utilitarians; and there were other symptoms of the growth of enlightenment. George Birkbeck (1776-1841) had started some popular lectures upon science at Glasgow about 1800, and having settled as a physician in London, started the 'Mechanics' Institution' in 1824. Brougham was one of the first trustees; and the institution, though exposed to a good deal of ridicule, managed to take root and become the parent of others. In 1827 was started the Society for the Diffusion of Useful Knowledge, of which Brougham was president, and the committee of which included James Mill. In the course of its twenty years' existence it published or sanctioned the publication by Charles Knight of a great mass of popular literature. The *Penny Magazine* (1832-1845) is said to have had two hundred thousand subscribers at the end of its first year of existence. Crude and superficial as were some of these enterprises, they clearly marked a very important change. Cobbett and the Radical orators found enormous audiences ready to listen to their doctrine. Churchmen and Dissenters, Tories and Radicals were finding it necessary both to educate and to disseminate their principles by writing; and as new social strata were becoming accessible to such influences, their opinions began to exercise in turn a more distinct reaction upon political and ecclesiastical affairs.

No party felt more confidence at the tendency of this new intellectual fermentation than the Utilitarians. They had a definite, coherent, logical creed. Every step which increased the freedom of discussion increased the influence of the truth. Their doctrines were the truth, if not the whole truth. Once allow them to get a fulcrum and they would move the world. Bit by bit their principles of legislation, of economy, of politics were being accepted in the most different quarters; and even the more intelligent of their opponents were applying them, though the application might be piecemeal and imperfect. It was in vain that an adversary protested that he was not bound by logic, and appealed to experience instead of theory. Let him justify his action upon what grounds he pleased, he was, in point of fact, introducing the leaven of true doctrine, and it might be trusted to work out the desirable results.

I must now deal more in detail with the Utilitarian theories. I will only observe in general terms that their triumph was not likely to be accepted without a struggle. Large classes regarded them with absolute abhorrence. Their success, if they did succeed, would mean the destruction of religious belief, of sound philosophy, of the great important ecclesiastical and political institutions, and probably general confiscation of property and the ruin of the foundations of society. And, meanwhile, in spite of the progress upon which I have dwelt, there were two problems, at least, of enormous importance, upon which it could scarcely be said that any progress had been made. The church, in the first place, was still where it had been. No change had been made in its constitution; it was still the typical example of corrupt patronage; and the object of the hatred of all thoroughgoing Radicals. And, in the second place, pauperism had grown to appalling dimensions during the war; and no effectual attempt had been made to deal with it. Behind pauperism there were great social questions, the discontent and misery of great masses of the labouring population. Whatever reforms might be made in other parts of the natural order, here were difficulties enough to task the wisdom of legislators and speculators upon legislative principles.

FOOTNOTES:

[32] *Life of Macaulay*, p. 114. (Popular Edition).

[33] Canning's *Political Correspondence*, i. 71-76.

[34] 12th December 1826.

[35] Bentham's *Works*, v. p. 370.

[36] Romilly's attempts to improve the criminal law began in 1808. For various notices of his efforts, see his *Life* (3 vols. 1860), especially vol. ii. 243-54, 309, 321, 331, 369, 371, 389-91. Romilly was deeply interested in Dumont's *Théorie des Peines Légales* (1811), which he read in ms. and tried to get reviewed in the *Quarterly* (ii. 258, 391; iii. 136). The remarks (ii. 2-3) on the 'stupid dread of innovation' and the savage spirit infused into Englishmen by the horrors of the French revolution are worth notice in this connection.

[37] Bentham's *Works*, x. p. 574.

[38] Brougham's *Speeches* (1838), ii. 287-486.

[39] An interesting summary of the progress of law reforms and of Bentham's share in them is given in Sir R. K. Wilson's *History of Modern English Law* (1875).

[40] Bentham's *Works*, x. 571.

[41] In Cambridge Pryme was the first professor in 1828, but had only the title without endowment. The professorship was only salaried in 1863.

[42] Ricardo's *Works* (1888), p. 407.

[43] Printed in Porter's *Progress of the Nation* and elsewhere.

[44] See sixth volume of *History of Prices* by Tooke and Newmarch, and privately printed *Minutes of Political Economy Club* (1882).

[45] *Speeches*, 3 vols. 8vo, 1831.

[46] *Ibid.* ii. 465-530.

[47] *Ibid.* ii. 477.

[48] Bentham's *Works*, ii. 459. We may remember how J. S. Mill in his boyhood was abashed because he could not explain to his father the force of the distinction.

[49] *Speeches*, ii. 246, 332.

[50] *Ibid.* i. 102-108 (Currency Pamphlet of 1810).

[51] *Ibid.* ii. 397.

[52] *Speeches*, iii. 257.

[53] Ricardo indeed made a reservation as to the necessity of counterbalancing by a moderate duty the special burthens upon agriculture.

[54] In the *History of Trades-Unionism* by Sidney and Beatrice Webb (1894), pp. 88-98. The history of Place's agitation is fully given in Mr. Graham Wallas's *Life*, chap. viii.

[55] Wallas's Francis *Place*, p. 217.

[56] First published in 1807-8.

[57] *Letter* iii.

[58] *Ibid.* vi.

[59] Sydney Smith put very ingeniously the advantages of what he called the 'lottery' system: of giving, that is, a few great prizes, instead of equalising the incomes of the clergy. Things look so different from opposite points of views.

[60] *Church of Englandism*, ii. 199.

[61] See especially his review of Southey's *Book of the Church*.

[62] Romilly's *Memoirs*, iii. 33.

[63] 57 George iii. caps. 60-67.

[64] Edition of 1828, p. 24.

[65] *Ibid.*

[66] A Mr. Gray proposed at a county meeting in 1816 that the cry of 'retrenchment and reform' should be raised in every corner of the island (Henry Jephson's *Platform*, p. 378). I do not know whether this was the first appearance of the formula.

[67] Hume had been introduced to Place by James Mill, who thought him worth 'nursing.' Place found him at first 'dull and selfish,' but 'nursed him' so well that by 1836 he had become the 'man of men,'—Wallas's *Francis Place*, p. 181, 182.

[68] Torrens's *Life of Graham*, i. 250-72, where his great speech of 14th May 1830 is given.

[69] 2 and 3 William iv. cap. 111 (passed 15 August 1832).

[70] 4 and 5 William iv. cap. 15.

[71] *The Platform, its Origin and Progress*, by Henry Jephson (1892), gives a very interesting historical account of the process.

[72] 57 George iii. cap. 19, and 60 George iii. cap. 6.

[73] See Jephson's *Platform*, pp. 167-70.

[74] See Jephson's *Platform*, i. 348, 455, 517.

[75] See *Ibid.* ii. 129-40 for some interesting passages as to this.

[76] *Official Correspondence* (1887), 308.

[77] Greville's *George IV. and William IV.*, iii. 155, 167-69, 171.

[78] Bentham's *Works*, x. 571.

[79] Romilly's *Memoirs*, ii. 67, 222.

CHAPTER III
POLITICAL THEORY

I. MILL ON GOVERNMENT

I now turn to the general political theory of which Mill was the authoritative exponent. The *Encyclopædia* article upon 'Government' (1820) gives the pith of their doctrine. It was, as Professor Bain [80] thinks, an 'impelling and a guiding force' in the movement which culminated in the Reform Bill. The younger Utilitarians regarded it, says J. S. Mill, as 'a masterpiece of political wisdom'; [81] while Macaulay [82] taunts them for holding it to be 'perfect and unanswerable.' This famous article is a terse and energetic summary of the doctrine implied in Bentham's *Works*, but there obscured under elaboration of minute details. It is rather singular, indeed, that so vigorous a manifesto of Utilitarian dogma should have been accepted by Macvey Napier—a sound Whig—for a publication which professed scientific impartiality. It has, however, in the highest degree, the merits of clearness and condensation desirable in a popular exposition. The reticence appropriate to the place excuses the omission of certain implicit conclusions. Mill has to give a complete theory of politics in thirty-two 8vo pages. He has scanty room for qualifying statement or historical illustration. He speaks as from the chair of a professor laying down the elementary principles of a demonstrated science. [83]

Mill starts from the sacred principle. The end of government, as the end of all conduct, must be the increase of human happiness. The province of government is limited by another consideration. It has to deal with one class of happiness, that is, with the pains and pleasures 'which men derive from one another.' By a 'law of nature' labour is requisite for procuring the means of happiness. Now, if 'nature' produced all that any man desired, there would be no need of government, for there would be no conflict of interest. But, as the material produced is finite, and can be appropriated by individuals, it becomes necessary to insure to every man his proper share. What, then, is a man's proper share? That which he himself produces; for, if you give to one man more than the produce of his labour, you must take away the produce of another man's labour. The greatest happiness, therefore, is produced by 'assuring to every man the greatest possible quantity of the produce of his own labour.' How can this be done? Will not the strongest take the share of the weakest? He can be prevented in one and apparently only in one way. Men must unite and delegate to a few the power necessary for protecting all. 'This is government.' [84]

The problem is now simple. Government is essentially an association of men for the protection of property. It is a delegation of the powers necessary for that purpose to the guardians, and 'all the difficult questions of government relate to the means' of preventing the guardians from themselves becoming plunderers.

How is this to be accomplished? The power of protection, says Mill, following the old theory, may be intrusted to the whole community, to a few, or to one; that is, we may have a democracy, an aristocracy, or a monarchy. A democracy, or direct government of all by all, is for the ordinary reasons pronounced impracticable. But the objections to the other systems are conclusive. The need of government, he has shown, depends upon 'the law of human nature' [85] that 'a man, if able, will take from others anything which they have and he desires.' The very principle which makes government necessary, therefore, will prompt a government to defeat its own proper end. Mill's doctrine is so far identical with the doctrine of Hobbes; men are naturally in a state of war, and government implies a tacit contract by which men confer upon a sovereign the power necessary for keeping the peace. But here, though admitting the force of Hobbes's argument, he diverges from its conclusion. If a democracy be impossible, and an aristocracy or monarchy necessarily oppressive, it might seem, he admits, as it actually seemed to Hobbes and to the French economists, that the fewer the oppressors the better, and that therefore an absolute monarchy is the best. Experience, he thinks, is 'on the surface' ambiguous. Eastern despots and Roman emperors have been the worst scourges to mankind; yet the Danes preferred a despot to an aristocracy, and are as 'well governed as any people in Europe.' In Greece, democracy, in spite of its defects, produced the most brilliant results. [86] Hence, he argues, we must go 'beyond the surface,' and 'penetrate to the springs within.' The result of the search is discouraging. The hope of glutting the rulers is illusory. There is no 'point of saturation' [87] with the objects of desire, either for king or aristocracy. It is a 'grand governing law of human nature' that we desire such power as will make 'the persons and properties of human beings subservient to our pleasures.' [88] This desire is indefinitely great. To the number of men whom we would force into subservience, and the degree in which we would make them subservient, we can assign no limits. Moreover, as pain is a more powerful instrument for securing obedience than pleasure, a man will desire to possess 'unlimited power of inflicting pain upon others.' Will he also desire, it may be asked, to make use of it? The 'chain of inference,' he replies, in this case is close and strong 'to a most unusual degree.' A man desires the actions of others to be in correspondence with his own wishes. 'Terror' will be the 'grand instrument.' [89] It thus follows that the very principle upon which government is founded leads, in the absence of checks, 'not only to that degree of plunder which leaves the members (of a community) ... the bare means of subsistence, but to that degree of cruelty which is necessary to keep in existence the most intense terror.' An English gentleman, he says, is a favourable specimen of civilisation, and yet West Indian slavery shows of what cruelty he could be guilty when unchecked. If equal cruelty has not been exhibited elsewhere, it is, he seems to think, because men were not 'the same as sheep in respect to their shepherd,' [90] and may therefore resist if driven too far. The difficulty upon this showing is to understand how any government, except the most brutal tyranny, ever has been, or ever can be, possible. What is the combining principle which can weld together such a mass of hostile and mutually repellent atoms? How they can even form the necessary compact is difficult to understand, and the view seems to clash with his own avowed purpose. It is Mill's aim, as it was Bentham's, to secure the greatest happiness of the greatest number; and yet he seems to set out by proving as a 'law of human nature' that nobody can desire the happiness of any one except himself. He quotes from Montesquieu the saying, which shows an 'acute sense of this important truth,' 'that every one who has power is led to abuse it.' [91] Rather it would seem, according to Mill, all power implies abuse in its very essence. The problem seems to be how to make universal cohesion out of universal repulsion.

Mill has his remedy for this deeply seated evil. He attacks, as Bentham had already done, the old-fashioned theory, according to which the British Constitution was an admirable mixture of the three 'simple forms.' Two of the powers, he argues, will always agree to 'swallow up the third.' [92] 'The monarchy and aristocracy have all possible motives for endeavouring to obtain unlimited power over the persons and property of the community,' though the democracy, as he also says, has every possible motive for preventing them. And in England, as he no doubt meant his readers to understand, the monarchy and aristocracy had to a great extent succeeded. Where, then, are we to look? To the 'grand discovery of modern times,' namely, the representative system. If this does not solve all difficulties we shall be forced to the conclusion that good government is impossible. Fortunately, however, the representative system may be made perfectly effective. This follows easily. It would, as he has said, [93] be a 'contradiction in terms' to suppose that the community at large can 'have an interest opposite to its interest,' In the Bentham formula, it can have 'no sinister interest.' It cannot desire its own misery. Though the community cannot act as a whole, it can act through representatives. It is necessary to intrust power to a governing body; but that body can be prevented by adequate checks from misusing its powers. Indeed, the common theory of the British Constitution was precisely that the House of Commons was 'the checking body.' [94] The whole problem is to secure a body which shall effectively discharge the function thus attributed in theory to the House of Commons. That will be done when the body is chosen in such a way that its interests are necessarily coincident with those of the community at large. Hence there is of course no difficulty in deducing the actual demands of reformers. Without defining precise limits, he shows that representatives must be elected for brief periods, and that the right to a vote must at least be wide enough to prevent the electoral body from forming a class with 'sinister interests.' He makes some remarkable qualifications, with the view apparently of not startling his readers too much by absolute and impracticable claims. He thinks that the necessary identity of interest would still be secured if classes were unrepresented whose interests are 'indisputably included in those of others.' Children's interests are involved in those of their parents, and the interests of 'almost all women' in those of their fathers or husbands. [95] Again, all men under forty might be omitted without mischief, for 'the great majority of old men have sons whose interests they regard as an essential part of their own. This is a law of human nature.' [96] There would, he observes, be no danger that men above forty would try to reduce the 'rest of the community to the state of abject slaves.' Mill, as his son tells us, [97] disowned any intention of positively advocating these exclusions. He only meant to say that they were not condemned by his general principle. The doctrine, however, about women, even as thus understood, scandalised his younger followers.

Mill proceeds to argue at some length that a favourite scheme of some moderate reformers, for the representation of classes, could only lead to 'a motley aristocracy,' and then answers two objections. The first is that his scheme would lead to the abolition of the monarchy and the House of Lords. The reply is simple and significant. It would only lead to that result if a monarchy or a House of Lords were favourable to bad government. He does not inquire whether they are so in fact. The second objection is that the people do not understand their own interest, and to this his answer is more remarkable. If the doctrine be true, he says, we are in 'deplorable' position: we have to choose between evils which will be designedly produced by those who have both the power to oppress and an interest in oppression; and the evils which will be accidentally produced by men who would act well if they recognised their own interests. [98] Now the first evil is in any case the worst, for it supposes an 'invariable' evil; while in the other case, men may at least act well by accident. A governing class, that is with interests separate from those of the government, *must* be bad. If the interests be identical, the government *may* be bad. It will be bad if ignorant, but ignorance is curable. Here he appeals for once to a historical case. The priesthood at the Reformation argued on behalf of their own power from the danger that the people would make a bad use of the Bible. The Bible should therefore be kept for the sacred caste. They had, Mill thinks, a stronger case in appearance than the Tories, and yet the effect of allowing the people to judge for themselves in religious matters has been productive of good effects 'to a degree which has totally altered the condition of human nature.' [99] Why should not the people be trusted to judge for themselves in politics? This implies a doctrine which had great influence with the Utilitarians. In the remarkable essay upon 'Education,' which is contained in the volume of reprints, Mill discusses the doctrine of Helvétius that all the differences between men are due to education. Without pronouncing positively upon the differences between individuals, Mill observes that, at any rate, the enormous difference between classes of men is wholly due to education. [100] He takes education, it must be observed, in the widest possible sense, as meaning what would now be called the whole action of the 'environment' upon the individual. This includes, as he shows at length, domestic education, all the vast influence exercised upon a child in his family, 'technical education,' by which he means the ordinary school teaching, 'social education,' that is the influences which we imbibe from the current opinions of our neighbours, and finally, 'political education,' which he calls the 'keystone of the arch.' The means, he argues, by which the 'grand objects of desire may be attained, depend almost wholly upon the political machine.' [101] If that 'machine' be so constituted as to make the grand objects of desire the 'natural prizes of just and virtuous conduct, of high services to mankind and of the generous and amiable sentiments from which great endeavours in the service of mankind naturally proceed, it is natural to see diffused among mankind a generous ardour in the acquisition of those admirable qualities which prepare a man for admirable action, great intelligence, perfect self-command, and over-ruling benevolence.' The contrary will be the case where the political machine prompts to the flattery of a small ruling body.

This characteristic passage betrays an enthusiasm which really burned under Mill's stern outside. He confines himself habitually to the forms of severe logic, and scorns anything like an appeal to sentiment. The trammels of his scientific manner impede his utterance a little, even when he is speaking with unwonted fervour. Yet the prosaic Utilitarian who has been laying down as a universal law that the strong will always plunder the weak, and that all rulers will reduce their subjects to abject slavery, is absolutely convinced, it seems, of the possibility of somehow transmuting selfishness into public spirit, justice, generosity, and devotion to truth. Equally characteristic is the faith in the 'political machine.' Mill speaks as if somebody had 'discovered' the representative system as Watt (more or less) discovered the steam-engine; that to 'discover' the system is the same thing as to set it to work; and that, once at work, it will be omnipotent. He is not less certain that a good constitution will make men virtuous, than was Bentham that he could grind rogues honest by the Panopticon. The indefinite modifiability of character was the ground upon which the Utilitarians based their hopes of progress; and it was connected in their minds with the doctrine of which his essay upon education is a continuous application. The theory of 'association of ideas' appeared to him to be of the utmost importance in education and in politics, because it implied almost unlimited possibilities of moulding human beings to fit them for a new order. In politics this implied, as J. S. Mill says, [102] 'unbounded confidence' in the influence of 'reason.' Teach the people and let them vote freely, and everything would follow.

This gives Mill's answer to one obvious objection. The Conservative who answered him by dwelling upon the ignorance of the lower classes was in some respects preaching to a convert. Nobody was more convinced than Mill of the depths of popular ignorance or, indeed, of the stupidity of mankind in general. The labourers who cheered Orator Hunt at Peterloo were dull enough; but so were the peers who cheered Eldon in the House of Lords; and the labourers at least desired general prosperity, while the peers were content if their own rents were kept up. With general education, however, even the lower orders of the people would be fit for power, especially when we take into account one other remarkable conclusion. The 'wise and good,' he says, 'in any class of men do, for all general purposes, govern the rest.' [103] Now, the class in which wisdom and virtue are commonest is not the aristocracy, but the middle rank. Another truth follows 'from the principles of human nature in general.' That is the rather surprising truth that the lower orders take their opinions from the middle class; apply to the middle class for help in sickness and old age; hold up the same class as a model to be imitated by their children, and 'account it an honour' to adopt its opinions. Consequently, however far the franchise were extended, it is this class which has produced the most distinguished ornaments of art, science, and even of legislation, which will ultimately decide upon political questions. 'The great majority of the people,' is his concluding sentence, 'never cease to be guided by that rank; and we may with some confidence challenge the adversaries of the people to produce a single instance to the contrary in the history of the world.'

This article upon 'Government' gives the very essence of Utilitarian politics. I am afraid that it also suggests that the political theory was chiefly remarkable for a simple-minded audacity. Good political treatises are rare. They are apt to be pamphlets in disguise, using 'general principles' for showy perorations, or to be a string of platitudes with no definite application to facts. They are fit only for the platform, or only for the professor's lecture-room. Mill's treatise, according to his most famous antagonist, was a mere bundle of pretentious sophistry.

Macaulay came forth like a Whig David to slay the Utilitarian Goliath. The *Encyclopædia* articles, finished in 1824, were already in 1825, [104] as Mill says, text-books of the young men at the Cambridge Union. Macaulay, who won his Trinity fellowship in 1824, had there argued the questions with his friend Charles Austin, one of Bentham's neophytes. In the next year Macaulay made his first appearance as an Edinburgh Reviewer; and in 1829 he took the field against Mill. In the January number he attacked the essay upon 'Government'; and in two articles in the succeeding numbers of the *Review* replied to a defence made by some Utilitarian in the *Westminster*. Mill himself made no direct reply; and Macaulay showed his gratitude for Mill's generosity in regard to the Indian appointment by declining to republish the articles. [105] He confessed to have treated his opponent with a want of proper respect, though he retracted none of his criticisms. The offence had its excuses. Macaulay was a man under thirty, in the full flush of early success; nor was Mill's own treatment of antagonists conciliatory. The dogmatic arrogance of the Utilitarians was not unnaturally met by an equally arrogant countercheck. Macaulay ridicules the Utilitarians for their claim to be the defenders of the true political faith. He is afraid not of them but of the 'discredit of their alliance'; he wishes to draw a broad line between judicious reformers and a 'sect which having derived all its influence from the countenance which they imprudently bestowed upon it, hates them with the deadly hatred of ingratitude.' No party, he says, was ever so unpopular. It had already disgusted people with political economy; and would disgust them with parliamentary reform, if it could associate itself in public opinion with the cause [106] . This was indeed to turn the tables. The half-hearted disciple was insulting the thoroughbred teacher who had borne the heat and burthen of the day, and from whom he had learned his own doctrine. Upon this and other impertinences—the assertion, for example, that Utilitarians were as incapable of understanding an argument as any 'true blue baronet after the third bottle at a Pitt Club'—it is needless to dwell. They illustrate, however, the strong resentment with which the Utilitarians were regarded by the classes from whom the Whigs drew their most cultivated supporters. Macaulay's line of argument will show what was the real conflict of theory.

His view is, in fact, a long amplification of the charge that Mill was adopting a purely *a priori* method. Mill's style is as dry as Euclid, and his arguments are presented with an affectation of logical precision. Mill has inherited the 'spirit and style of the Schoolmen. He is an Aristotelian of the fifteenth century.' He writes about government as though he was unaware that any actual governments had ever existed. He deduces his science from a single assumption of certain 'propensities of human nature.' [107] After dealing with Mill's arguments, Macaulay winds up with one of his characteristic purple patches about the method of induction. He invokes the authority of Bacon—a great name with which in those days writers conjured without a very precise consideration of its true significance. By Bacon's method we are to construct in time the 'noble science of politics,' which is equally removed from the barren theories of Utilitarian sophists and the petty craft of intriguing jobbers. The Utilitarians are schoolmen, while the Whigs are the true followers of Bacon and scientific induction. J. S. Mill admitted within certain limits the relevancy of this criticism, and was led by the reflections which it started to a theory of his own. Meanwhile, he observes that his father ought to have justified himself by declaring that the book was not a 'scientific treatise on politics,' but an 'argument for parliamentary reform.' [108] It is not quite easy to see how James Mill could have made such a 'justification' and distinguished it from a recantation.

If Mill really meant what Macaulay took him to mean, it would be superfluous to argue the question gravely. The reasoning is only fit, like the reasoning of all Macaulay's antagonists, for the proverbial schoolboy. Mill, according to Macaulay, proposes to discover what governments are good; and, finding that experience gives no clear answer, throws experience aside and appeals to absolute laws of human nature. One such 'law' asserts that the strong will plunder the weak. Therefore all governments except the representative must be oppressive, and rule by sheer terror. Mill's very reason for relying upon this argument is precisely that the facts contradict it. Some despotisms work well, and some democracies ill; therefore we must prove by logic that all despotisms are bad, and all democracies good. Is this really Mill's case?

An answer given by Mill's champion, to which Macaulay replies in his last article, suggests some explanation of Mill's position. Macaulay had paid no attention to one highly important phrase. The terrible consequences which Mill deduces from the selfishness of rulers will follow, he says, 'if nothing checks.' [109] Supplying this qualification, as implied throughout, we may give a better meaning to Mill's argument. A simple observation of experience is insufficient. The phenomena are too complex; governments of the most varying kinds have shown the same faults; and governments of the same kind have shown them in the most various degrees. Therefore the method which Macaulay suggests is inapplicable. We should reason about government, says Macaulay, [110] as Bacon told us to reason about heat. Find all the circumstances in which hot bodies agree, and you will determine the principle of heat. Find all the circumstances in which good governments agree, and you will find the principles of good government. Certainly; but the process, as Macaulay admits, would be a long one. Rather, it would be endless. What 'circumstances' can be the same in all good governments in all times and places? Mill held in substance, that we could lay down certain broad principles about human nature, the existence of which is of course known from 'experience', and by showing how they would work, if restrained by no distinct checks, obtain certain useful conclusions. Mill indicates this line of reply in his own attack upon Mackintosh. [111] There he explains that what he really meant was to set forth a principle recognised by Berkeley, Hume, Blackstone, and, especially, in Plato's *Republic*. Plato's treatise is a development of the principle that 'identity of interests affords the only security for good government.' Without such identity of interest, said Plato, the guardians of the flock become wolves. Hume [112] had given a pithy expression of the same view in the maxim 'established,' as he says, 'by political writers,' that in framing the 'checks and controls of the constitution, every man ought to be supposed a knave and to have no other end in his actions than private interest.' Mill points this by referring to the 'organs of aristocratical opinion' for the last fifty years. The incessant appeal has been for 'confidence in public men,' and confidence is another name for scope for misrule. [113] This, he explains, was what he meant by the statement (which Mackintosh considered to have been exploded by Macaulay) that every man pursued his own interest. [114] It referred to the class legislation of the great aristocratic ring: kings, nobles, church, law, and army. Utilitarianism, in its political relations, was one continuous warfare against these sinister 'interests,' The master-evil of the contemporary political state undoubtedly implied a want of responsibility. A political trust was habitually confounded with private property. Moreover, whatever else may be essential to good government, one essential is a strong sense of responsibility in the governors. That is a very sound principle, though not an axiom from which all political science can be deduced. If the essay on 'Government' was really meant as a kind of political Euclid—as a deduction of the best system of government from this single principle of responsibility—it was as grotesque as Macaulay asserted. Mill might perhaps have met the criticism by lowering his claims as his son suggests. He certainly managed to express his argument in such terms that it has an uncomfortable appearance of being intended for a scientific exposition.

This deserves notice because the position is characteristic of the Utilitarians' method. Their appeals to experience always end by absolute assertions. We shall find the same difficulty in their economic inquiries. When accused, for example, of laying down absolute principles in such cases, they reply that they are only speaking of 'tendencies,' and recognise the existence of 'checks.' They treat of what would be, if certain forces acted without limit, as a necessary step towards discovering what is when the limits exist. They appear to their opponents to forget the limits in their practical conclusions. This political argument is an instance of the same method. The genesis of his theory is plain. Mill's 'government,' like Bentham's, is simply the conception of legal 'sovereignty' transferred to the sphere of politics. Mill's exposition is only distinguished from his master's by the clearness with which he brings out the underlying assumptions. The legal sovereign is omnipotent, for what he declares to be the law is therefore the law. The law is his commands enforced by 'sanctions,' and therefore by organised force. The motives for obedience are the fear of the gallows on one side, and, on the other, the desire of protection for life and property. Law, again, is the ultimate social bond, and can be made at will by the sovereign. He thus becomes so omnipotent that it is virtually assumed that he can even create himself. Not only can the sovereign, once constituted, give commands enforced by coercive sanctions upon any kind of conduct, but he can determine his own constitution. He can at once, for example, create a representative system in practice, when it has been discovered in theory, and can by judicious regulations so distribute 'self-interest' as to produce philanthropy and public spirit. Macaulay's answer really makes a different assumption. He accepts the purely 'empirical' or 'rule of thumb' position. It is idle, he says, to ask what would happen if there were no 'checks.' It is like leaving out the effect of friction in a problem of mechanics. The logic may be correct, but the conclusions are false in practice. [115] Now this 'friction' was precisely the favourite expedient of the Utilitarians in political economy. To reason about facts, they say, you must analyse, and therefore provisionally disregard the 'checks,' which must be afterwards introduced in practical applications. Macaulay is really bidding us take 'experience' in the lump, and refrains from the only treatment which can lead to a scientific result. His argument, in fact, agrees with that of his famous essay on Bacon, where we learn that philosophy applied to moral questions is all nonsense, and that science is simply crude common-sense. He is really saying that all political reasoning is impossible, and that we must trust to unreasoned observation. Macaulay, indeed, has good grounds of criticism.

He shows very forcibly the absurdity of transferring the legal to the political sovereignty. Parliament might, as he says, make a law that every gentleman with £2000 a year might flog a pauper with a cat-of-nine-tails whenever he pleased. But, as the first exercise of such a power would be the 'last day of the English aristocracy,' their power is strictly limited in fact. [116] That gives very clearly the difference between legal and political sovereignty. What parliament makes law is law, but is not therefore enforceable. We have to go behind the commands and sanctions before we understand what is the actual power of government. It is very far from omnipotent. Macaulay, seeing this, proceeds to throw aside Mill's argument against the possibility of a permanent division of power. The *de facto* limitation of the sovereign's power justifies the old theory about 'mixed forms of government.' 'Mixed governments' are not impossible, for they are real. All governments are, in fact, 'mixed.' Louis xiv. could not cut off the head of any one whom he happened to dislike. An oriental despot is strictly bound by the religious prejudices of his subjects. If 'sovereignty' means such power it is a chimera in practice, or only realised approximately when, as in the case of negro slavery, a class is actually ruled by force in the hands of a really external power. And yet the attack upon 'mixed governments,' which Bentham had expounded in the *Fragment*, has a real force which Macaulay seems to overlook. Mill's argument against a possible 'balance' of power was, as Macaulay asserted, equally applicable to the case of independent sovereigns; yet France might be stronger at Calais and England at Dover. [117] Mill might have replied that a state is a state precisely because, and in so far as, there is an agreement to recognise a common authority or sovereign. Government does not imply a 'mixture,' but a fusion of power. There is a unity, though not the abstract unity of the Utilitarian sovereign. The weakness of the Utilitarians is to speak as though the sovereign, being external to each individual, could therefore be regarded as external to the whole society. He rules as a strong nation may rule a weak dependency. When the sovereign becomes also the society, the power is regarded as equally absolute, though now applied to the desirable end of maximising happiness. The whole argument ignores the simple consideration that the sovereign is himself in all cases the product of the society over which he rules, and his whole action, even in the most despotic governments, determined throughout by organic instincts, explaining and not ultimately explicable by coercion. Macaulay's doctrine partially recognises this by falling back upon the Whig theory of checks and balances, and the mixture of three mysterious entities, monarchy, aristocracy, and democracy. But, as Bentham had sufficiently shown in the *Fragment*, the theory becomes hopelessly unreal when we try to translate it into facts. There are not three separate forces, conflicting like three independent forces, but a complex set of social institutions bound together into a whole. It is impossible really to regard government as a permanent balance of antagonistic forces, confronting each other like the three duellists in Sheridan's *Critic*. The practical result of that theory is to substitute for the 'greatest happiness' principle the vague criterion of the preservation of an equilibrium between indefinable forces; and to make the ultimate end of government the maintenance as long as possible of a balance resting on no ulterior principle, but undoubtedly pleasant for the comfortable classes. Nothing is left but the rough guesswork, which, if a fine name be wanted, may be called Baconian induction. The 'matchless constitution,' as Bentham calls it, represents a convenient compromise, and the tendency is to attach exaggerated importance to its ostensible terms. When Macaulay asserted against Mill [118] that it was impossible to say which element—monarchy, aristocracy, or democracy—had gained strength in England in the last century, he is obviously looking at the formulæ and not at the social body behind.

This leads to considerations really more important than the argumentation about *a priori* and inductive methods. Mill in practice knew very well the qualifications necessary before his principles applied. He showed it in his Indian evidence; and Place could have told him, had it required telling, that the actual political machinery worked by very strange and tortuous methods. Yet he was content to override such considerations when he is expounding his theory, and laid himself open to Macaulay's broad common-sense retort. The nation at large cannot, he says, have a 'sinister interest.' It must desire legislation which is beneficial to the whole. This is to make the vast assumption that every individual will desire what is good for all, and will be a sufficient judge of what is good. But is it clear that a majority will even desire what is good for the whole? May they not wish to sacrifice both other classes and coming generations to their own instantaneous advantages? Is it plain that even enlightenment of mind would induce a poor man to see his own advantage in the policy which would in the long run be best for the whole society? You are bound, said Macaulay, to show that the poor man will not believe that he personally would benefit by direct plunder of the rich; and indeed that he would not be right in so believing. The nation, no doubt, would suffer, but in the immediate period which alone is contemplated by a selfish pauper, the mass of the poor might get more pleasure out of confiscation. Will they not, on your own principles, proceed to confiscation? Shall we not have such a catastrophe as the reign of terror?

The Westminster Reviewer retorted by saying that Macaulay prophesied a reign of terror as a necessary consequence of an extended franchise. Macaulay, skilfully enough, protested against this interpretation. 'We say again and again,' he declares, 'that we are on the defensive. We do not think it necessary to prove that a quack medicine is poison. Let the vendor prove it to be sanative. We do not pretend to show that universal suffrage is an evil. Let its advocates show it to be a good.' [119] Mill rests his whole case upon the selfishness of mankind. Will not the selfishness lead the actual majority at a given moment to plunder the rich and to disregard the interests of their own successors?

Macaulay's declaration that he was only 'upon the defensive' might be justifiable in an advocate. His real thought may be inferred from a speech on the charter made in 1842. The chartists' petition of that year had asked for universal suffrage. Universal suffrage, he replies, would be incompatible with the 'institution of property.' [120] If the chartists acted upon their avowed principles, they would enforce 'one vast spoliation.' Macaulay could not say, of course, what would actually result, but his 'guess' was that we should see 'something more horrible than can be imagined—something like the siege of Jerusalem on a far larger scale.' The very best event he could anticipate—'and what must the state of things be, if an Englishman and a Whig calls such an event the very best?'—would be a military despotism, giving a 'sort of protection to a miserable wreck of all that immense glory and prosperity.' [121] So in the criticism of Mill he had suggested that if his opponent's principles were correct, and his scheme adopted, 'literature, science, commerce, manufactures' would be swept away, and that a 'few half-naked fishermen would divide with the owls and foxes the ruins of the greatest of European cities.' [122]

Carefully as Macaulay guards himself in his articles upon Mill, the speech shows sufficiently what was his 'guess'; that is, his real expectation. This gives the vital difference. What Macaulay professes to deduce from Mill's principles he really holds himself, and he holds it because he argues, as indeed everybody has to argue, pretty much on Mill's method. He does not really remain in the purely sceptical position which would correspond to his version of 'Baconian induction.' He argues, just as Mill would have argued, from general rules about human nature. Selfish and ignorant people will, he thinks, be naturally inclined to plunder; therefore, if they have power, they will plunder. So Mill had argued that a selfish class would rule for its own sinister interests and therefore not for the happiness of the greatest number. The argument is the same, and it is the only line of argument which is possible till, if that should ever happen, a genuine science of politics shall have been constituted. The only question is whether it shall take the pomp of *a priori* speculation or conceal itself under a show of 'Baconian induction.'

On one point they agree. Both Mill and Macaulay profess unbounded confidence in the virtue and wisdom of the middle, that is, of their own class. Macaulay hopes for a reform bill which will make the votes of the House of Commons 'the express image of the opinion of the middle orders of Britain.' [123] Mill holds that the middle class will retain this moral authority, however widely the franchise be extended; while Macaulay fears that they will be swamped by its extension to the masses. The reform bill which they joined in supporting was regarded by the Radicals as a payment on account; while the Whig hoped that it would be a full and final discharge. The Radical held that no barriers against democracy were needed; he took for granted that a democracy would find its natural leaders in the educated and intelligent. The Whig, to whom such confidence appeared to be altogether misplaced, had to find some justification for the 'checks' and 'balances' which he thought essential.

II. WHIGGISM

I have spoken of Macaulay's articles because they represent the most pointed conflict between the Utilitarian and the Whig. Macaulay belongs properly to the next generation, but he appeared as the mouthpiece of the earlier group of writers who in Mill's time delivered through the *Edinburgh Review* the true oracles of the Whig faith. Upon that ground Mill had assailed them in his article. Their creed, he said, was a 'see-saw.' The Whigs were aristocrats as much as the Tories. They were simply the 'outs' who hoped to be the 'ins.' They trimmed their sails to catch public opinion, but were careful not to drift into the true popular currents. They had no desire to limit the power which they hoped one day to possess. They would attack abuses—the slave-trade or the penal laws—to gain credit for liberality and enlightenment, when the abuses were such as could be removed without injuring the power of the aristocracy. They could use 'vague generalities' about liberty and so forth, but only to evade definite applications. When any measure was proposed which really threatened the power of the privileged classes, they could bring out a contradictory set of fine phrases about Jacobinism and democracy. Their whole argument was a shuffle and they themselves mere selfish trimmers. [124] To this Jeffrey replied (in December 1826) by accepting the position. [125] He pleaded guilty to a love of 'trimming,' which meant a love of the British Constitution. The constitution was a compromise—a balance of opposing forces—and the only question could be whether they were properly balanced. The answer was fair enough. Mill was imputing motives too easily, and assuming that the Reviewers saw the abuses in the same light as he did, and were truckling to public robbers in hopes of sharing the plunder. He was breaking a butterfly upon a wheel. The Edinburgh Reviewers were not missionaries of a creed. They were a set of brilliant young men, to whom the *Review* was at first a mere pastime, occupying such leisure as was allowed by their professional pursuits. They were indeed men of liberal sympathies, intelligent and independent enough to hold by a party which was out of power. They had read Hume and Voltaire and Rousseau; they had sat at the feet of Dugald Stewart; and were in sympathy with intellectual liberalism. But they were men who meant to become judges, members of parliament, or even bishops. Nothing in their social atmosphere had stimulated the deep resentment against social injustice which makes the fanatic or the enthusiast. We may take as their interpreter the Whig philosopher James Mackintosh (1765-1832), a man of wide reading, both in history and philosophy, an eloquent orator, and a very able writer. Mackintosh, said Coleridge, [126] is the 'king of the men of talent'; by which was intimated that, as a man of talent, he was not, like some people, a man of genius. Mackintosh, that is, was a man to accept plausible formulæ and to make them more plausible; not a man to pierce to the heart of things, or reveal fruitful germs of thought. His intellect was judicial; given to compromises, affecting a judicious *via media*, and endeavouring to reconcile antagonistic tendencies. Thoroughgoing or one-sided thinkers, and Mill in particular, regarded him with excessive antipathy as a typical representative of the opposite intellectual tendencies. Mackintosh's political attitude is instructive. At the outbreak of the French revolution he was a struggling young Scot, seeking his fortune in London, just turning from medicine to the bar, and supporting himself partly by journalism. He became secretary to the Society of the 'Friends of the People,' the Whig rival of the revolutionary clubs, and in April 1791 sprang into fame by his *Vindiciæ Gallicæ*. The Whigs had not yet lost the fervour with which they had welcomed the downfall of the Bastille. Burke's *Reflections*, the work of a great thinker in a state of irritation bordering upon frenzy, had sounded the note of alarm. The revolution, as Burke maintained, was in fact the avatar of a diabolic power. It meant an attack upon the very organic principles of society. It therefore implied a complete breach of historical continuity, and a war against the reverence for 'prescription' and tradition which is essential to all healthy development. To his extreme opponents the same theory afforded the justification of the revolution. It meant that every institution was to be thrown into the crucible, and a new world to arise governed only by reason. The view very ably defended by Mackintosh was opposed to both. He looks upon the French revolution as a more complete application of the principles of Locke and the English Whigs of 1688. The revolutionists are, as he urges, [127] applying the principles which had been worked out by the 'philosophers of Europe' during the preceding century. They were not, as Burke urged, rejecting experience for theory. The relation between their doctrine and politics is analogous to the relation between geometry and mechanics. [128] We are now in the position of a people who should be familiar with Newton, but in shipbuilding be still on a level with the Esquimaux. The 'rights of man' appear to him to mean, not, as Burke and Bentham once agreed, a set of 'anarchical fallacies,' but a set of fundamental moral principles; and the declaration of them a most wise and 'auspicious' commencement of the 'regenerating labours' of the new legislators. The French revolution represented what Somers would now approve if he had our advantages. [129] A thoroughgoing change had become necessary in France. The church, army, and law were now 'incorrigible.' [130] Burke had seen, in the confiscation of church property, an attempt to abolish Christianity. To Mackintosh it seemed to be a reform justifiable in principle, which, though too roughly carried out, would reduce 'a servile and imperious priesthood to humble utility.' [131] A poor priesthood, indeed, might incline to popular superstition. We could console ourselves by reflecting that the power of the church, as a corporation, was broken, and that toleration and philosophy would restrain fanaticism. [132] The assignats were still 'almost at par.' [133] The sale of the national property would nearly extinguish the debt. France had 'renounced for ever the idea of conquest,' [134] and had no temptations to war, except her colonies. Their commercial inutility and political mischievousness had been so 'unanimously demonstrated,' that the French empire must soon be delivered from 'this cumbrous and destructive appendage.' An armed people, moreover, could never be used like a mercenary army to suppress liberty. There was no danger of military despotism, and France would hereafter seek for a pure glory by cultivating the arts of peace and extending the happiness of mankind. [135]

No wonder that Mackintosh, with these views, thought that the history of the fall of the Bastille would 'kindle in unborn millions the holy enthusiasm of freedom'; [136] or that, in the early disorders, he saw temporary aberrations of mobs, destined to be speedily suppressed by the true leaders of the revolution. Mackintosh saw, I take it, about as far as most philosophers, that is, about as far as people who are not philosophers. He observes much that Burke ought to have remembered, and keeps fairly to the philosophical principle which he announces of attributing the revolution to general causes, and not to the schemes of individuals. [137] When assignats became waste paper, when the guillotine got to work, when the religion of reason was being set up against Christianity, when the French were conquering Europe, when a military despotism was arising, when, in short, it became quite clear that the French revolution meant something very different from a philosophical application of the principles of Locke and Adam Smith, Mackintosh began to see that Burke had not so far missed the mark. Burke, before dying, received his penitent opponent at Beaconsfield; and in 1800 Mackintosh took the opportunity of publicly declaring that he 'abhorred, abjured, and for ever renounced the French revolution, with its sanguinary history, its abominable principles, and its ever execrable leaders.' He hoped to 'wipe off the disgrace of having been once betrayed into that abominable conspiracy against God and man.' [138] In his famous defence of Peltier (1803), he denounced the revolution in a passage which might have been adopted from Burke's *Letters on a Regicide Peace*. [139]

In a remarkable letter to Windham [140] of 1806, Mackintosh gives his estimate of Burke, and takes some credit to himself for having discovered, even in the time of his youthful errors, the consistency of Burke's principles, as founded upon an abhorrence of 'abstract politics.' [141] Politics, he now thought, must be made scientific by recognising with Burke the supreme importance of prescription and historic continuity, and by admitting that the philosophers had not yet constructed a science bearing to practical politics the same relation as geometry to mechanics. He applied his theory to the question of parliamentary reform in the *Edinburgh Review*. [142] Here he accepts the doctrine, criticised by James Mill, that a proper representative system must be judged, not, as Mill maintained, solely by the identity of its interest with that of the community at large, but by its fitness to give power to different classes. It follows that the landowners, the professional classes, and the populace should all be represented. And he discovers that the variety of the English system was calculated to secure this end. Though it was only in a few constituencies that the poorest class had a voice, their vote in such places represented the same class elsewhere. It was as well that there should be some extreme Radicals to speak for the poorest. But he thinks that any uniform suffrage would be bad, and that universal suffrage would be the most mischievous of all systems. [143] That would mean the swamping of one class by all—a tyranny more oppressive, perhaps, than any other tyranny. If one class alone were to be represented, it should be the favourite middle class, which has the 'largest share of sense and virtue,' and is most connected in interest with other classes. [144] A legitimate aim of the legislator is, therefore, to prevent an excess of democracy. With Mackintosh it seems essential not simply to suppress 'sinister interests,' but to save both the aristocracy and the middle class from being crushed by the lower classes. The opposition is vital; and it is plain that the argument for the aristocracy, that is, for a system developed from all manner of historical accidents and not evolved out of any simple logical principles, must be defended upon empirical grounds.

Mackintosh was in India during the early period of the *Edinburgh Review*. Jeffrey, as editor for its first quarter of a century, may be taken more fully to represent its spirit. Jeffrey's trenchant, if not swaggering style, covered a very timid, sensitive, and, in some respects, a very conservative temperament. His objection to the 'Lake Poets' was the objection of the classical to the romantic school. Jeffrey's brightness of intellect may justify Carlyle's comparison of him to Voltaire,—only a Voltaire qualified by dislike to men who were 'dreadfully in earnest.' Jeffrey was a philosophical sceptic; he interpreted Dugald Stewart as meaning that metaphysics, being all nonsense, we must make shift with common-sense; and he wrote a dissertation upon taste, to prove that there are no rules about taste whatever. He was too genuine a sceptic to sacrifice peace to the hopeless search for truth. One of the most striking passages in his *Essays* [145] is an attack upon 'perfectibility.' He utterly disbelieves that progress in knowledge will improve morals or diminish war, or cure any of the evils that flesh is heir to. Such a man is not of the material of which enthusiastic reformers are made. Throughout the war he was more governed by his fear than by his zeal. He was in constant dread of failure abroad and ruin at home. The *Review* provoked the Tories, and induced them to start its rival, not by advocacy of political principles, but by its despairing view of the war. [146] He was still desiring at that time (1808) to avoid 'party politics' in the narrower sense.

The political view corresponding to this is given in the articles, some of which (though the authorship was not yet avowed) were assailed by Mill in the *Westminster*. In an early article [147] he defends the French philosophers against the imputation of responsibility for the reign of terror. Their excellent and humane doctrines had been misapplied by the 'exasperation' and precipitation of inexperienced voters. His most characteristic article is one published in January 1810. The failure of the Walcheren expedition had confirmed his disbelief in our military leaders; the rise of English Radicalism, led by Burdett in the House of Commons, and Cobbett in the press, the widely spread distress and the severity of oppressive measures, roused his keenest alarm. [148] We are, he declared, between two violent and pernicious factions—the courtiers of arbitrary power and the democrats. If the Whig leaders did not first conciliate and then restrain the people, the struggle of the extreme parties would soon sweep away the constitution, the monarchy, and the Whig aristocracy by which that monarchy 'is controlled, confirmed, and exalted above all other forms of polity.' Democracy, it was plain, was increasing with dangerous rapidity. A third of every man's income was being taken by taxes, and after twenty years' boastful hostility we were left without a single ally. Considering all this, it seems as though 'the wholesome days of England were numbered,' and we are on the 'verge of the most dreadful of all calamities'—a civil war.

Jeffrey has learned from Hume that all government is ultimately founded upon opinion. The great thing is to make the action of public opinion regular and constituted. The whole machinery of the constitution, he says, is for the express purpose of 'preventing the kingly power from dashing itself to pieces against the more radical power of the people.' [149] The merit of a representative body is not to be tested simply by the goodness of its legislation, but by its diminishing the intensity of the struggle for the supreme power. Jeffrey in fact is above all preoccupied with the danger of revolution. The popular will is, in fact, supreme; repression may force it into explosion; but by judicious management it may be tamed and tempered. Then we need above all things that it should, as he says in his reply to Mill (December 1826), give their 'natural and wholesome influence to wealth and rank.' The stability of the English Constitution depends, as he said in 1810, upon the monarchy and aristocracy, and their stability on their being the natural growth of ages and having 'struck their roots deep into every stratum of the political soil.'

The Whigs represent the view implied in Macaulay's attack upon Mill—the view of cultivated men of sense, with their eyes open to many difficulties overlooked by zealots, but far too sceptical and despondent to rouse any enthusiasm or accept any dogmas absolutely. By the time of the Reform Bill the danger was obviously on the side of dogged obstructionism, and then the 'middle party,' as Jeffrey calls it, inclined towards the Radical side and begged them to join its ranks and abandon the attempt to realise extreme views. They could also take credit as moderate men do for having all along been in the right. But to both extremes, as Jeffrey pathetically complains, they appeared to be mere trimmers. [150]

The Utilitarian held the Whig to be a 'trimmer'; the Whig thought the Utilitarian a fanatic; they agreed in holding that the Tory was simply stupid. And yet, when we look at the Tory creed, we shall find that both Whig and Utilitarian overlooked some very vital problems. The Tories of course represent the advocates of strong government; and, as their opponents held, had no theories—only prejudices. The first article of the creed of an Eldon or a Sidmouth was, 'I believe in George iii.';—not a doctrine capable of philosophical justification. Such Toryism meant the content of the rich and powerful with the system by which their power and wealth were guaranteed. Their instincts had been sharpened by the French revolution; and they saw in any change the removal of one of the safeguards against a fresh outburst of the nether fires. The great bulk of all political opinion is an instinct, not a philosophy; and the obstructive Tories represented little more than class prejudice and the dread of a great convulsion. Yet intelligent Tories were being driven to find some reasons for their creed, which the Utilitarians might have considered more carefully.

III. CONSERVATISM

A famous man of letters represents certain tendencies more clearly than the average politician. Robert Southey (1777-1843), the 'ultra servile sack-guzzler,' as Bentham pleasantly calls him in 1823, [151] was probably the best abused man, on his own side at least, among Mill's contemporaries. He was attacked by Mill himself, and savagely denounced by Byron and Hazlitt. He was not only a conspicuous writer in the *Quarterly Review* but, as his enemies thought, a renegade bought by pensions. It is, I hope, needless to defend him against this charge. He was simply an impatient man of generous instincts and no reflective power, who had in his youth caught the revolutionary fever, and, as he grew up, developed the patriotic fever.

Later views are given in the *Colloquies on the Progress and Prospects of Society* (1829), chiefly known to modern readers by one of Macaulay's essays. Southey was as assailable as Mill. His political economy is a mere muddle; his political views are obviously distorted by accidental prejudices; and the whole book is desultory and disjointed. In a dialogue with the ghost of Sir Thomas More, he takes the opportunity of introducing descriptions of scenery, literary digressions, and quaint illustrations from his vast stores of reading to the confusion of all definite arrangement. Southey is in the awkward position of a dogmatist defending a compromise. An Anglican claiming infallibility is necessarily inconsistent. His view of toleration, for example, is oddly obscure. He would apparently like to persecute infidels; [152] and yet he wishes to denounce the Catholic church for its persecuting principles. He seems to date the main social evils to the changes which began at the Reformation, and yet he looks back to the period which succeeded the Reformation as representing the ideal state of the British polity. His sympathy with the literature of the sixteenth and seventeenth centuries predisposed him to this position. He would have been more intelligible if he had been more distinctly reactionary. For all that, his views show the presence of a leaven which was materially to affect the later development of English opinions. That Jacobinism meant anarchy, and that anarchy led irresistibly to military despotism were propositions which to him, as to so many others, seemed to be established by the French revolution. What, then, was the cause of the anarchy? Sir Thomas More comes from the grave to tell us this, because he had witnessed the past symptoms of the process. The transition from the old feudal system to the modern industrial organisation had in his day become unmistakably developed. In feudal times, every man had his definite place in society; he was a member of a little group; supported, if controlled and disciplined, by an elaborate system of spiritual authority. The Reformation was the period at which the 'masterless man' made his appearance. The conversion of pastures into arable land, the growth of commerce and of pauperism, were marks of the coming change. It proceeded quietly for some generations; but the development of the modern manufacturing system represents the operation of the same process on a far larger scale, and with far greater intensity. The result may be described by saying that we have instead of a legitimate development a degeneration of society. A vast populace has grown up outside of the old order. It is independent indeed, but at the heavy price of being rather an inorganic mass than a constituent part of the body politic. It is, briefly, to the growth of a huge 'proletariate' outside the church, and hostile to the state, that Southey attributes all social evils.

The view has become familiar enough in various shapes; and in the reproaches which Southey brings against the manufacturing system we have an anticipation of other familiar lamentations. Our manufacturing wealth is a 'wen,' a 'fungous excrescence from the body politic'; [153] it is no more a proof of real prosperity than the size of a dropsical patient is a proof of health; [154] the manufacturer worships mammon instead of Moloch; [155] and wrings his fortune from the degradation of his labourers as his warlike ancestors wrung wealth from their slaves; he confines children in a tainted atmosphere, physical and moral, from morning till night, and a celebrated minister (Pitt) boasts of this very evil; [156] he treats his fellow-creatures as machines, [157] and wealth, though accumulated, is not diffused; the great capitalists, 'like pikes in a fishpond,' devour the weaker fish; [158] competition is not directed to providing the best goods, but the cheapest; [159] every man oppresses his neighbour; the landlord racks his tenant, the farmer grinds the labourer; all the little centres of permanent life are broken up; not one man in a thousand is buried with his fathers, and the natural ties and domestic affections are prematurely dissolved. [160]

Here, too, is to be found the source of the infidel opinions which call for suppression. London is a hotbed of corruption; [161] a centre of wealth; and yet, in spite of poor-laws, a place where wretches are dying of starvation, and which could collect a mob capable of producing the most appalling catastrophes. In such a place, men become unbelievers like savages, because removed from all humanising influences, and booksellers can carry on a trade in blasphemy. Infidelity is bred in 'the filth and corruption of large towns and manufacturing districts.' [162] The disappearance of clerical influence has led to 'a mass of ignorance, vice, and wretchedness which no generous heart can contemplate without grief.' [163] It is not surprising that, in Southey's opinion, it is doubtful whether the bulk of the people has gained or lost in the last thousand years. [164] Macaulay takes all this as mere sentimentalism and preference of a picturesque outside to solid comfort. But whatever Southey's errors of fact, they show at least a deeper insight than his opponent into some social evils. His proposed remedies explain his diagnosis of the evil. In the first place, it is not surprising, though it surprised Macaulay, that he had many sympathies with the socialist, Robert Owen. He saw Owen in 1816, [165] and was much impressed by his views. In the *Colloquies*, [166] Owen is called the 'happiest, most beneficent, and most practical of all enthusiasts'; an account is given of one of the earliest co-operative schemes, [167] and Southey believes in the possibility of the plan. He makes, however, one significant remark. Owen, he thinks, could not succeed without enlisting in his support some sectarian zeal. As Owen happened to object to all religious sects, this defect could not be remedied.

Southey, in fact, held that the absence of religious discipline was at the root of the whole evil. Religion, he declares, much to the scorn of Macaulay, 'is the basis upon which civil government rests.' [168] There must, as he infers, be an established religion, and the state which neglects this duty is preparing its own ruin. 'Nothing,' he declares, 'in abstract science can be more certain than these propositions,' though they are denied by 'our professors of the arts babblative and scribblative' — that is, by Benthamites and Whigs. For here, in fact, we come to the irreconcilable difference. Government is not to be a mere machinery for suppressing violence, but an ally of the church in spreading sound religion and morality. The rulers, instead of merely reflecting the popular will, should lead and direct all agencies for suppressing vice and misery. Southey, as his son takes pains to show, [169] though he was for upholding authority by the most stringent measures, was convinced that the one way to make government strong was to improve the condition of the people. He proposed many measures of reform; national education on the principles, of course, of Dr. Bell; state-aided colonisation and the cultivation of waste lands at home; Protestant sisterhoods to reproduce the good effects of the old order which he regretted and yet had to condemn on Anglican principles. The English church should have made use of the Wesleyans as the church of Rome had used the Franciscans and Dominicans; and his *Life of Wesley* was prompted by his fond belief that this might yet be done. Government, he said, ought to be 'paternal'; [170] and his leading aspirations have been adopted by Socialists on the one hand, and the converts to Catholicism on the other.

For his philosophy, Southey was in the habit of referring to Coleridge; and Coleridge's *Constitution of Church and State* is perhaps the book in which Coleridge comes nearest to bringing an argument to a conclusion. Though marked by his usual complexities of style, his parentheses and irrelevant allusions and glances at wide metaphysical discussions, he succeeds in laying down a sufficient sketch of his position. The book was originally published in 1830, and refers to the Catholic emancipation of the previous year. Unlike Southey, he approves of the measure, only regretting the absence of certain safeguards; and his general purpose may be said to be to give such a theory of the relations of church and state as may justify an establishment upon loftier grounds than those of the commonplace Tory.

His method, as he explains, is to find the true 'idea' of a constitution and a national church. The 'idea,' he explains, does not mean the conscious aim of the persons who founded or now constitute the bodies in question. An 'idea' is the subjective counterpart of an objective law. [171] It corresponds to the vital force which moulds the structure of the social organism, although it may never have been distinctly formulated by any one of the actors. In this sense, therefore, we should have to proceed by a historical method. We should study the constitution as we study the physiology of a physical body; [172] and he works out the analogy at some length. So far, Coleridge is expressing the characteristic view that Nature in general is to be regarded as an evolution; only that evolution is to be understood in the sense of Schelling not in the sense of either Darwin. Of course, when Coleridge professes to find the 'idea' of the church and state, what he really finds is not the idea so much as his idea of the idea—which may be a very different thing. His theory of 'evolution' is compatible with assuming that evolutions are illegitimate whenever he happens to dislike them.

He coincides rather curiously with James Mill in asserting that the 'social bond' was originally formed to protect property, not to protect life. [173] He discovers accordingly that the ancient races, Jews, Goths, and Kelts alike, divided the land into two parts, one to be inherited by separate families, the other to be set apart for the nation. From the latter or the 'nationalty' springs the church establishment. This property belongs rightfully and inalienably to the nation itself. It is held by what he calls the 'clerisy.' Its functions are, in the first place, to provide a career by which the poorest classes may rise to a higher position; and secondly, to provide for the development of all the qualities which distinguish the civilised man from the savage. [174] Briefly, then, the church is that part of the national organism which is devoted to educating the people to be 'obedient, free, useful organisable subjects, citizens, and patriots, living to the benefit of the estate, and prepared to die for its defence.' Henry viii. would have surpassed Alfred if he had directed the 'nationalty' to its true purposes; that is, especially to the maintenance of universities, of a parochial clergy, and of schools in every parish. Unluckily, Henry viii.'s 'idea' of a national church was vague. Ideas were not his strong point. Coleridge appears to be especially troubled to work the principles into conformity with his views of Catholic emancipation. The peculiarity of the theory is that the church, according to him, seems to be simply a national institution. It might exist, and in fact, did exist before Christianity, as is proved not only by the Jewish but by the Druidical church. [175] That it should be Christian in England is a 'blessed accident,' or 'providential boon' — or, as he puts it, 'most awfully a godsend.' Hence it follows that a primary condition of its utility is that the clerisy should contribute to the support of the other organs of the community. They must not be the subjects of a foreign power, nor, as he argues at length, subject to the desocialising influence of celibacy. It follows that the Roman church is unfitted to be ever a national church, although, if that danger be sufficiently obviated, no political disqualifications should be imposed upon Romanists. And thus, too, the Church Catholic is essentially a body which has no relations to any particular state. It is opposed to the world, not to the nation, and can have no visible head or 'personal centre of unity.' [176] The church which makes such claims is the revelation of Antichrist.

We need not inquire into the prophecies. It is enough to say that to Coleridge as to Southey the preservation of an established church seemed to be an essential condition of morality and civilisation. They differed from the ordinary Tory, who was content to defend any of the abuses by the cry of sacrilege and confiscation. The church was to be made worthy of its position, and rendered capable of discharging its high functions effectually. Coleridge, it may be said, would fully admit that an organ which had ceased to correspond to its idea must die. It could not continue to preserve itself by mere force of obstruction, but must arouse, throw off its abuses, and show itself to be worthy of its high claims. Meanwhile, however, he was perhaps more anxious to show the Utilitarians that in assailing the institution on account of its abuses, they were really destroying the most essential guarantee of progress. He sums up, in a curious passage, the proofs of modern degradation. [177] The wicked eighteenth century is of course responsible for everything. The 'mechanic corpuscular theory'; the consequent decay of philosophy, illustrated by such phrases as an excellent 'idea' of cooking; 'the ourang-outang theology of the origin of the human species substituted for the first ten chapters of the book of Genesis; rights of nature for the duties and privileges of citizens; idealess facts, misnamed proofs from history, for principles and the insight derived from them': all these and other calamitous results of modern philosophy are connected with a neglect of the well-being of the people, the mistaking of a large revenue for prosperity, and the consumption of gin by paupers to the 'value of eighteen millions yearly.' He appeals pathetically to the leaders of the Utilitarians. They will scorn him for pronouncing that a 'natural clerisy' is 'an essential element of a rightly constituted nation.' All their tract societies and mechanics' institutes and 'lecture bazaars under the absurd name of universities' are 'empiric specifics' which feed the disease. Science will be plebified, not popularised. The morality necessary for a state 'can only exist for the people in the form of religion. But the existence of a true philosophy, or the power and habit of contemplating particulars in the unity and fontal mirror of the idea, — this in the rulers and teachers of a nation is indispensable to a sound state of religion in all classes. In fact, religion, true or false, is and ever has been the centre of gravity in a realm to which all other things must and will accommodate themselves.'

The existence of the eighteenth century always remained a hopeless puzzle for Coleridge and his followers. Why at that period everything went wrong in the higher regions of thought remained a mystery. 'God is above,' says Sir Thomas More to Southey, [178] 'but the devil is below; evil principles are in their nature more active than good.' The devil seemed to have got into the upper air, and was working with his allies, Bentham and Mill and Paine and Cobbett, with remarkable success. But, whatever the theories of conservatives in church and state, the fact that the theories were held is important. The diametrical opposition between two schools, one of which regarded the church as a simple abuse, and its doctrines as effete superstitions, while the other looked to the church and its creed as giving the sole hope for suppressing the evil principle, was a critical point in later movements, political as well as religious.

IV. SOCIALISM

I have spoken of Southey's sympathy for Robert Owen. Owen (1771-1858) is one of the characteristic figures of the time. He was the son of a village tradesman in Wales, and had risen to prosperity by the qualities of the virtuous apprentice. Industry, patience, an imperturbably good temper, and sagacity in business matters had raised him to high position as a manufacturer at the time of the rapid advance of the cotton trade. Many poor men have followed the same path to wealth. Owen's peculiarity was that while he became a capitalist he preserved his sympathy with the working classes. While improving machinery, he complained that the 'living machinery' was neglected. One great step in his career was his marriage to the daughter of David Dale of New Lanark, a religious and worthy manufacturer. [179] Dale had employed a number of pauper children who were in that day to be disposed of by their parishes; and had done his best to make their position more tolerable. Owen took up this scheme, and carried it out more systematically. New Lanark, in his hands, became a model village; he provided in various ways for the encouragement of sobriety, industry, and honesty among his workmen, set up stores to supply cheap and good provisions, and especially provided infant schools and a systematic education. 'The children,' he declares, 'were the happiest human beings he ever saw.' When his partners interfered with his plans, Owen bought them out and started the company to which Bentham and Allen belonged. New Lanark rapidly became famous. It was visited by all the philanthropists of the day. The royal dukes not only of England but of Russia were interested; and Owen even believed that he had converted Napoleon at Elba. So far, Owen was a benevolent capitalist, exercising a paternal sway over his people. He became convinced, however, that he had discovered the key to the great social problems of the day. When the distresses followed the peace, he was prepared to propound his remedy, and found many willing hearers in all classes. Liverpool and Sidmouth listened to him with favour, and the duke of Kent became president of a committee started to carry out his views. He gave the impetus to the movement by which the Factory Act of 1819 was carried, although it was far from embodying his proposals in their completeness.

Owen's diagnosis of the social disease explains Southey's partiality. Like Southey, he traced the evil to the development of the manufacturing system. That system involved, as he held, what later Socialists have called the 'exploitation' of the labouring classes by the capitalists. With singularly crude notions of political economy, Owen assumed that the 'dead machinery' was in competition with the 'living machinery.' He made startling calculations as to the amount of human labour represented by steam-engines; and took for granted that the steam-engine displaced an equal number of workmen. His remedy for poverty was to set up a number of communities, which should maintain themselves by cultivating the soil with the spade, and in which every man should labour for all. Thus New Lanarks were to be spread over the country, with the difference that the employer was to be omitted. Owen, in short, became properly a Socialist, having been simply a paternal philanthropist. For a time Owen met with considerable support. A great meeting was held in London in 1817, and a committee was started two years afterwards, of which Ricardo was a member. Ricardo, indeed, took pains to let it be known that he did not believe in the efficacy of Owen's plans. Meanwhile Owen was breaking off his connection with New Lanark, and becoming the apostle of a new social creed. His missionary voyages took him to Ireland, to the United States and Mexico, and attempts were made to establish communities in Scotland and in the State of Illinois.

Owen and his followers became natural antagonists of the Utilitarians. He agreed with Southey in tracing distress to the development of the great manufacturing system, though he went much further. The principles essentially involved in the whole industrial system were, according to him, pernicious. He held the essential doctrine of his modern successors that property is theft. Between such a man and the men who took the *Wealth of*

Nations for their gospel, and Ricardo as its authorised commentator, there was an impassable gulf. On the other hand, Owen was equally far from the Tory view of religious principles. Southey's remark that he could only succeed by allying himself with some religious fanaticism was just to the point.

Owen was a man of very few ideas, though he held such as he had with extraordinary tenacity, and enforced them by the effective if illogical method of incessant repetition. Among them was the idea which, as he declares, had occurred to him before he was ten years old that there was something radically wrong in all religions. Whether this opinion had come to him from the diffused rationalism of his time, or was congenial to the practical and prosaic temperament which was disquieted by the waste of energy over futile sectarian squabbles, or was suggested by his early study of Seneca—the only author of whom he speaks as having impressed him in early years—it became a fixed conviction. He had been an early supporter of Lancaster and 'unsectarian' education. When his great meeting was to be held in 1817 it occurred to him that he might as well announce his views. He accordingly informed his hearers that the religions of the world were the great obstacles to progress. He expected, as he assures us, that this candid avowal would cause him to be 'torn in pieces.' It provoked on the contrary general applause, and Owen congratulated himself rather hastily on having struck the deathblow of superstition.

Owen's position, at any rate, was a significant symptom. It showed that the Socialist movement sprang from motives outside the sphere of the churches. Owen's personal simplicity and calmness seems to have saved him from any bitter animosity. He simply set aside Christianity as not to the purpose, and went on calmly asserting and re-asserting his views to Catholics and Protestants, Whigs, Radicals, and Tories. They agreed in considering him to be a bore, but were bored rather than irritated. Owen himself, like later Socialists, professed indifference to the political warfare of Whigs and Tories. When, at the height of the Reform movement, he published a paper called the *Crisis*, the title referred not to the struggle in which all the upper classes were absorbed, but to the industrial revolution which he hoped to bring about. He would have been equally ready to accept help from Whig, Tory, or Radical; but his position was one equally distasteful to all. The Tory could not ally himself with the man who thought all religions nonsense; nor any of the regular parties with the man who condemned the whole industrial system and was opposed to all the cherished prejudices of the respectable middle classes.

Owen's favourite dogma is worth a moment's notice. He was never tired of repeating that 'character is formed by circumstances'; from which he placidly infers that no man deserves praise or blame for his conduct. The inference, it must be admitted, is an awkward one in any ethical system. It represents, probably, Owen's most serious objection to the religions of the world. The ultimate aim of the priest is to save men's souls; and sin means conduct which leads to supernatural punishment. Owen, on the contrary, held that immorality was simply a disease to be cured, and that wrath with the sinner was as much out of place as wrath with a patient. In this sense Owen's view, as I at least should hold, defines the correct starting-point of any social reformer. He has to consider a scientific problem, not to be an agent of a supernatural legislator. He should try to alter the general conditions from which social evils spring, not to deal in pardons or punishment. Owen was acting with thoroughly good sense in his early applications of this principle. The care, for example, which he bestowed upon infant education recognised the fact that social reform implied a thorough training of the individual from his earliest years. Owen's greatest error corresponds to the transformation which this belief underwent in his mind. Since circumstances form character, he seems to have argued, it is only necessary to change the circumstances of a grown-up man to alter his whole disposition. His ambitious scheme in America seemed to suppose that it was enough to bring together a miscellaneous collection of the poor and discontented people, and to invite them all to behave with perfect unselfishness. At present I need only remark that in this respect there was a close coincidence between Owen and the Utilitarians. Both of them really aimed at an improvement of social conditions on a scientific method; and both justified their hopes by the characteristic belief in the indefinite modifiability of human nature by external circumstances.

I turn to a man who was in some ways the most complete antithesis to Owen. William Cobbett (1762-1835), unlike Owen, took a passionate and conspicuous part in the political struggles of the day. Cobbett, declares the *Edinburgh Review* in July 1807, has more influence than all the other journalists put together. He had won it, as the reviewer thought, by his force of character, although he had changed his politics completely 'within the last six months.' The fact was more significant than was then apparent. Cobbett, son of a labourer who had risen to be a small farmer, had in spite of all obstacles learned to read and write and become a great master of the vernacular. His earliest model had been Swift's *Tale of a Tub,* and in downright vigour of homely language he could scarcely be surpassed even by the author of the *Drapier's Letters.* He had enlisted as a soldier, and had afterwards drifted to America. There he had become conspicuous as a typical John Bull. Sturdy and pugnacious in the highest degree, he had taken the English side in American politics when the great question was whether the new power should be bullied by France or by England. He had denounced his precursor, Paine, in language savouring too much, perhaps, of barrack-rooms, but certainly not wanting in vigour. He defied threats of tar and feathers; put a portrait of George iii. in his shop-window; and gloried in British victories, and, in his own opinion, kept American policy straight. He had, however, ended by making America too hot to hold him; and came back to declare that republicanism meant the vilest and most corrupt of tyrannies, and that, as an Englishman, he despised all other nations upon earth. He was welcomed on his return by Pitt's government as likely to be a useful journalist, and became the special adherent of Windham, the ideal country-gentleman and the ardent disciple of Burke's principles. He set up an independent paper and heartily supported the war. On the renewal of hostilities in 1803 Cobbett wrote a manifesto [180] directed by the government to be read in every parish church in the kingdom, in order to rouse popular feeling. When Windham came into office in 1806, Cobbett's friends supposed that his fortune was made. Yet at this very crisis he became a reformer. His conversion was put down, of course, to his resentment at the neglect of ministers. I do not think that Cobbett was a man to whose character one can appeal as a conclusive answer to such charges. Unfortunately he was not free from weaknesses which prevent us from denying that his political course was affected by personal motives. But, in spite of weaknesses and of countless inconsistencies, Cobbett had perfectly genuine convictions and intense sympathies which sufficiently explain his position, and make him more attractive than many less obviously imperfect characters. He tells us unconsciously what were the thoughts suggested to a man penetrated to the core by the strongest prejudices—they can hardly be called opinions—of the true country labourer.

The labourer, in the first place, if fairly represented by Cobbett, had none of the bitter feeling against the nobility which smouldered in the French peasantry. Cobbett looked back as fondly to the surroundings of his youth as any nobleman could look back to Eton or to his country mansion. He remembered the 'sweet country air' round Crooksbury Hill, the song of birds, and the rambles through heather and woodland. He loved the rough jovial sports; bull-baiting and prize-fighting and single-stick play. He had followed the squire's hounds on foot, and admired without jealousy the splendid gardens of the bishop's palace at Farnham. Squire and parson were an intrinsic part of the general order of things. The state of the English working classes was, he often declares, the happiest that could be imagined, [181] and he appeals in confirmation to his own memories. Although, upon enlisting, he had found the army corrupt, he not only loved the soldier for the rest of his life, but shared to the full the patriotic exultation which welcomed the 1st of June and the Nile. Even to the last, he could not stomach the abandonment of the title 'King of France'; for so long as it was retained, it encouraged the farmer to tell his son the story of Crecy and Agincourt. [182]

What, then, alienated Cobbett? Briefly, the degradation of the class he loved. 'I wish,' he said, 'to see the poor men of England what the poor men of England were when I was born, and from endeavouring to accomplish this task, nothing but the want of means shall make me desist.' [183] He had a right to make that boast, and his ardour in the cause was as unimpeachable as honourable. It explains why Cobbett has still a sympathetic side. He was a mass of rough human nature; no prig or bundle of abstract formulæ, like Paine and his Radical successors. Logic with him is not in excess, but in defect. His doctrines are hopelessly inconsistent, except so far as they represent his stubborn prejudices. Any view will serve his purpose which can be made a weapon of offence in his multitudinous quarrels. Cobbett, like the Radicals of the time, was frightened by the gigantic progress of the debt. He had advocated war; but the peasant who was accustomed to reckon his income by pence, and had cried like a child when he lost the price of a red herring, was alarmed by the reckless piling up of millions of indebtedness. In 1806 he calmly proposed to his patron Windham to put matters straight by repudiating the interest. 'The nation must destroy the debt, or the debt will destroy the nation,' as he argued in the *Register*. [184] The proposal very likely caused the alienation of a respectable minister, though propounded with an amusing air of philosophical morality. Cobbett's alarm developed until it became to him a revelation of the mystery of iniquity. His Radical friends were denouncing placemen and jobbery, and Cobbett began to perceive what was at the bottom of the evil. The money raised to carry on the war served also to support a set of bloodsuckers, who were draining the national strength. Already, in 1804, he was lamenting a change due to Pitt's funding system. The old families, he said, were giving way to 'loanjobbers, contractors, and nabobs'; and the country people amazed to find that their new masters had been 'butchers, bakers, bottle-corkers, and old-clothesmen.' [185] Barings and Ricardos and their like were swallowing up the old country gentry wholesale; and in later years he reckons up, as he rides, the changes in his own neighbourhood. [186] His affection for the old country-gentleman might be superficial; but his lamentations over the degradation of the peasantry sprang from his heart. It was all, in his eyes, part of one process. Paper money, he found out, was at the bottom of it all; for paper money was the outward and visible symbol of a gigantic system of corruption and jobbery. It represented the device by which the hard-earned wages of the labourer were being somehow conjured away into the pockets of Jews and stockjobbers. The classes which profited by this atrocious system formed what he called the 'Thing'—the huge, intricate combination of knaves which was being denounced by the Radicals—though with a difference. Cobbett could join the reformers in so far as, like them, he thought that the rotten boroughs were a vital part of the system. He meets a miserable labourer complaining of the 'hard times.' The harvest had been good, but its blessings were not for the labourer. That 'accursed hill,' says Cobbett, pointing to old Sarum, 'is what has robbed you of your supper.' [187] The labourer represented the class whose blood was being sucked.

So far, then, as the Radicals were assailing the borough-mongers, Cobbett could be their cordial ally. Two years' imprisonment for libel embittered his feelings. In the distress which succeeded the peace, Cobbett's voice was for a time loudest in the general hubbub. He reduced the price of his *Register*, and his 'two-penny trash' reached a circulation of 25,000 or 30,000 copies. He became a power in the land, and anticipated the immediate triumph of reform. The day was not yet. Sidmouth's measures of repression frightened Cobbett to America (March 1819), where he wrote his history of the 'last hundred days of English liberty.' He returned in a couple of years, damaged in reputation and broken in fortune; but only to carry on the war with indomitable energy, although with a recklessness and extravagance which alienated his allies and lowered his character. He tried to cover his errors by brags and bombast, which became ridiculous, and which are yet not without significance.

Cobbett came back from America with the relics of Paine. Paine, the object of his abuse, had become his idol, not because Cobbett cared much for any abstract political theories, or for religious dogmas. Paine's merit was that he had attacked paper money. To Cobbett, as to Paine, it seemed that English banknotes were going the way of French assignats and the provincial currency of the Americans. This became one main topic of his tirades, and represented, as he said, the 'Alpha and Omega' of English politics. The theory was simple. The whole borough-mongering system depended upon the inflated currency. Prick that bubble and the whole would collapse. It was absolutely impossible, he said, that the nation should return to cash payments and continue to pay interest on the debt. Should such a thing happen, he declared, he would 'give his poor body up to be broiled on one of Castlereagh's widest-ribbed gridirons.' [188] The 'gridiron prophecy' became famous; a gridiron was for long a frontispiece to the *Register*; and Cobbett, far from retracting, went on proving, in the teeth of facts, that it had been fulfilled. His inference was, not that paper should be preserved, but that the debt should be treated with a 'sponge.'

Cobbett, therefore, was an awkward ally of political economists, whose great triumph was the resumption of cash payments, and who regarded repudiation as the deadly sin. The burthen of the debt, meanwhile, was so great that repudiation was well within the limits of possibility. [189] Cobbett, in their eyes, was an advocate of the grossest dishonesty, and using the basest incentives. Cobbett fully retorted their scorn. The economists belonged to the very class whom he most hated. He was never tired of denouncing Scottish 'feelosophers'; he sneers at Adam Smith, [190] and Ricardo was to him the incarnation of the stock-jobbing interest. Cobbett sympathised instinctively with the doctrine of the French economists that agriculture was the real source of all wealth. He nearly accepts a phrase, erroneously attributed to Windham, 'Perish Commerce'; and he argues that commerce was, in fact, of little use, and its monstrous extension at the bottom of all our worst evils. [191] Nobody could be more heartily opposed to the spirit which animated the political economists and the whole class represented by them. At times he spoke the language of modern Socialists. He defines Capital as 'money taken from the labouring classes, which, being given to army tailors and suchlike, enables them to keep foxhounds and trace their descent from the Normans.' [192]

The most characteristic point of his speculations is his view of the poor-laws. Nobody could speak with more good sense and feeling of the demoralisation which they were actually producing, of the sapping of the spirit of independence, and of all the devices by which the agricultural labourer was losing the happiness enjoyed in early years. But Cobbett's deduction from his principles is peculiar. 'Parson Malthus' is perhaps the favourite object of his most virulent abuse. 'I have hated many men,' he says, 'but never any one so much as you,' 'I call you parson,' he explains, 'because that word includes "boroughmonger" among other meanings, though no single word could be sufficient.' [193] Cobbett rages against the phrase 'redundant population.' There would be plenty for all if the borough-mongers and stockjobbers could be annihilated, taxes abolished, and the debt repudiated. The ordinary palliatives suggested were little to the taste of this remarkable Radical. The man who approved bull-fighting and supported the slave-trade naturally sneered at 'heddekashun,' and thought savings-banks a mean device to interest the poor in the keeping up of the funds. His remedy was always a sponge applied to the debt, and the abolition of taxes.

This leads, however, to one remarkable conclusion. Cobbett's attack upon the church establishment probably did more to cause alarm than any writings of the day. For Paine's attacks upon its creed he cared little enough. 'Your religion,' said a parson to him, 'seems to be altogether political.' It might well be, was Cobbett's retort, since his creed was made for him by act of parliament. [194] In fact, he cared nothing for theology, though he called himself a member of the church of England, and retained an intense dislike for Unitarians, dissenters in general, 'saints' as he called the Evangelical party, Scottish Presbyterians, and generally for all religious sects. He looked at church questions solely from one point of view. He had learned, it seems, from a passage in Ruggles's *History of the Poor*, [195] that the tithes had been originally intended to support the poor as well as the church. Gradually, as he looked back upon the 'good old times,' he developed the theory expounded in his *History of the Reformation*. It is a singular performance, written at the period of his most reckless exasperation (1824-27), but with his full vigour of style. He declares [196] in 1825 that he has sold forty-five thousand copies, and it has been often reprinted. The purpose is to show that the Reformation was 'engendered in beastly lust, brought forth in hypocrisy, and cherished and fed by plunder and devastation, and by rivers of English and Irish blood.' [197] Briefly, it is the cause of every evil that has happened since, including 'the debt, the banks, the stockjobbers, and the American revolution.' [198] In proving this, Cobbett writes in the spirit of some vehement Catholic bigot, maddened by the penal laws. Henry viii., Elizabeth, and William iii. are his monsters; the Marys of England and Scotland his ideal martyrs. He almost apologises for the massacre of St. Bartholomew and the Gunpowder Plot; and, in spite of his patriotism, attributes the defeat of the Armada to a storm, for fear of praising Elizabeth. The bitterest Ultramontane of to-day would shrink from some of this Radical's audacious statements. Cobbett, in spite of his extravagance, shows flashes of his usual shrewdness. He remarks elsewhere that the true way of studying history is to examine acts of parliament and lists of prices of labour and of food; [199] and he argues upon such grounds for the prosperity of the agricultural labourer under Edward iii., 'when a dung-cart filler could get a fat goose and a half for half a day's work.' He makes some telling hits, as when he contrasts William of Wykeham with Brownlow North, the last bishop of Winchester. Protestants condemned celibacy. Well, had William been married, we should not have had Winchester school, or New College; had Brownlow North been doomed to celibacy, he would not have had ten sons and sons-in-law to share twenty-four rich livings, besides prebends and other preferments; and perhaps he would not have sold small beer from his episcopal palace at Farnham. Cobbett's main doctrine is that when the Catholic church flourished, the population was actually more numerous and richer, that the care of the priests and monks made pauperism impossible, and that ever since the hideous blunder perpetrated by the reformers everything has been going from bad to worse. When it was retorted that the census proved the population to be growing, he replied that the census was a lie. Were the facts truly stated, he declares, we should have a population of near twenty-eight million in England by the end of this century, [200] a manifest *reductio ad absurdum*. If it were remarked that there was a Catholic church in France, and that Cobbett proves his case by the superiority of the English poor to the French poor, he remarked summarily that the French laws were different. [201]

Thus, the one monster evil is the debt, and the taxes turn out to have been a Protestant invention made necessary by the original act of plunder. That was Cobbett's doctrine, and, however perverse might be some of his reasonings, it was clearly to the taste of a large audience. The poor-law was merely a partial atonement for a vast and continuous process of plunder. Corrupt as might be its actual operation, it was a part of the poor man's patrimony, extorted by fear from the gang of robbers who fattened upon their labours.

Cobbett's theories need not be discussed from the logical or historical point of view. They are the utterances of a man made unscrupulous by his desperate circumstances, fighting with boundless pugnacity, ready to strike any blow, fair or foul, so long as it will vex his enemies, and help to sell the *Register*. His pugnacity alienated all his friends. Not only did Whigs and Tories agree in condemning him, but the Utilitarians hated and despised him, and his old friends, Burnett and Hunt, were alienated from him, and reviled by him. His actual followers were a small and insignificant remnant. Yet Cobbett, like Owen, represented in a crude fashion blind instincts of no small importance in the coming years. And it is especially to be noted that in one direction the philosophic Coleridge and the keen Quarterly Reviewer Southey, and the Socialist Owen and the reactionary Radical Cobbett, were more in agreement than they knew. What alarmed them was the vast social change indicated by the industrial revolution. In one way or another they connected all the evils of the day with the growth of commerce and manufactures, and the breaking up of the old system of domestic trade and village life. [202] That is to say, that in a dumb and inarticulate logic, though in the loudest tones of denunciation, Tories and Socialists, and nondescript Radicals were raging against the results of the great social change, which the Utilitarians regarded as the true line of advance of the day. This gives the deepest line of demarcation, and brings us to the political economy, which shows most fully how the case presented itself to the true Utilitarian.

FOOTNOTES:

[80] Bain's *James Mill*, p. 215.

[81] *Autobiography*, p. 104.

[82] *Miscellaneous Works* (Popular Edition), p. 131.

[83] The articles from the *Encyclopædia* upon Government, Jurisprudence, Liberty of the Press, Prisons and Prison Discipline, Colonies, Law of Nations, Education, were reprinted in a volume 'not for sale,' in 1825 and 1828. I quote from a reprint not dated.

[84] 'Government,' pp. 3-5.

[85] 'Government,' p. 8.

[86] 'Government,' p. 9.

[87] *Ibid.*

[88] *Ibid.*

[89] *Ibid.*

[90] 'Government,' p. 9.

[91] C'est une expérience éternelle que tout homme qui a du pouvoir est porté à en abuser; il va jusqu'à ce qu'il trouve des limites.—*Esprit des Lois*, Bk. xi. chap 4.

[92] 'Government,' p. 15.

[93] 'Government,' p. 7.

[94] *Ibid.*

[95] 'Government,' p. 21.

[96] *Ibid.*

[97] *Autobiography*, p. 104.

[98] 'Government,' p. 28.

[99] *Ibid.* p. 30. Mill especially refers to the exposure of clerical artifices in Father Paul's *Council of Trent*.

[100] 'Education,' p. 20

[101] *Ibid.*

[102] *Autobiography*, p. 106.

[103] 'Government,' p. 31.

[104] Bain's *James Mill*, p. 392.

[105] They were reprinted in the *Miscellaneous Works* after Macaulay's death. I quote from the 'popular edition' of that work (1875).

[106] *Miscellaneous Works*, p. 166.

[107] *Miscellaneous Works*, p. 132.

[108] Mill's *Autobiography*, p. 158.

[109] 'Government,' p. 12.

[110] *Miscellaneous Works*, p. 169.

[111] *Fragment on Mackintosh* (1870), pp. 275-94.

[112] Essay on the 'Independency of Parliament.'

[113] *Fragment*, p. 292.

[114] *Ibid.*

[115] *Miscellaneous Works*, p. 170.

[116] *Miscellaneous Works*, p. 173.

[117] *Miscellaneous Works*, p. 138.

[118] *Miscellaneous Works*, pp. 135-40.

[119] *Miscellaneous Works*, p. 158, and see pp. 143-47.

[120] *Speeches* (Popular Edition), p. 125.

[121] *Ibid.*

[122] *Miscellaneous Works*, p. 146.

[123] *Miscellaneous Works*, p. 183.

[124] A full analysis of this article is in Bain's *James Mill*, pp. 265-75.

[125] Article upon Sheridan, reprinted in Jeffrey's *Essays*, iv. (1844).

[126] *Table-Talk*, 27th April 1823.

[127] *Vindiciæ Gallicæ*, in *Miscellaneous Works*, iii. (1846), p. 57.

[128] Mackintosh thinks it necessary to add that this parallel was suggested to him by William Thomson (1746-1837), a literary gentleman who continued Watson's *Philip III.*, and may, for anything I know, deserve Mackintosh's warm eulogy.

[129] *Vindiciæ Gallicæ*, p. 59.

[130] *Ibid.*

[131] *Ibid.*

[132] *Ibid.*

[133] *Ibid.*

[134] *Ibid.*

[135] *Vindiciæ Gallicæ*, p. 128.

[136] *Ibid.*

[137] *Ibid.*

[138] *Life of Mackintosh*, i. 125.

[139] *Miscellaneous Works*, iii. 261-65.

[140] *Life*, i. 309-16.

[141] See *Miscellaneous Works*, iii. 3.

[142] *Ibid.* iii. 203-38 (an article highly praised by Bagehot in his *Parliamentary Reform*).

[143] *Miscellaneous Works*, iii. 215-16.

[144] *Ibid.* iii. 226. Mackintosh in this article mentions the 'caucus,' and observes that the name implies that combinations have been already formed upon 'which the future government of the confederacy may depend more than on the forms of election, or the letter of the present laws.' He inclines to approve the system as essential to party government.

[145] *Essays* (1844), i. 84-106.

[146] The famous 'Cevallos' article of 1808, said to be written by Jeffrey and Brougham (Macvey Napier's *Correspondence*, p. 308), gave the immediate cause of starting the *Quarterly*; and, according to Brougham, first gave a distinctly Liberal character to the *Edinburgh*. For Jeffrey's desire to avoid 'party politics,' see Lockhart's *Life of Scott*, M. Napier's *Correspondence*, p. 435, and Homer's *Memoirs* (1853), i. 464.

[147] April 1805; reprinted in *Essays*, ii. 38, etc., to show, as he says, how early he had taken up his view of the French revolution.

[148] Sydney Smith complains in his correspondence of this article as exaggerating the power of the aristocracy.

[149] *Essays,* iv. 29.

[150] I need not speak of Brougham, then the most conspicuous advocate of Whiggism. He published in 1843 a *Political Philosophy,* which, according to Lord Campbell, killed the 'Society for the Diffusion of Useful Knowledge.' No such hypothesis is necessary to account for the death of a society encumbered by a 'Dictionary of Universal Biography.' But the book was bad enough to kill, if a collection of outworn platitudes can produce that effect.

[151] Bentham's *Works,* x. 536.

[152] *Colloquies,* i. 253.

[153] *Colloquies,* i. 171.

[154] *Ibid.* i. 178.

[155] *Ibid.* i. 169.

[156] *Ibid.* i. 167.

[157] *Ibid.* i. 170.

[158] *Ibid.* i. 194.

[159] *Ibid.* ii. 247.

[160] *Colloquies,* ii. 259.

[161] *Ibid.* i. 109.

[162] *Ibid.* ii. 105-7.

[163] *Ibid.* i. 106.

[164] *Ibid.* i. 47.

[165] *Life and Correspondence,* iv. 195; *Selections,* iii. 45.

[166] *Colloquies,* i. 62.

[167] *Colloquies,* i. 135.

[168] *Ibid.* ii. 147. Southey is here almost verbally following Burke's *Reflections.*

[169] *Life and Correspondence,* v. 4-6.

[170] *Colloquies,* i. 105.

[171] *On the Constitution of Church and State, according to the idea of each,* 1852 (fourth edition).

[172] *Church and State,* p. 100.

[173] *Ibid.* p. 97.

[174] *Church and State*, p. 85.

[175] *Ibid.*

[176] *Church and State*, p. 142.

[177] *Ibid.*

[178] *Colloquies*, i. 37.

[179] See an early account of Dale (in 1798) in Sydney Smith's *Life and Letters*, i. 35, and another in Wilberforce's *Correspondence* (1840), i. 137 (in 1796).

[180] Printed in *Political Works*, i. 302.

[181] *Political Works*, v. 313; vi. 579.

[182] *Political Works*, i. 473; v. 319.

[183] *Ibid.* ii. 285.

[184] *Political Works*, ii. 28; iv. 388.

[185] *Ibid.* i. 443.

[186] *Rural Rides* (1853), p. 311.

[187] *Rural Rides*, p. 386.

[188] *Political Works*, v. 436 (22nd July 1819).

[189] Even M'Culloch had recommended a partial repudiation.

[190] *Political Works*, iv. 237.

[191] *Ibid.* ii. 19, 107, 250, 346; and iii. 423. See *Parliamentary History*, xxx., where the first use of the phrase by Hardinge is reported.

[192] *Political Works*, vi. 176.

[193] *Ibid.* 395.

[194] *Rural Rides*, p. 446.

[195] He complains bitterly that Ruggles had suppressed this in a second edition. *Protestant Reformation* (1850), ii., Introduction.

[196] *Political Register*, 29th Jan. 1825.

[197] *Protestant Reformation*, p. 13.

[198] *Ibid.*

[199] *Advice to Young Men*, p. 8.

[200] *Political Works*, v. 405. If our census be not a lie, there were twenty-seven million Englishmen in 1891.

[201] *Protestant Reformation*, i. 311.

[202] Coleridge in a letter to Allsop (*Conversations*, etc., i. 20) approves one of Cobbett's articles, because it popularises the weighty truth of the 'hollowness of commercial wealth.' Cobbett, he sadly reflects, is an overmatch for Liverpool. See Cobbett's *Political Works*, v. 466 *n.*

CHAPTER IV
MALTHUS

I. MALTHUS'S STARTING-POINT

The political movement represented the confluence of many different streams of agitation. Enormous social changes had generated multifarious discontent. New wants and the new strains and stresses between the various parts of the political mechanism required new adaptations. But, if it were inquired what was the precise nature of the evils, and how the reform of parliament was to operate, the most various answers might be given. A most important line of division did not coincide with the line between the recognised parties. One wing of the Radicals agreed with many Conservatives in attributing the great evils of the day to the industrial movement and the growth of competition. The middle-class Whigs and the Utilitarians were, on the contrary, in thorough sympathy with the industrial movement, and desired to limit the functions of government, and trust to self-help and free competition. The Socialistic movement appeared for the present to be confined to a few dreamers and demagogues. The Utilitarians might approve the spirit of the Owenites, but held their schemes to be chimerical. Beneath the political controversies there was therefore a set of problems to be answered; and the Utilitarian answer defines their distinction from Radicals of a different and, as they would have said, unphilosophical school.

What, then, was the view really taken by the Utilitarians of these underlying problems? They not only had a very definite theory in regard to them, but in working it out achieved perhaps their most important contribution to speculation. Beneath a political theory lies, or ought to lie, what we now call a 'sociology'—a theory of that structure of society which really determines the character and the working of political institutions. The Utilitarian theory was embodied in their political economy. I must try to define as well as I can what were the essential first principles implied, without going into the special problems which would be relevant in a history of political economy.

The two leading names in the literature of political economy during the first quarter of this century were undoubtedly Malthus and Ricardo. Thomas Robert Malthus [203] (1766-1834) was not one of the Utilitarian band. As a clergyman, he could not share their opinion of the Thirty-nine Articles. Moreover, he was a Whig, not a Radical; and he was even tainted with some economic heresy. Still, he became one of the prophets, if not the leading prophet, of the Utilitarians. Belief in the Malthusian theory of population was the most essential article of their faith, and marked the line of cleavage between the two wings of the Radical party.

Malthus was the son of a country gentleman in Surrey. His father was a man of studious habits, and one of the enthusiastic admirers of Rousseau. His study of *Émile* probably led to the rather desultory education of his son. The boy, after being taught at home, was for a time a pupil of R. Graves (1715-1804), author of the *Spiritual Quixote*, a Whig clergyman who was at least orthodox enough to ridicule Methodism. Malthus was next sent to attend Gilbert Wakefield's lectures at the Warrington 'Academy,' the Unitarian place of education, and in 1784 went to Jesus College, Cambridge, of which Wakefield had been a fellow. For Wakefield, who had become a Unitarian, and who was afterwards a martyr to political Radicalism, he appears to have retained a strong respect. At Jesus, again, Malthus was under Frend, who also was to join the Unitarians. Malthus was thus brought up under the influences of the modified rationalism which was represented by the Unitarians outside the establishment and by Paley within. Coleridge was at Jesus while Malthus was still a fellow, and there became an ardent admirer of Priestley, Malthus remained within the borders of the church. Its yoke was light enough, and he was essentially predisposed to moderate views. He took his degree as ninth wrangler in 1788, became a fellow of his college in 1793, took orders, and in 1798 was curate of Albury, near his father's house in Surrey. Malthus's home was within a walk of Farnham, where Cobbett had been born and passed his childhood. He had, therefore, before his eyes the same agricultural labourer whose degradation excited Cobbett to Radicalism. Very different views were suggested to Malthus. The revolutionary doctrine was represented in England by the writings of Godwin, whose *Political Justice* appeared in 1793 and *Enquirer* in 1797. These books naturally afforded topics for discussion between Malthus and his father. The usual relations between senior and junior were inverted; the elder Malthus, as became a follower of Rousseau, was an enthusiast; and the younger took the part of suggesting doubts and difficulties. He resolved to put down his arguments upon paper, in order to clear his mind; and the result was the *Essay upon Population*, of which the first edition appeared anonymously in 1798.

The argument upon which Malthus relied was already prepared for him. The dreams of the revolutionary enthusiasts supposed either a neglect of the actual conditions of human life or a belief that those conditions could be radically altered by the proposed political changes. The cooler reasoner was entitled to remind them that they were living upon solid earth, not in dreamland. The difficulty of realising Utopia may be presented in various ways. Malthus took a point which had been noticed by Godwin. In the conclusion of his *Political Justice*, [204] while taking a final glance at the coming millennium, Godwin refers to a difficulty suggested by Robert Wallace. Wallace had [205] said that all the evils under which mankind suffers might be removed by a community of property, were it not that such a state of things would lead to an 'excessive population.' Godwin makes light of the difficulty. He thinks that there is some 'principle in human society by means of which everything tends to find its own level and proceed in the most auspicious way, when least interfered with by the mode of regulation.' Anyhow, there is plenty of room on the earth, at present. Population may increase for 'myriads of centuries.' Mind, as Franklin has said, may become 'omnipotent over matter'; [206] life may be indefinitely prolonged; our remote descendants who have filled the earth 'will probably cease to propagate'; [207] they will not have the trouble of making a fresh start at every generation; and in those days there will be 'no war, no crimes, no administration of justice'; and moreover, 'no disease, anguish, melancholy, or resentment.' Briefly, we shall be like the angels, only without the needless addition of a supreme ruler. Similar ideas were expressed in Condorcet's famous *Tableau historique des progrès de l'esprit humain*, [208] written while he was in daily fear of death by the guillotine, and so giving the most striking instance on record of the invincibility of an idealist conviction under the hardest pressure of facts.

The argument of Malthus is a product of the whole previous course of speculation. The question of population had occupied the French economists. The profound social evils of France gave the starting-point of their speculations; and one of the gravest symptoms had been the decay of population under the last years of Louis XIV. Their great aim was to meet this evil by encouraging agriculture. It could not escape the notice of the simplest observer that if you would have more mouths you must provide more food, unless, as some pious people assumed, that task might be left to Providence. Quesnay had laid it down as one of his axioms that the statesman should aim at providing sustenance before aiming simply at stimulating population. It follows, according to Gulliver's famous maxim, that the man who makes two blades of grass grow where one grew before deserves better of his country than the 'whole race of politicians put together.' Other writers, in developing this thesis, had dwelt upon the elasticity of population. The elder Mirabeau, for example, published his *Ami des hommes ou traité de la population* in 1756. He observes that, given the means of subsistence, men will multiply like rats in a barn. [209] The great axiom, he says, [210] is 'la mesure de la subsistance est celle de la population.' Cultivate your fields, and you will raise men. Mirabeau replies to Hume's essay upon the 'Populousness of ancient nations' (1752), of which Wallace's first treatise was a criticism. The problem discussed by Hume and Wallace had been comparatively academical; but by Malthus's time the question had taken a more practical shape. The sentimentalists denounced luxury as leading to a decay of the population. Their prevailing doctrine is embodied in Goldsmith's famous passage in the *Deserted Village* (1770):

'Ill
Fares the land, to hastening ills a prey, Where wealth accumulates and men decay.'

The poetical version only reflected the serious belief of Radical politicians. Although, as we are now aware, the population was in fact increasing rapidly, the belief prevailed among political writers that it was actually declining. Trustworthy statistics did not exist. In 1753 John Potter, son of the archbishop, proposed to the House of Commons a plan for a census. A violent discussion arose, [211] in the course of which it was pointed out that the plan would inevitably lead to the adoption of the 'canvas frock and wooden shoes.' Englishmen would lose their liberty, become French slaves, and, when counted, would no doubt be taxed and forcibly enlisted. The bill passed the House of Commons in spite of such reasoning, but was thrown out by the House of Lords. Till the first census was taken in 1801 — a period at which the absolute necessity of such knowledge had become obvious—the most elementary facts remained uncertain. Was population increasing or decreasing? That surely might be ascertainable.

Richard Price (1723-1791) was not only a distinguished moralist and a leading politician, but perhaps the best known writer of his time upon statistical questions. He had the credit of suggesting Pitt's sinking fund, [212] and spoke with the highest authority upon facts and figures. Price argued in 1780 [213] that the population of England had diminished by one-fourth since the revolution of 1688. A sharp controversy followed upon the few ascertainable data. The vagueness of the results shows curiously how much economists had to argue in the dark. Malthus observes in his first edition that he had been convinced by reading Price that population was restrained by 'vice and misery,' as results, not of political institutions, but of 'our own creation.' [214] This gives the essential point of difference. Mirabeau had declared that the population of all Europe was decaying.

Hume's essay, which he criticises, had been in answer to a similar statement of Montesquieu. Price had learned that other countries were increasing in number, though England, he held, was still declining. What, then, was the cause? The cause, replied both Price and Mirabeau, was 'luxury,' to which Price adds the specially English evils of the 'engrossment of farms' and the enclosure of open fields. Price had to admit that the English towns had increased; but this was an additional evil. The towns increased simply by draining the country; and in the towns themselves the deaths exceeded the births. The great cities were the graves of mankind. This opinion was strongly held, too, by Arthur Young, who ridiculed the general fear of depopulation, and declared that if money were provided, you could always get labour, but who looked upon the towns as destructive cancers in the body politic.

The prevalence of this view explains Malthus's position. To attribute depopulation to luxury was to say that it was caused by the inequality of property. The rich man wasted the substance of the country, became demoralised himself, and both corrupted and plundered his neighbours. The return to a 'state of nature,' in Rousseau's phrase, meant the return to a state of things in which this misappropriation should become impossible. The whole industry of the nation would then be devoted to supporting millions of honest, simple peasants and labourers, whereas it now went to increasing the splendour of the great at the expense of the poor. Price enlarges upon this theme, which was, in fact, the contemporary version of the later formula that the rich are growing richer and the poor poorer. The immediate effect of equalising property, then, would be an increase of population. It was the natural retort, adopted by Malthus, that such an increase would soon make everybody poor, instead of making every one comfortable. Population, the French economists had said, follows subsistence. Will it not multiply indefinitely? The rapid growth of population in America was noticed by Price and Godwin; and the theory had been long before expanded by Franklin, in a paper which Malthus quotes in his later editions. 'There is no bound,' said Franklin in 1751, [215] 'to the prolific nature of plants and animals but what is made by their crowding and interfering with each other's means of subsistence.' The whole earth, he infers, might be overspread with fennel, for example, or, if empty of men, replenished in a few ages with Englishmen. There were supposed to be already one million of Englishmen in North America. If they doubled once in twenty-five years, they would in a century exceed the number of Englishmen at home. This is identical with Mirabeau's principle of the multiplying of rats in a barn. Population treads closely on the heels of subsistence. Work out your figures and see the results. [216]

Malthus's essay in the first edition was mainly an application of this retort, and though the logic was effective as against Godwin, he made no elaborate appeal to facts. Malthus soon came to see that a more precise application was desirable. It was clearly desirable to know whether population was or was not actually increasing, and under what conditions. I have spoken of the contemporary labours of Sinclair, Young, Sir F. Eden, and others. To collect statistics was plainly one of the essential conditions of settling the controversy. Malthus in 1799 travelled on the continent to gather information, and visited Sweden, Norway, Russia, and Germany. The peace of Amiens enabled him in 1802 to visit France and Switzerland. He inquired everywhere into the condition of the people, collected such statistical knowledge as was then possible, and returned to digest it into a elaborate treatise. Meanwhile, the condition of England was giving a fresh significance to the argument. The first edition had been published at the critical time when the poor-law was being relaxed, and disastrous results were following war and famine. The old complaint that the poor-law was causing depopulation was being changed for the complaint that it was stimulating pauperism. The first edition already discussed this subject, which was occupying all serious thinkers; it was now to receive a fuller treatment. The second edition, greatly altered, appeared in 1803, and made Malthus a man of authority. His merits were recognised by his appointment in 1805 to the professorship of history and political economy at the newly founded East India College at Haileybury. There he remained till the end of his life, which was placid, uneventful, and happy. He made a happy marriage in 1804; and his calm temperament enabled him to bear an amount of abuse which might have broken the health of a more irritable man. Cobbett's epithet, 'parson Malthus,' strikes the keynote. He was pictured as a Christian priest denouncing charity, and proclaiming the necessity of vice and misery. He had the ill luck to be the centre upon which the antipathies of Jacobin and anti-Jacobin converged. Cobbett's language was rougher than Southey's; but the poet-laureate and the author of 'two-penny trash' were equally vehement in sentiment. Malthus, on the other hand, was accepted by the political economists, both Whig and Utilitarian. Horner and Mackintosh, lights of the Whigs, were his warm friends as well as his disciples. He became intimate with Ricardo, and he was one of the original members of the Political Economy Club. He took abuse imperturbably; was never vexed 'after the first fortnight' by the most unfair attack; and went on developing his theories, lecturing his students, and improving later editions of his treatise. Malthus died on 23rd December 1834.

II. THE RATIOS

The doctrine marks a critical point in political economy. Malthus's opponents, as Mr. Bonar remarks, [217] attacked him alternately for propounding a truism and for maintaining a paradox. A 'truism' is not useless so long as its truth is not admitted. It would be the greatest of achievements to enunciate a law self-evident as soon as formulated, and yet previously ignored or denied. Was this the case of Malthus? Or did he really startle the world by clothing a commonplace in paradox, and then explain away the paradox till nothing but the commonplace was left?

Malthus laid down in his first edition a proposition which continued to be worried by all his assailants. Population, he said, when unchecked, increases in the geometrical ratio; the means of subsistence increase only in an arithmetical ratio. Geometrical ratios were just then in fashion. [218] Price had appealed to their wonderful ways in his arguments about the sinking fund; and had pointed out that a penny put out to 5 per cent. compound interest at the birth of Christ would, in the days of Pitt, have been worth some millions of globes of solid gold, each as big as the earth. Both Price and Malthus lay down a proposition which can easily be verified by the multiplication-table. If, as Malthus said, population doubles in twenty-five years, the number in two centuries would be to the present number as 256 to 1, and in three as 4096 to 1. If, meanwhile, the quantity of subsistence increased in 'arithmetical progression,' the multipliers for it would be only 9 and 13. It follows that, in the year 2003, two hundred and fifty-six persons will have to live upon what now supports nine. So far, the case is clear. But how does the argument apply to facts? For obvious reasons, Price's penny could not become even one solid planet of gold. Malthus's population is also clearly impossible. That is just his case. The population of British North America was actually, when he wrote, multiplying at the assigned rate. What he pointed out was that such a rate must somehow be stopped; and his question was, how precisely will it be stopped? The first proposition, he says [219] (that is, that population increased geometrically), 'I considered as proved the moment that the American increase was related; and the second as soon as enunciated.' To say that a population increases geometrically, in fact, is simply to say that it increases at a fixed rate. The arithmetical increase corresponds to a statement which Malthus, at any rate, might regard as undeniable; namely, that in a country already fully occupied, the possibility of increasing produce is restricted within much narrower limits. In a 'new country,' as in the American colonies, the increase of food might proceed as rapidly as the increase of population. Improved methods of cultivation, or the virtual addition of vast tracts of fertile territory by improved means of communication, may of course add indefinitely to the resources of a population. But Malthus was contemplating a state of things in which the actual conditions limited the people to an extraction of greater supplies from a strictly limited area. Whether Malthus assumed too easily that this represented the normal case may be questionable. At any rate, it was not only possible but actual in the England of the time. His problem was very much to the purpose. His aim was to trace the way in which the population of a limited region is prevented from increasing geometrically. If the descendants of Englishmen increase at a certain rate in America, why do they not increase equally in England? That, it must be admitted, is a fair scientific problem. Finding that two races of similar origin, and presumably like qualities, increase at different rates, we have to investigate the causes of the difference.

Malthus answered the problem in the simplest and most consistent way in his first edition. What are the checks? The ultimate check would clearly be starvation. A population might multiply till it had not food. But before this limit is actually reached, it will suffer in various ways from scarcity. Briefly, the checks may be distinguished into the positive, that is, actual distress, and the preventive, or 'foresight.' We shall actually suffer unless we are restrained by the anticipation of suffering. As a fact, however, he thinks that men are but little influenced by the prudence which foresees sufferings. They go on multiplying till the consequences are realised. You may be confined in a room, to use one of his illustrations, [220] though the walls do not touch you; but human beings are seldom satisfied till they have actually knocked their heads against the wall. He sums up his argument in the first edition in three propositions. [221] Population is limited by the means of subsistence; that is obvious; population invariably increases when the means of subsistence are increased; that is shown by experience to be practically true; and therefore, finally, the proportion is maintained by 'misery and vice.' That is the main conclusion which not unnaturally startled the world. Malthus always adhered in some sense to the main doctrine, though he stated explicitly some reserves already implicitly involved. A writer must not be surprised if popular readers remember the unguarded and dogmatic utterances which give piquancy to a theory, and overlook the latent qualifications which, when fully expressed, make it approximate to a commonplace. The political bearing of his reasoning is significant. The application of Godwin's theories of equality would necessarily, as he urges, stimulate an excessive population. To meet the consequent evils, two measures would be obviously necessary; private property must be instituted in order to stimulate prudence; and marriage must be instituted to make men responsible for the increase of the population. These institutions are necessary, and they make equality impossible. Weak, then, as foresight may be with most men, the essential social institutions have been developed by the necessity of enabling foresight to exercise some influence; and thus indirectly societies have in fact grown in wealth and numbers through arrangements which have by one and the same action strengthened prudence and created inequality. Although this is clearly implied, the main impression produced upon Malthus's readers was that he held 'vice and misery' to be essential to society; nay, that in some sense he regarded them as blessings. He was accused, as he tells us, [222] of objecting to vaccination, because it tended to prevent deaths from small-pox, and has to protest against some one who had declared his principles to be favourable to the slave trade. [223] He was represented, that is, as holding depopulation to be good in itself. These perversions were grotesque, but partly explain the horror with which Malthus was constantly regarded; and we must consider what made them plausible.

I must first notice the maturer form of his doctrine. In the second edition he turns to account the result of his later reading, his personal observations, and the statistical results which were beginning to accumulate. The remodelled book opens with a survey of the observed action of the checks; and it concludes with a discussion of the 'moral restraint' which is now added to 'vice and misery.' Although considerable fragments of the old treatise remained to the last, the whole book was altered both in style and character. The style certainly suffers, for Malthus was not a master of the literary art; he inserts his additions with little care for the general effect. He tones down some of the more vivid phrases which had given offence, though he does not retract the substance. A famous passage [224] in the second edition, in which he speaks of 'nature's mighty feast,' where, unluckily, the 'table is already full,' and therefore unbidden guests are left to starve, was suppressed in the later editions. Yet the principle that no man has a claim to subsistence as of right remains unaltered. The omission injures the literary effect without altering the logic; and I think that, where the argument is amended, the new element is scarcely worked into the old so as to gain thorough consistency.

Malthus's survey of different countries showed how various are the 'checks' by which population is limited in various countries. We take a glance at all nations through all epochs of history. In the South Sea we find a delicious climate and a fertile soil, where population is mainly limited by vice, infanticide, and war; and where, in spite of these influences, the population multiplies at intervals till it is killed off by famine. In China, a vast and fertile territory, inhabited by an industrious race, in which agriculture has always been encouraged, marriage stimulated, and property widely diffused, has facilitated the production of a vast population in the most abject state of poverty, driven to expose children by want, and liable at intervals to destructive famines. In modern Europe, the checks appear in the most various forms; in Switzerland and Norway a frugal population in small villages sometimes instinctively understands the principle of population, and exhibits the 'moral restraint,' while in England the poor-laws are producing a mass of hopeless and inert pauperism. Consideration of these various cases, and a comparison of such records as are obtainable of the old savage races, of the classical states of antiquity, of the Northern barbarians and of the modern European nations, suggests a natural doubt. Malthus abundantly proves what can hardly be denied, that population has everywhere been found to press upon the means of subsistence, and that vice and misery are painfully abundant. But does he establish or abandon his main proposition? He now asserts the 'tendency' of population to outrun the means of subsistence. Yet he holds unequivocally that the increase of population has been accompanied by an increased comfort; that want has diminished although population has increased; and that the 'preventive' check is stronger than of old in proportion to the positive check. Scotland, he says, [225] is 'still overpeopled, but not so much as when it contained fewer inhabitants.' Many nations, as he points out in general terms, have been most prosperous when most populous. [226] They could export food when crowded, and have ceased to import it when thinned. This, indeed, expresses his permanent views, though the facts were often alleged by his critics as a disproof of them. Was not the disproof real? Does not a real evasion lurk under the phrase 'tendency'? You may say that the earth has a tendency to fall into the sun, and another 'tendency' to move away from the sun. But it would be absurd to argue that we were therefore in danger of being burnt or of being frozen. To explain the law of a vital process, we may have to analyse it, and therefore to regard it as due to conflicting forces; but the forces do not really exist separately, and in considering the whole concrete phenomenon we must take them as mutually implied. A man has a 'tendency' to grow too fat; and another 'tendency' to grow too thin. That surely means that on the whole he has a 'tendency' to preserve the desirable mean. The phrase, then, can only have a distinct meaning when the conflicting forces represent two independent or really separable forces. To use an illustration given by Malthus, we might say that a man had a 'tendency' to grow upwards; but was restrained by a weight on his head. The man has the 'tendency,' because we may regard the weight as a separable accident. When both forces are of the essence, the separate 'tendencies' correspond merely to our way of analysing the fact. But if one can be properly regarded as relatively accidental, the 'tendency' means the way in which the other will manifest itself in actual cases.

In 1829, Senior put this point to Malthus. [227] What, he asked, do you understand by a 'tendency' when you admit that the tendency is normally overbalanced by others? Malthus explains his meaning to be that every nation suffers from evils 'specifically arising from the pressure of population against food.' The wages of the labourer in old countries have never been sufficient to enable him to maintain a large family at ease. There is overcrowding, we may say, in England now as there was in England at the Conquest; though food has increased in a greater proportion than population; and the pressure has therefore taken a milder form. This, again, is proved by the fact that, whenever a relaxation of the pressure has occurred, when plagues have diminished population, or improvements in agriculture increased their supply of food, the gap has been at once filled up. The people have not taken advantage of the temporary relaxation of the check to preserve the new equilibrium, but have taken out the improvement by a multiplication of numbers. The statement then appears to be that at any given time the population is in excess. Men would be better off if they were less numerous. But, on the other hand, the tendency to multiply does not represent a constant force, an irresistible instinct which will always bring men down to the same level, but something which, in fact, may vary materially. Malthus admits, in fact, that the 'elasticity' is continually changing; and therefore repudiates the interpretation which seemed to make all improvement hopeless. Why, then, distinguish the 'check' as something apart from the instinct? If, in any case, we accept this explanation, does not the theory become a 'truism,' or at least a commonplace, inoffensive but hardly instructive? Does it amount to more than the obvious statement that prudence and foresight are desirable and are unfortunately scarce?

III. MORAL RESTRAINT

The change in the theory of 'checks' raises another important question. Malthus now introduced a modification upon which his supporters laid great stress. In the new version the 'checks' which proportion population to means of subsistence are not simply 'vice and misery,' but 'moral restraint, vice, and misery.' [228] How, precisely, does this modify the theory? How are the different 'checks' related? What especially is meant by 'moral' in this connection? Malthus takes his ethical philosophy pretty much for granted, but is clearly a Utilitarian according to the version of Paley. [229] He agrees with Paley that 'virtue evidently consists in educing from the materials which the Creator has placed under our guidance the greatest sum of human happiness.' [230] He adds to this that our 'natural impulses are, abstractedly considered, good, and only to be distinguished by their consequences.' Hunger, he says, as Bentham had said, is the same in itself, whether it leads to stealing a loaf or to eating your own loaf. He agrees with Godwin that morality means the 'calculation of consequences,' [231] or, as he says with Paley, implies the discovery of the will of God by observing the effect of actions upon happiness. Reason then regulates certain innate and practically unalterable instincts by enabling us to foretell their consequences. The reasonable man is influenced not simply by the immediate gratification, but by a forecast of all the results which it will entail. In these matters Malthus was entirely at one with the Utilitarians proper, and seems to regard their doctrine as self-evident.

He notices briefly one logical difficulty thus introduced. The 'checks' are vice, misery, and moral restraint. But why distinguish vice from misery? Is not conduct vicious which causes misery, [232] and precisely because it causes misery? He replies that to omit 'vice' would confuse our language. Vicious conduct may cause happiness in particular cases; though its general tendency would be pernicious. The answer is not very clear; and Malthus, I think, would have been more logical if he had stuck to his first theory, and regarded vice as simply one form of imprudence. Misery, that is, or the fear of misery, and the indulgence in conduct which produces misery are the 'checks' which limit population; and the whole problem is to make the ultimate sanction more operative upon the immediate conduct. Man becomes more virtuous simply as he becomes more prudent, and is therefore governed in his conduct by recognising the wider and more remote series of consequences. There is, indeed, the essential difference that the virtuous man acts (on whatever motives) from a regard to the 'greatest happiness of the greatest number,' and not simply from self-regard. Still the ultimate and decisive criterion is the tendency of conduct to produce misery; and if Malthus had carried this through as rigorously as Bentham, he would have been more consistent. The 'moral check' would then have been simply a department of the prudential; including prudence for others as well as for ourselves. One reason for the change is obvious. His assumption enables him to avoid coming into conflict with the accepted morality of the time. On his exposition 'vice' occasionally seems not to be productive of misery but an alternative to misery; and yet something bad in itself. Is this consistent with his Utilitarianism? The vices of the South Sea Islanders, according to him, made famine less necessary; and, if they gave pleasure at the moment, were they not on the whole beneficial? Malthus again reckons among vices practices which limit the population without causing 'misery' directly. [233] Could he logically call them vicious? He wishes to avoid the imputation of sanctioning such practices, and therefore condemns them by his moral check; but it would be hard to prove that he was consistent in condemning them. Or, again, there is another familiar difficulty. The Catholic church encourages marriage as a remedy for vice; and thereby stimulates both population and poverty. How would Malthus solve the problem: is it better to encourage chastity and a superabundance of people, or to restrict marriage at the cost of increasing temptation to vice? He seems to evade the point by saying that he recommends both chastity and abstinence from marriage. By 'moral restraint,' as he explains, he means 'restraint from marriage from prudential motives, with a conduct strictly moral during the period of this restraint.' 'I have never,' he adds, 'intentionally deviated from this sense.' [234] A man, that is, should postpone taking a wife, and should not console himself by taking a mistress. He is to refrain from increasing the illegitimate as well as from increasing the legitimate population. It is not surprising that Malthus admits that this check has 'in past ages operated with inconsiderable force.' [235] In fact Malthus, as a thoroughly respectable and decent clergyman, manages by talking about the 'moral restraint' rather to evade than to answer some awkward problems of conduct; but at the cost of some inconsequence.

But another result of this mode of patching up his argument is more important. The 'vices of mankind,' he says in an unusually rhetorical summary of his historical inquiry, [236] 'are active and able ministers of depopulation. They are the precursors in the great army of destruction, and often finish the dreadful work themselves. But should they fail in the war of extermination, sickly seasons, epidemics, pestilence, and plague advance in terrific array, and sweep off their thousands and ten thousands. Should success still be incomplete, gigantic inevitable famine stalks in the rear, and at one mighty blow levels the population with the food of the world.' The life of the race, then, is a struggle with misery; its expansion is constantly forcing it upon this array of evils; and in proportion to the elasticity is the severity of the evils which follow. This is not only a 'gloomy view,' but again seems to suggest that 'vice' is an alternative to 'misery.' Vices are bad, it would seem, but at least they obviate the necessity for disease and famine. Malthus probably suppressed the passage because he thought it liable to this interpretation. It indicates, however, a real awkwardness, if not something more, in his exposition. He here speaks as if there was room for a fixed number of guests at his banquet. Whatever, therefore, keeps the population to that limit must be so far good. If he had considered his 'moral check' more thoroughly, he might have seen that this does not correspond to his real meaning. The 'moral' and the prudential checks are not really to be contrasted as alternative, but co-operative. Every population, vicious or virtuous, must of course proportion its numbers to its means of support. That gives the prudential check. But the moral check operates by altering the character of the population itself. From the purely economic point of view, vice is bad because it lowers efficiency. A lazy, drunken, and profligate people would starve where an industrious, sober, and honest people would thrive. The check of vice thus brings the check of misery into play at an earlier stage. It limits by lowering the vitality and substituting degeneration for progress. The check, therefore, is essentially mischievous. Though it does not make the fields barren, it lowers the power of cultivation. Malthus had recognised this when he pointed out, as we have seen, that emergence from the savage state meant the institution of marriage and property and, we may infer, the correlative virtues of chastity, industry, and honesty. If men can form large societies, and millions can be supported where once a few thousands were at starvation point, it is due to the civilisation which at every stage implies 'moral restraint' in a wider sense than Malthus used the phrase. An increase of population by such means was, of course, to be desired. If Malthus emphasises this inadequately, it is partly, no doubt, because the Utilitarian view of morality tended to emphasise the external consequences rather than the alteration of the man himself. Yet the wider and sounder view is logically implied in his reasoning—so much so that he might have expressed his real aim more clearly if he had altered the order of his argument. He might have consistently taken the same line as earlier writers and declared that he desired, above all things, the increase of population. He would have had indeed to explain that he desired the increase of a sound and virtuous population; and that hasty and imprudent increase led to misery and to a demoralisation which would ultimately limit numbers in the worst way. We shall see directly how nearly he accepts this view. Meanwhile, by insisting upon the need of limitation, he was led to speak often as if limitation by any means was good and the one thing needful, and the polemic against Godwin in the first edition had given prominence to this side of the question. Had he put his views in a different shape, he would perhaps have been so edifying that he would have been disregarded. He certainly avoided that risk, and had whatever advantage is gained by stating sound doctrine paradoxically.

We shall, I think, appreciate his real position better by considering his approximation to the theory which, as we know, was suggested to Darwin by a perusal of Malthus. [237] There is a closer resemblance than appears at first. The first edition concludes by two chapters afterwards omitted, giving the philosophical application of his theory. He there says that the 'world is a mighty process of God not for the trial but for the creation and formation of the mind.' [238] It is not, as Butler thought, a place of 'probation,' but a scene in which the higher qualities are gradually developed. Godwin had quoted Franklin's view that 'mind' would become 'omnipotent over matter.' Malthus holds that, as he puts it, 'God is making matter into mind.' The difference is that Malthus regards evil in general not as a sort of accident of which we can get rid by reason; but as the essential stimulus which becomes the efficient cause of intellectual activity. The evils from which men suffer raise savage tribes from their indolence, and by degrees give rise to the growth of civilisation. The argument, though these chapters were dropped by Malthus, was taken up by J. B. Sumner, to whom he refers in later editions. [239] It is, in fact, an imperfect way of stating a theory of evolution. This appears in his opening chapters upon the 'moral restraint.' [240] He explains that moral and physical evils are 'instruments employed by the Deity' to admonish us against such conduct as is destructive of happiness. Diseases are indications that we have broken a law of nature. The plague of London was properly interpreted by our ancestors as a hint to improve the sanitary conditions of the town. Similarly, we have to consider the consequences of obeying our instincts. The desire of food and necessaries is the most powerful of these instincts, and next to it the passion between the sexes. They are both good, for they are both natural; but they have to be properly correlated. To 'virtuous love' in particular we owe the 'sunny spots' in our lives, where the imagination loves to bask. Desire of necessaries gives us the stimulus of the comfortable fireside; and love adds the wife and children, without whom the fireside would lose half its charm. Now, as a rule, the sexual passion is apt to be in excess. The final cause of this excess is itself obvious. We cannot but conceive that it is an object of 'the Creator that the earth should be replenished.' [241] To secure that object, it is necessary that 'there should be a tendency in the population to increase faster than food.' If the two instincts were differently balanced, men would be content though the population of a fertile region were limited to the most trifling numbers. Hence the instinct has mercifully been made so powerful as to stimulate population, and thus indirectly and eventually to produce a population at once larger and more comfortable. On the one hand, it is of the very utmost importance to the happiness of mankind that they should not increase too fast, [242] but, on the other hand, if the passion were weakened, the motives which make a man industrious and capable of progress would be diminished also. It would, of course, be simpler to omit the 'teleology'; to say that sanitary regulations are made necessary by the plague, not that the plague is divinely appointed to encourage sanitary regulations. Malthus is at the point of view of Paley which becomes Darwinism when inverted; but the conclusion is much the same. He reaches elsewhere, in fact, a more precise view of the value of the 'moral restraint.' In a chapter devoted for once to an ideal state of things, [243] he shows how a race thoroughly imbued with that doctrine would reconcile the demands of the two instincts. Population would in that case increase, but, instead of beginning by an increase, it would begin by providing the means of supporting. No man would become a father until he had seen his way to provide for a family. The instinct which leads to increasing the population would thus be intrinsically as powerful as it now is; but when regulated by prudence it would impel mankind to begin at the right end. Food would be ready before mouths to eat it.

IV. SOCIAL REMEDIES

This final solution appears in Malthus's proposed remedies for the evils of the time. Malthus [244] declares that 'an increase of population when it follows in its natural order is both a great positive good in itself, and absolutely necessary' to an increase of wealth. This natural order falls in, as he observes, with the view to which Mirabeau had been converted, that 'revenue was the source of population,' and not population of revenue. [245] Malthus holds specifically that, 'in the course of some centuries,' the population of England might be doubled or trebled, and yet every man be 'much better fed and clothed than he is at present.' [246] He parts company with Paley, who had considered the ideal state to be 'that of a laborious frugal people ministering to the demands of an opulent luxurious nation.' [247] That, says Malthus, is 'not an inviting prospect.' Nothing but a conviction of absolute necessity could reconcile us to the 'thought of ten millions of people condemned to incessant toil, and to the privation of everything but absolute necessaries, in order to minister to the excessive luxuries of the other million.' But he denies that any such necessity exists. He wishes precisely to see luxury spread among the poorer classes. A desire for such luxury is the best of all checks to population, and one of the best means of raising the standard. It would, in fact, contribute to his 'moral restraint.' So, too, he heartily condemns the hypocrisy of the rich, who professed a benevolent desire to better the poor, and yet complained of high wages. [248] If, he says elsewhere, [249] a country can 'only be rich by running a successful race for low wages, I should be disposed to say, Perish such riches!' No one, in fact, could see more distinctly than Malthus the demoralising influence of poverty, and the surpassing importance of raising the people from the terrible gulf of pauperism. He refers to Colquhoun's account of the twenty thousand people who rose every morning in London without knowing how they were to be supported; and observes that 'when indigence does not produce overt acts of vice, it palsies every virtue.' [250]

The temptations to which the poor man is exposed, and the sense of injustice due to an ignorance of the true cause of misery, tend to 'sour the disposition, to harden the heart, and deaden the moral sense.' Unfortunately, the means which have been adopted to lessen the evil have tended to increase it. In the first place, there was the master-evil of the poor-laws. Malthus points out the demoralising effects of these laws in chapters full of admirable common sense, which he was unfortunately able to enforce by fresh illustrations in successive editions. He attends simply to the stimulus to population. He thinks that if the laws had never existed, the poor would now have been much better off. [251] If the laws had been fully carried out, every labourer might have been certain that all his children would be supported, or, in other words, every check to population would have been removed. [252] Happily, the becoming pride of the English peasantry was not quite extinct; and the poor-law had to some extent counteracted itself, or taken away with one hand what it gave with the other, by placing the burthen upon the parishes. [253] Thus landlords have been more disposed to pull down than to build cottages, and marriage has been checked. On the whole, however, Malthus could see in the poor-laws nothing but a vast agency for demoralising the poor, tempered by a system of petty tyrannical interference. He proposes, therefore, that the poor-law should be abolished. Notice should be given that no children born after a certain day should be entitled to parish help; and, as he quaintly suggests, the clergyman might explain to every couple, after publishing the banns, the immorality of reckless marriage, and the reasons for abolishing a system which had been proved to frustrate the intentions of the founders. [254] Private charity, he thinks, would meet the distress which might afterwards arise, though humanity imperiously requires that it should be 'sparingly administered.' Upon this duty he writes a sensible chapter. [255] To his negative proposals Malthus adds a few of the positive kind. He is strongly in favour of a national system of education, and speaks with contempt of the 'illiberal and feeble' arguments opposed to it. The schools, he observes, might confer 'an almost incalculable benefit' upon society, if they taught 'a few of the simplest principles of political economy.' [256] He had been disheartened by the prejudices of the ignorant labourer, and felt the incompatibility of a free government with such ignorance. A real education, such as was given in Scotland, would make the poor not, as alarmists had suggested, more inflammable, but better able to detect the sophistry of demagogues. [257] He is, of course, in favour of savings banks, [258] and approves friendly societies, though he is strongly opposed to making them compulsory, as they would then be the poor-law in a new form. [259] The value of every improvement turns upon its effect in encouraging the 'moral restraint.' Malthus's ultimate criterion is always, Will the measure make people averse to premature marriage?

He reaches the apparently inconsistent result that it might be desirable to make an allowance for every child beyond six. [260] But this is on the hypothesis that the 'moral restraint' has come to be so habitual that no man marries until he has a fair prospect of maintaining a family of six. If this were the practical code, the allowance in cases where the expectation was disappointed would not act as an encouragement to marriage, but as a relief under a burthen which could not have been anticipated. Thus all Malthus's teaching may be said to converge upon this practical point. Add to the Ten Commandments the new law, 'Thou shalt not marry until there is a fair prospect of supporting six children.' Then population will increase, but sufficient means for subsistence will always be provided beforehand. We shall make sure that there is a provision for additional numbers before, not after, we add to our numbers. Food first and population afterwards gives the rule; thus we achieve the good end without the incidental evils.

Malthus's views of the appropriate remedy for social evils undoubtedly show an imperfect appreciation of the great problems involved. Reckless propagation is an evil; but Malthus regards it as an evil which can be isolated and suppressed by simply adding a new article to the moral code. He is dealing with a central problem of human nature and social order. Any modification of the sexual instincts or of the constitution of the family involves a profound modification of the whole social order and of the dominant religious and moral creeds. Malthus tacitly assumes that conduct is determined by the play of two instincts, unalterable in themselves, but capable of modification in their results by a more extensive view of consequences. To change men's ruling motives in regard to the most important part of their lives is to alter their whole aims and conceptions of the world, and of happiness in every other relation. It supposes, therefore, not a mere addition of knowledge, but a transformation of character and an altered view of all the theories which have been embodied in religious and ethical philosophy. He overlooks, too, considerations which would be essential to a complete statement. A population which is too prudent may suffer itself to be crowded out by more prolific races in the general struggle for existence; and cases may be suggested such as that of the American colonies, in which an increase of numbers might be actually an advantage by facilitating a more efficient organisation of labour.

The absence of a distinct appreciation of such difficulties gives to his speculation that one-sided character which alienated his more sentimental contemporaries. It was natural enough in a man who was constantly confronted by the terrible development of pauperism in England, and was too much tempted to assume that the tendency to reckless propagation was not only a very grave evil, but the ultimate source of every evil. The doctrine taken up in this unqualified fashion by some of his disciples, and preached by them with the utmost fervour as the one secret of prosperity, shocked both the conservative and orthodox whose prejudices were trampled upon, and such Radicals as inherited Godwin's or Condorcet's theory of perfectibility. Harsh and one-sided as it might be, however, we may still hold that it was of value, not only in regard to the most pressing difficulty of the day, but also as calling attention to a vitally important condition of social welfare. The question, however, recurs whether, when the doctrine is so qualified as to be admissible, it does not also become a mere truism.

An answer to this question should begin by recognising one specific resemblance between his speculations and Darwin's. Facts, which appear from an older point of view to be proofs of a miraculous interposition, become with Malthus, as with Darwin, the normal results of admitted conditions. Godwin had admitted that there was some 'principle which kept population on a level with subsistence.' 'The sole question is,' says Malthus, [261] 'what is this principle? Is it some obscure and occult cause? a mysterious interference of heaven,' inflicting barrenness at certain periods? or 'a cause open to our researches and within our view?' Other writers had had recourse to the miraculous. One of Malthus's early authorities was Süssmilch, who had published his *Göttliche Ordnung* in 1761, to show how Providence had taken care that the trees should not grow into the sky. The antediluvians had been made long-lived in order that they might have large families and people an empty earth, while life was divinely shortened as the world filled up. Süssmilch, however, regarded population as still in need of stimulus. Kings might help Providence. A new Trajan would deserve to be called the father of his people, if he increased the marriage-rate. Malthus replies that the statistics which the worthy man himself produced showed conclusively that the marriages depended upon the deaths. The births fill up the vacancies, and the prince who increased the population before vacancies arose would simply increase the rate of mortality. [262] If you want to increase your birth-rate without absolutely producing famine, as he remarks afterwards, [263] make your towns unhealthy, and encourage settlement by marshes. You might thus double the mortality, and we might all marry prematurely without being absolutely starved. His own aim is not to secure the greatest number of births, but to be sure that the greatest number of those born may be supported. [264] The ingenious M. Muret, again, had found a Swiss parish in which the mean life was the highest and the fecundity smallest known. He piously conjectures that it may be a law of God that 'the force of life in each country should be in the inverse ratio of its fecundity.' He needs not betake himself to a miracle, says Malthus. [265] The case is simply that in a small and healthy village, where people had become aware of the importance of the 'preventive check,' the young people put off marriage till there was room for them, and consequently both lowered the birth-rate and raised the average duration of life.

Nothing, says Malthus very forcibly, has caused more errors than the confusion between 'relative and positive, and between cause and effect.' [266] He is here answering the argument that because the poor who had cows were the most industrious, the way to make them industrious was to give them cows. Malthus thinks it more probable that industry got the cow than that the cow produced industry. This is a trifling instance of a very general truth. People had been content to notice the deaths caused by war and disease, and to infer at once that what caused death must diminish population. Malthus shows the necessity of observing other collateral results. The gap may be made so great as to diminish population; but it may be compensated by a more rapid reproduction; or, the rapidity of reproduction may itself be the cause of the disease; so that to remove one kind of mortality may be on some occasion to introduce others. The stream is dammed on one breach to flow more strongly through other outlets. [267]

This is, I conceive, to say simply that Malthus was introducing a really scientific method. The facts taken in the true order became at once intelligible instead of suggesting mysterious and irregular interferences. Earlier writers had been content to single out one particular set of phenomena without attending to its place in the more general and complex processes, of which they formed an integral part. Infanticide, as Hume had pointed out, might tend to increase population. [268] In prospect, it might encourage people to have babies; and when babies came, natural affection might prevent the actual carrying out of the intention. To judge of the actual effect, we have to consider the whole of the concrete case. It may be carried out, as apparently in the South Sea Islands, so generally as to limit population; or it may be, as in China, an indication that the pressure is so great that a number of infants become superfluous. Its suppression might, in the one case, lead to an increase of the population; in the other, to the increase of other forms of mortality. Malthus's investigations illustrate the necessity of referring every particular process to its place in the whole system, of noting how any given change might set up a set of actions and reactions in virtue of the general elasticity of population, and thus of constantly referring at every step to the general conditions of human life. He succeeded in making many points clear, and of showing how hastily many inferences had been drawn. He explained, for example, why the revolutionary wars had not diminished the population of France, in spite of the great number of deaths, [269] and thus gave an example of a sound method of inquiry which has exercised a great influence upon later observers. Malthus was constantly misunderstood and misrepresented, and his opponents often allege as fatal objections to his doctrine the very facts by which it was really supported. But we may, I think, say, that since his writing no serious economical writer has adopted the old hasty guesses, or has ventured to propose a theory without regard to the principles of which he first brought out the full significance.

V. POLITICAL APPLICATION

This I take to indicate one real and permanent value of Malthus's writings. He introduced a new method of approaching the great social problems. The value of the method may remain, however inaccurate may be the assumptions of facts. The 'tendency,' if interpreted to mean that people are always multiplying too rapidly, may be a figment. If it is taken as calling attention to one essential factor in the case, it is a most important guide to investigation. This brings out another vital point. The bearing of the doctrine upon the political as well as upon the economical views of the Utilitarians is of conspicuous importance. Malthus's starting-point, as we have seen, was the opposition to the doctrine of 'perfectibility.' Hard facts, which Godwin and Condorcet had neglected, were fatal to their dreams. You have, urged Malthus, neglected certain undeniable truths as to the unalterable qualities of human nature, and, therefore, your theories will not work. The revolutionists had opposed an ideal 'state of nature' to the actual arrangements of society. They imagined that the 'state of nature' represented the desirable consummation, and that the constitution of the 'natural' order could be determined from certain abstract principles. The equality of man, and the absolute rights which could be inferred by a kind of mathematical process, supplied the necessary dogmatic basis. The antithesis to the state of nature was the artificial state, marked by inequality, and manifesting its spirit by luxury. Kings, priests, and nobles had somehow established this unnatural order; and to sweep them away summarily was the way of bringing the natural order into full activity. The ideal system was already potentially in existence, and would become actual when men's minds were once cleared from superstition, and the political made to correspond to the natural rights of man. To this Malthus had replied, as we have seen, that social inequality was not a mere arbitrary product of fraud and force, but an expedient necessary to restrain the primitive instincts of mankind. He thus coincides with Bentham's preference of 'security' to 'equality,' and illustrates the real significance of that doctrine. Property and marriage, though they involve inequality, were institutions of essential importance. Godwin had pushed his theories to absolute anarchy; to the destruction of all law, for law in general represented coercion or an interference with the state of nature.

Malthus virtually asserted that the metaphysical doctrine was inapplicable because, men being what they are, these conclusions were incompatible with even the first stages of social progress. This means, again, that for the metaphysical method Malthus is substituting a scientific method. Instead of regarding all government as a kind of mysterious intervention from without, which has somehow introduced a fatal discord into the natural order, he inquires what are the facts; how law has been evolved; and for what reason. His answer is, in brief, that law, order, and inequality have been absolutely necessary in order to limit tendencies which would otherwise keep men in a state of hopeless poverty and depression.

This gives the 'differentia' of the Utilitarian considered as one species of the genus 'Radical.' Malthus's criticism of Paine is significant. [270] He agrees with Paine that the cause of popular risings is 'want of happiness.' But Paine, he remarks, was 'in many important points totally ignorant of the structure of society'; and has fallen into the error of attributing all want of happiness to government. Consequently, Paine advocates a plan for distributing taxes among the poorest classes, which would aggravate the evils a hundredfold. He fully admits with Paine that man has rights. The true line of answer would be to show what those rights are. To give this answer is not Malthus's present business; but there is one right, at any rate, which a man does not and cannot possess: namely, the 'right to subsistence when his labour will not fairly purchase it.' He does not possess it because he cannot possess it; to try to secure it is to try to 'reverse the laws of nature,' and therefore to produce cruel suffering by practising an 'inhuman deceit.' The Abbé Raynal had said that a man had a right to subsist 'before all social laws.' Man had the same right, replied Malthus, as he had to live a hundred or a thousand years. He may live, *if he can* without interfering with others. Social laws have, in fact, enlarged the power of subsistence; but neither before nor after their institution could an unlimited number subsist. Briefly, the question of fact comes before the question of right, and the fault of the revolutionary theorists was to settle the right without reference to the possibility of making the right correspond to the fact.

Hence Malthus draws his most emphatic political moral. The admission that all evil is due to government is the way to tyranny. Make men believe that government is the one cause of misery, and they will inevitably throw the whole responsibility upon their rulers; seek for redress by cures which aggravate the disease; and strengthen the hands of those who prefer even despotism to anarchy. This, he intimates, is the explanation of the repressive measures in which the country-gentlemen had supported Pitt. The people had fancied that by destroying government they would make bread cheap; government was forced to be tyrannical in order to resist revolution; while its supporters were led to 'give up some of the most valuable privileges of Englishmen.' [271] It is then of vital importance to settle what is and what is not to be set down to government. Malthus, in fact, holds that the real evils are due to underlying causes which cannot be directly removed, though they may be diminished or increased, by legislators. Government can do something by giving security to property, and by making laws which will raise the self-respect of the lower classes. But the effect of such laws must be slow and gradual; and the error which has most contributed to that delay in the progress of freedom, which is 'so disheartening to every liberal mind,' [272] is the confusion as to the true causes of misery. Thus, as he has already urged, professed economists could still believe, so long after the publication of Adam Smith's work, that it was 'in the power of the justices of the peace or even of the omnipotence of parliament to alter by a *fiat* the whole circumstances of the country.' [273] Yet men who saw the absurdity of trying to fix the price of provisions were ready to propose to fix the rate of wages. They did not see that one term of the proportion implied the other. Malthus's whole criticism of the poor-law, already noticed, is a commentary upon this text. It is connected with a general theory of human nature. The author of nature, he says, has wisely made 'the passion of self-love beyond expression stronger than the passion of benevolence.' [274] He means, as he explains, that every man has to pursue his own welfare and that of his family as his primary object. Benevolence, of course, is the 'source of our purest and most refined pleasures,' and so forth; but it should come in as a supplement to self-love. Therefore we must never admit that men have a strict right to relief. That is to injure the very essential social force. 'Hard as it may seem in individual instances, dependent poverty ought to be held disgraceful.' [275] The spirit of independence or self-help is the one thing necessary. 'The desire of bettering our condition and the fear of making it worse, like the *vis medicatrix* in physics, is the *vis medicatrix naturae* in politics, and is continually counteracting the disorders arising from narrow human institutions.' [276] It is only because the poor-laws have not quite destroyed it, that they have not quite ruined the country. The pith of Malthus's teaching is fairly expressed in his last letter to Senior. [277] He holds that the improvement in the condition of the great mass of the labouring classes should be considered as the main interest of society. To improve their condition, it is essential to impress them with the conviction that they can do much more for themselves than others can do for them, and that the *only* source of permanent improvement is the improvement of their moral and religious habits. What government can do, therefore, is to maintain such institutions as may strengthen the *vis medicatrix*, or 'desire to better our condition,' which poor-laws had directly tended to weaken. He maintains in his letter to Senior, that this desire is 'perfectly feeble' compared with the tendency of the population to increase, and operates in a very slight degree upon the great mass of the labouring class. [278] Still, he holds that on the whole the 'preventive checks' have become stronger relatively to the positive, [279] and, at any rate, all proposals must be judged by their tendency to strengthen the preventive.

Malthus was not a thoroughgoing supporter of the 'do-nothing' doctrine. He approved of a national system of education, and of the early factory acts, though only as applied to infant labour. So, as we shall see, did all the Utilitarians. The 'individualism,' however, is not less decided; and leads him to speak as though the elasticity of population were not merely an essential factor in the social problem, but the sole principle from which all solutions must be deduced. He is thus led, as I have tried to show, to a narrow interpretation of his 'moral check.' He is apt to take 'vice' simply as a product of excessive pressure, and, in his general phrases at least, to overlook its reciprocal tendency to cause pressure. The 'moral check' is only preventive or negative, not a positive cause of superior vigour. A similar defect appears in his theory of the *vis medicatrix*. He was, I hold, perfectly right in emphasising the importance of individual responsibility. No reform can be permanent which does not raise the morality of the individual. His insistence upon this truth was of the highest importance, and it is to be wished that its importance might be more fully recognised to-day. The one-sidedness appears in his proposal to abolish the poor-law simply. That became the most conspicuous and widely accepted doctrine. All men of 'sense,' said Sydney Smith—certainly a qualified representative of the class—in 1820, agree, first, that the poor-law must be abolished; and secondly, that it must be abolished very gradually. [280] That is really to assume that by refusing to help people at all, you will force them to help themselves. There is another alternative, namely, that they may, as Malthus himself often recognises, become demoralised by excessive poverty. To do simply nothing may lead to degeneration instead of increased energy. The possibility of an improved law, which might act as a moral discipline instead of a simply corrupting agency, is simply left out of account; and the tendency to stimulate reckless population is regarded not only as one probable consequence, but as the very essence of all poor-laws. Upon Malthus's assumptions, the statement that sound political and social theories must be based upon systematic inquiry into facts, meant that the individual was the ultimate unalterable unit, whose interest in his own welfare gave the one fulcrum for all possible changes. The ideal 'state of nature' was a fiction. The true basis of our inquiries is the actual man known to us by observation. The main fault of this being was the excess of the instinct of multiplication, and the way to improve him was to show how it might conflict with the instinct of self-preservation. In this shape the doctrine expressed the most characteristic tendency of the Utilitarians, and divided them from the Socialists or believers in abstract rights of man.

VI. RENT

Here, then, we are at a central point of the Utilitarian creed. The expansive force of population is, in a sense, the great motive power which moulds the whole social structure; or, rather, it forces together the independent units, and welds them into an aggregate. The influence of this doctrine upon other economical speculations is of the highest importance. One critical stage in the process is marked by the enunciation of the theory of rent, which was to become another essential article of the true faith. The introduction of this doctrine is characteristic, and marks the point at which Ricardo superseded Malthus as chief expositor of the doctrine.

Malthus's views were first fully given in his *Inquiry into Rent*, the second of three pamphlets which he published during the corn-law controversy of 1814-15. [281] The opinions now stated had, he says, been formed in the course of his lecturing at Haileybury; and he made them public on account of their bearing upon the most absorbing questions of the time. The connection of the theory with Malthus's speculations and with the contemporary difficulties is indeed obvious. The landlord had clearly one of the reserved seats at the banquet of nature. He was the most obvious embodiment of 'security' as opposed to equality. Malthus, again, had been influenced by the French economists and their theory of the 'surplus fund,' provided by agriculture. According to them, as he says, [282] this fund or rent constitutes the whole national wealth. In his first edition he had defended the economists against some of Adam Smith's criticisms; and though he altered his views and thought that they had been led into preposterous errors, he retained a certain sympathy for them. Agriculture has still a certain 'pre-eminence.' God has bestowed upon the soil the 'inestimable quality of being able to maintain more persons than are necessary to work it.' [283] It has the special virtue that the supply of necessaries generates the demand. Make more luxuries and the price may fall; but grow more food and there will be more people to eat it. This, however, seems to be only another way of stating an unpleasant fact. The blessing of 'fertility' counteracts itself. As he argues in the essay, [284] an equal division of land might produce such an increase of population as would exhaust any conceivable increase of food. These views—not, I think, very clear or consistently worked out—lead apparently to the conclusion that the fertility is indeed a blessing, but on condition of being confined to a few. The result, in any case, is the orthodox theory of rent. The labourer gets less than he would if the products of the soil were equally distributed. Both wages and profits must fall as more is left to rent, and that this actually happens, he says, with unusual positiveness, is an 'incontrovertible truth.' [285] The fall enables the less fertile land to be cultivated, and gives an excess of produce on the more fertile. 'This excess is rent.' [286] He proceeds to expound his doctrine by comparing land to a set of machines for making corn. [287] If, in manufacture, a new machine is introduced every one adopts it. In agriculture the worst machines have still to be used; and those who have the best and sell at the same price, can appropriate the surplus advantage. This, he declares, is a law 'as invariable as the action of the principle of gravity.' [288] Yet Smith and others have overlooked a 'principle of the highest importance' [289] and have failed to see that the price of corn, as of other things, must conform to the cost of production. The same doctrine was expounded in the same year by Sir Edward West; [290] and, as it seems to me, more clearly and simply. West, like Malthus, says that he has to announce a principle overlooked by Adam Smith. This is briefly that 'each equal additional quantity of work bestowed on agriculture yields an actually diminished return.' He holds that profits fall as wealth increases, but he denies Adam Smith's view that this is a simple result of increased competition. [291] Competition would equalise, but would not lower profits, for 'the productive powers of manufactures are constantly increasing.' In agriculture the law is the opposite one of diminishing returns. Hence the admitted fall of profits shows that the necessity of taking inferior soils into cultivation is the true cause of the fall.

Such coincidences as that between Malthus and West are common enough, for very obvious reasons. In this case, I think, there is less room for surprise than usual. The writer generally credited with the discovery of the rent doctrine is James Anderson, who had stated it as early as 1777. [292] The statement, however, did not attract attention until at the time of West and Malthus it was forced upon observers by the most conspicuous facts of the day. Adam Smith and other economists had, as Malthus notices, observed what is obvious enough, that rent in some way represented a 'net produce'—a something which remained after paying the costs of production. So much was obvious to any common-sense observer. In a curious paper of December 1804, [293] Cobbett points out that the landlords will always keep the profits of farmers down to the average rate of equally agreeable businesses. This granted, it is a short though important step to the theory of rent. The English system had, in fact, spontaneously analysed the problem. The landlord, farmer, and labourer represented the three interests which might elsewhere be combined. Prices raised by war and famine had led to the enclosure of wastes and the breaking up of pastures. The 'margin of cultivation' was thus illustrated by facts. Farmers were complaining that they could not make a profit if prices were lowered. The landed classes were profiting by a rise of price raised, according to a familiar law, in greater proportion than the deficiency of the harvest. Facts of this kind were, one must suppose, familiar to every land-agent; and to discover the law of rent, it was only necessary for Malthus and West to put them in their natural order. The egg had only to be put on its end, though that, as we know, is often a difficult task. When the feat was accomplished consequences followed which were fully developed by Ricardo.

FOOTNOTES:

[203] Mr. James Bonar's *Malthus and his Work* (1885) gives an admirable account of Malthus. The chief original authorities are a life by Bishop Otter, prefixed to a second edition of the *Political Economy* (1831), and an article by Empson, Malthus's colleague, in the *Edinburgh Review* for January 1837.

[204] *Political Justice* (3rd edition, 1798), ii. bk. viii. chap. ix., p. 514.

[205] Wallace wrote in answer to Hume, *A Dissertation on the Numbers of Mankind in Ancient and Modern Times* (1753), and *Various Prospects of Mankind*, and *Nature and Providence* (1761). Godwin refers to the last.

[206] *Political Justice*, ii. 520.

[207] *Ibid.* ii. 528.

[208] First published in 1795, after the first edition, as Godwin remarks, of the *Political Justice*.

[209] *Ami des hommes* (reprint of 1883), p. 15.

[210] *Ami des hommes*, p. 26.

[211] See the curious debate in *Parl. Hist.* xiv. 1318-1365.

[212] The seventh edition of Price's *Observations on Reversionary Payments*, etc. (1812), contains a correspondence with Pitt (i. 216, etc.). The editor, W. Morgan, accuses Pitt of adopting Price's plans without due acknowledgment and afterwards spoiling them.

[213] *Essay on Population*, p. 18. In *Observations*, ii. 141, he estimates the diminution at a million and a half. Other books referring to the same controversy are Howlett's *Examination of Dr. Price's Essay* (1781); *Letter to Lord Carlisle*, by William Eden (1744-1814), first Lord Auckland; William Wales's *Enquiry into Present State of Population*, etc. (1781); and Geo. Chalmers's *Estimate of the Comparative Strength of Great Britain* (1782 and several later editions).

[214] *Essay* (first edition), p. 339.

[215] *Memoirs*, etc. (1819), ii. 10.

[216] So Sir James Stewart, whose light was extinguished by Adam Smith, begins his *Enquiry into the Principles of Political Economy* (1767) by discussing the question of population, and compares the 'generative faculty' to a spring loaded with a weight, and exerting itself in proportion to the diminution of resistance (*Works*, 1805, i. 22). He compares population to 'rabbits in a warren.' Joseph Townsend, in his *Journey Through Spain* (1792), to whom Malthus refers, had discussed the supposed decay of the Spanish population, and illustrates his principles by a geometric progression: see ii. 213-56, 386-91. Eden, in his book on the poor (i. 214), quotes a tract attributed to Sir Matthew Hale for the statement that the poor increase on 'geometrical progression.'

[217] *Malthus and his Work*, p. 85.

[218] Voltaire says in the *Dictionnaire Philosophique* (art. 'Population'): 'On ne propage point en Progression Géométrique. Tous les calculs qu'on a faits sur cette prétendue multiplication sont des chimères absurdes.' They had been used to reconcile the story of the deluge with the admitted population of the world soon afterwards.

[219] *Essay* (1826), ii 453 *n.* I cite from this, the last edition published in Malthus's lifetime, unless otherwise stated.

[220] *Essay*, ii. 251 (bk. iii. ch. xiv.).

[221] *Ibid.* (1798), p. 141.

[222] *Essay*, ii. 449 (Appendix).

[223] *Essay*, ii. 473 (Appendix).

[224] *Ibid.* (Second Edition), p. 400. The passage is given in full in *Malthus and his Work*, p. 307.

[225] *Essay*, i. 469 (bk. ii. ch. x.). Eden had made the same remark.

[226] *Ibid.* ii. 229 (bk. iii. ch. xiv.).

[227] Correspondence in Senior's *Three Essays on Population* (1829).

[228] *Essay*, i. 234 (bk. i. ch. ii.).

[229] Mr. Bonar thinks (*Malthus and his Work*, p. 324) that Malthus followed Paley's predecessor, Abraham Tucker, rather than Paley. The difference is not for my purpose important. In any case, Malthus's references are to Paley.

[230] *Essay*, ii. 266 (bk. iv. ch. i.).

[231] *Essay* (first edition), p. 212.

[232] *Ibid.* i. 16 *n.* (bk. i. ch. ii.).

[233] See *e.g.* his remarks upon Condorcet in *Essay*, ii. 8 (bk. iii. ch. i.); and Owen in *Ibid.* ii. 48 (bk. iii ch. ii.).

[234] *Essay*, i. 15 *n.* (bk. i. ch. ii.); and see *Ibid.* (edit. of 1807) ii. 128.

[235] *Ibid.* (1807) ii. 128.

[236] *Ibid.* (1807) ii. 3 (bk. ii. ch. ii.). (Omitted in later editions.)

[237] Mr. A. R. Wallace, Darwin's fellow-discoverer of the doctrine, also learned it from Malthus. See Clodd's *Pioneers of Evolution.* Malthus uses the phrase 'struggle for existence' in relation to a fight between two savage tribes in the first edition of his *Essay*, p. 48. In replying to Condorcet, Malthus speaks (*Essay*, ii. 12, bk. iii. ch. i.) of the possible improvement of living organisms. He argues that, though a plant may be improved, it cannot be indefinitely improved by cultivation. A carnation could not be made as large as a tulip. It has been said that this implies a condemnation by anticipation of theories of the development of species. This is hardly correct. Malthus simply urges against Condorcet that our inability to fix limits precisely does not imply that there are no limits. This, it would seem, must be admitted on all hands. Evolution implies definite though not

precisely definable limits. Life may be lengthened, but not made immortal.

[238] *Essay* (first edition), 353.

[239] *Ibid.* 42 *n.* (bk. iii. ch. iii.)

[240] *Essay*, ii. 301-36 (bk. iv. ch. i. and ii.). Sumner's *Treatise on the Records of the Creation, and on the Moral Attributes of the Creator: with Particular Reference to the Jewish History and the Consistency of the Principle of Population with the Wisdom and Goodness of the Creator* (1815), had gained the second Burnett prize. It went through many editions; and shows how Cuvier confirms Genesis, and Malthus proves that the world was intended to involve a competition favourable to the industrious and sober. Sumner's view of Malthus is given in Part ii., chaps, v. and vi. In previous chapters he has supported Malthus's attack on Godwin and Condorcet.

[241] *Essay*, ii. 266 (bk. iv. ch. i.).

[242] *Essay*, ii 268 (bk. iv. ch. i.).

[243] *Ibid.* (bk. iv. ch. ii.).

[244] *Essay*, 241 (bk. iii. ch. iv.).

[245] *Ibid.* ii. 241 (bk. iii. ch. xiv.).

[246] *Ibid.* ii. 293 (bk. iv. ch. iv.).

[247] *Ibid.* ii. 425 (bk. iv. ch. xiii.). Malthus expresses a hope that Paley had modified his views upon population, and refers to a passage in the *Natural Theology.*

[248] *Essay*, ii. 292 (bk. iv. ch. iv.).

[249] *Political Economy* (1836), p. 214.

[250] *Essay*, ii. 298 (bk. iv. ch. iv.).

[251] *Ibid.* ii. 86 (bk. iii. ch. vi.).

[252] *Ibid.* ii. 87 (bk. iii. ch. vi.).

[253] *Essay*, ii. 90 (bk. iii. ch. vi.).

[254] *Ibid.* ii. 338 (bk. iv. ch. viii.).

[255] *Ibid.* ii. (bk. iv. ch. x.).

[256] *Ibid.* ii. 353 (bk. iv. ch. ix.).

[257] *Essay*, ii. 356 (bk. iv. ch. ix.).

[258] *Ibid.* ii. 407 (bk. iv. ch. xii.).

[259] *Ibid.* ii. 375 (bk. iv. ch. xi.).

[260] *Ibid.* ii. 429 (bk. iv. ch. xiii.).

[261] *Essay of 1807* (bk. iii. ch. ii., and vol. ii. p. 111). The phrases quoted are toned down in later editions.

[262] *Essay,* i. 330 (bk. ii. ch. iv.).

[263] *Ibid.* ii. 300 (bk. iv. ch. v.).

[264] *Ibid.* ii. 405 (bk. iv. ch. xiii.).

[265] *Ibid.* i. 343 (bk. ii. ch. v.).

[266] *Essay,* ii. 424 (bk. iv. ch. xiii.).

[267] *Ibid.* ii. 304 (bk. iv. ch. v.).

[268] *Essay,* i. 75 (bk. i. ch. v.).

[269] *Ibid.* (bk. ii. ch. vi.).

[270] *Essay,* ii. 318 (bk. iv. ch. vi.).

[271] *Essay,* ii. 315 (bk. iv. ch. v.).

[272] *Ibid.* ii. 326 (bk. iv. ch. vi.).

[273] *Ibid.* ii. 78 (bk. iii. ch. v.).

[274] *Essay,* ii. 454 (Appendix).

[275] *Ibid.* ii. 82 (bk. iii. ch. vi.).

[276] *Ibid.* ii. 90 (bk. iii. ch. vi.).

[277] Senior's *Three Lectures,* p. 86.

[278] Senior's *Three Lectures,* p. 60.

[279] *Essay,* i. 534 (bk. ii. ch. xiii.).

[280] Smith's *Works* (1859), i. 295.

[281] *Observations on the Effects of the Corn-laws, 1814; Inquiry into the Nature and Progress of Rent, 1815*; and *The Grounds of an Opinion on the Policy of restricting the Importation of Foreign Corn,* intended as an appendix to the *Observations on the Corn-laws,* 1815.

[282] *Inquiry into Rent,* p. 1.

[283] *Ibid*

[284] *Essay*, ii. 35 (bk. iii. ch. ii.).

[285] *Inquiry into Rent*, p. 20.

[286] *Ibid.*

[287] *Ibid.*

[288] *Inquiry into Rent*, p. 20.

[289] *Ibid*

[290] *Essay on the Application of Capital to Land, by a Fellow of University College, Oxford, 1815.*

[291] *Essay*, p. 19.

[292] *In An Inquiry into the Nature of the Corn-laws,* and again (1801) in *Observations on Agriculture,* etc., vol. v. 401-51.

[293] *Political Works*, i. 485, etc. In this paper, I may add, Cobbett, not yet a Radical, accepts Malthus's view of the tendency of the human species to multiply more quickly than its support. He does not mention Malthus, but speaks of the belief as universally admitted, and afterwards illustrates it amusingly by saying that, in his ploughboy days, he used to wonder that there was always just enough hay for the horses and enough horses for the hay.

CHAPTER V
RICARDO

I. RICARDO'S STARTING-POINT

David Ricardo, [294] born 19th April 1772, was the son of a Dutch Jew who had settled in England, and made money upon the Stock Exchange. Ricardo had a desultory education, and was employed in business from his boyhood. He abandoned his father's creed, and married an Englishwoman soon after reaching his majority. He set up for himself in business, and, at a time when financial transactions upon an unprecedented scale were giving great opportunities for speculators, he made a large fortune, and about 1814 bought an estate at Gatcombe Park, Gloucestershire. He withdrew soon afterwards from business, and in 1819 became member of parliament. His death on 11th September 1823 cut short a political career from which his perhaps too sanguine friends anticipated great results. His influence in his own department of inquiry had been, meanwhile, of the greatest importance. He had shown in his youth some inclination for scientific pursuits; he established a laboratory, and became a member of scientific societies. The perusal of Adam Smith's *Wealth of Nations* in 1799 gave him an interest in the application of scientific methods to the questions with which he was most conversant. Accepting Adam Smith as the leading authority, he proceeded to think out for himself certain doctrines, which appeared to him to have been insufficiently recognised by his teacher. The first result of his speculations was a pamphlet published in 1809 upon the depreciation of the currency. Upon that topic he spoke as an expert, and his main doctrines were accepted by the famous Bullion Committee. Ricardo thus became a recognised authority on one great set of problems of the highest immediate interest. Malthus's *Inquiry into Rent* suggested another pamphlet; and in 1817, encouraged by the warm pressure of his friend, James Mill, he published his chief book, the *Principles of Political Economy and Taxation*. This became the economic Bible of the Utilitarians. The task of a commentator or interpreter is, for various reasons, a difficult one.

There is a certain analogy between Ricardo and a very different writer, Bishop Butler. Each of them produced a great effect by a short treatise, and in each case the book owed very little to the ordinary literary graces. Ricardo's want of literary training, or his natural difficulty of utterance, made his style still worse than Butler's; but, like Butler, he commands our respect by his obvious sincerity and earnestness. He is content when he has so expressed his argument that it can be seized by an attentive reader. He is incapable of, or indifferent to, clear and orderly exposition of principles. The logic is there, if you will take the trouble to look for it. Perhaps we ought to be flattered by this tacit reliance upon our patience. 'You,' Ricardo, like Butler, seems to say to us, 'are anxious for truth: you do not care for ornament, and may be trusted to work out the full application of my principles.' In another respect the two are alike. Butler's argument has impressed many readers as a demolition of his own case. It provokes revolt instead of adhesion. Ricardo, an orthodox economist, laid down principles which were adopted by Socialists to upset his own assumptions. Such a God as you worship, said Butler's opponents, is an unjust being, and therefore worse than no God. Such a system as you describe, said Ricardo's opponents, is an embodiment of injustice, and therefore to be radically destroyed. Admitting the logic, the argument may be read as a *reductio ad absurdum* in both cases.

Ricardo has involved himself in certain special difficulties. In the first place, he presupposes familiarity with Adam Smith. The *Principles* is a running comment upon some of Smith's theories, and no attempt is made to reduce them to systematic order. He starts by laying down propositions, the proof of which comes afterwards, and is then rather intimated than expressly given. He adopts the terminology which Smith had accepted from popular use, [295] and often applies it in a special significance, which is at least liable to be misunderstood by his readers, or forgotten by himself. It is difficult, again, to feel sure whether some of his statements are to be taken as positive assertions of fact, or merely as convenient assumptions for the purposes of his argument. Ricardo himself, as appears in his letters, was painfully aware of his own awkwardness of expression, and upon that point alone all his critics seem to be in tolerable agreement. Happily, it will be enough for my purpose if I can lay down his essential premises without following him to the remoter deductions.

Ricardo's pamphlet upon Malthus (1815) gives a starting-point. Ricardo cordially adopts Malthus's theory of rent, but declares that it is fatal to some of Malthus's conclusions. Malthus, we have seen, wished to regard rent as in some sense a gift of Providence—a positive blessing due to the fertility of the soil. Ricardo maintains, on the contrary, that 'the interest of the landlord is necessarily opposed to the interest of every other class in the community.' [296] The landlord is prosperous when corn is scarce and dear; all other persons when it is plentiful and cheap. This follows upon Malthus's own showing. As men are forced to have recourse to inferior soils, the landlord obtains a larger share of the whole produce; and, moreover, since corn also becomes more valuable, will have a larger share of a more valuable product. The question apparently in dispute—whether we should be glad that some land is better than the worst, or sorry because all is not equal to the best—seems rather idle. The real question, however, is whether rent, being a blessing, should be kept up by protection, [297] or, being a curse, should be brought down by competition? What is the real working of the system? Set the trade free, says Ricardo, and the capital will be withdrawn from the poor land and employed upon manufactures, to be exchanged for the corn of other countries. [298] The change must correspond to a more advantageous distribution of capital, or it would not be adopted. The principle involved in this last proposition is, he adds, one of the 'best established in the science of political economy, and by no one is more readily admitted than by Mr. Malthus.' To enforce protection would be, on Malthus's illustration, to compel us to use the 'worst machines, when, at a less expense, we could hire the very best from our neighbours.' [299] Briefly, then, the landlord's interest is opposed to the national interest, because it enforces a worse distribution of capital. He compels us to get corn from his worst land, instead of getting it indirectly, but in greater quantity, from our spinning-jennies.

For Ricardo, as for Malthus, the ultimate driving force is the pressure of population. The mass of mankind is always struggling to obtain food, and is able to multiply so rapidly as to exhaust any conceivable increase of supplies. The landlord class alone profits. The greater the struggle for supply the greater will be the share of the whole produce which must be surrendered to it. Beyond this, however, lies the further problem which specially occupied Ricardo. How will the resulting strain affect the relations of the two remaining classes, the labourers and the capitalists? The ultimate evil of protection is the bad distribution of capital. But capital always acts by employing labour. The farmer's capital does not act by itself, but by enabling his men to work. Hence, to understand the working of the industrial machinery, we have to settle the relation of wages and profits. Ricardo states this emphatically in his preface. Rent, profit, and wages, he says, represent the three parts into which the whole produce of the earth is divided. 'To determine the laws which regulate this distribution is the principal problem in political economy'; and one, he adds, which has been left in obscurity by previous writers. [300] His investigations are especially directed by the purpose thus defined. He was the first writer who fairly brought under distinct consideration what he held, with reason, to be the most important branch of economical inquiry.

There was clearly a gap in the economic doctrine represented by the *Wealth of Nations*. Adam Smith was primarily concerned with the theory of the 'market.' He assumes the existence of the social arrangement which is indicated by that phrase. The market implies a constitution of industrial agencies such that, within it, only one price is possible for a given commodity, or, rather, such that a difference of price cannot be permanent. According to the accepted illustration, the sea is not absolutely level, but it is always tending to a level. [301] A permanent elevation at one point is impossible. The agency by which this levelling or equilibrating process is carried out is competition, involving what Smith called the 'higgling of the market.' The momentary fluctuation, again, supposes the action of 'supply and demand,' which, as they vary, raise and depress prices. To illustrate the working of this machinery, to show how previous writers had been content to notice a particular change without following out the collateral results, and had thus been led into fallacies such as that of the 'mercantile system,' was Smith's primary task.

Beyond or beneath these questions lie difficulties, which Smith, though not blind to their existence, treated in a vacillating and inconsistent fashion. Variations of supply and demand cause fluctuations in the price; but what finally determines the point to which the fluctuating prices must gravitate? We follow the process by which one wave propagates another; but there is still the question, What ultimately fixes the normal level? Upon this point Ricardo could find no definite statement in his teacher. 'Supply and demand' was a sacred phrase which would always give a verbal answer, or indicate the immediate cause of variations on the surface. Beneath the surface there must be certain forces at work which settle why a quarter of corn 'gravitates' to a certain price; why the landlord can get just so many quarters of corn for the use of his fields; and why the produce, which is due jointly to the labourer and the farmer, is divided in a certain fixed proportion. To settle such points it is necessary to answer the problem of distribution, for the play of the industrial forces is directed by the constitution of the classes which co-operate in the result. Ricardo saw in Malthus's doctrines of rent and of population a new mode of approaching the problem. What was wanted, in the first place, was to systematise the logic adopted by his predecessors. Rent, it was clear, could not be both a cause and an effect of price, though at different points of his treatise Smith had apparently accepted each view of the relation. We must first settle which is cause and which effect; and then bring our whole system into the corresponding order. For the facts, Ricardo is content to trust mainly to others. The true title of his work should be that which his commentator, De Quincey, afterwards adopted, the *Logic of Political Economy*. This aim gives a partial explanation of the characteristic for which Ricardo is most generally criticised. He is accused of being abstract in the sense of neglecting facts. He does not deny the charge.

'If I am too theoretical (which I really believe to be the case) you,' he says to Malthus, 'I think, are too practical.' [302] If Malthus is more guided than Ricardo by a reference to facts, he has of course an advantage. But so far as Malthus or Adam Smith theorised—and, of course, their statement of facts involved a theory—they were at least bound to be consistent. It is one thing to recognise the existence of facts which your theory will not explain, and to admit that it therefore requires modification. It is quite another thing to explain each set of facts in turn by theories which contradict each other. That is not to be historical but to be muddleheaded. Malthus and Smith, as it seemed to Ricardo, had occasionally given explanations which, when set side by side, destroyed each other. He was therefore clearly justified in the attempt to exhibit these logical inconsistencies and to supply a theory which should be in harmony with itself. He was so far neither more nor less 'theoretical' than his predecessors, but simply more impressed by the necessity of having at least a consistent theory.

There was never a time at which logic in such matters was more wanted, or its importance more completely disregarded. Rash and ignorant theorists were plunging into intricate problems and propounding abstract solutions. The enormous taxation made necessary by the war suggested at every point questions as to the true incidence of the taxes. Who really gained or suffered by the protection of corn? Were the landlords, the farmers, or the labourers directly interested? Could they shift the burthen upon other shoulders or not? What, again, it was of the highest importance to know, was the true 'incidence' of tithes, of a land-tax, of the poor-laws, of an income-tax, and of all the multitudinous indirect taxes from which the national income was derived? The most varying views were held and eagerly defended. Who really paid? That question interested everybody, and occupies a large part of Ricardo's book. The popular answers involved innumerable inconsistencies, and were supported by arguments which only required to be confronted in order to be confuted. Ricardo's aim was to substitute a clear and consistent theory for this tangle of perplexed sophistry. In that sense his aim was in the highest degree 'practical,' although he left to others the detailed application of his doctrines to the actual facts of the day.

II. THE DISTRIBUTION PROBLEM

The rent doctrine gives one essential datum. A clear comprehension of rent is, as he was persuaded, 'of the utmost importance to political economy.' [303] The importance is that it enables him to separate one of the primary sources of revenue from the others. It is as though, in the familiar illustration, we were considering the conditions of equilibrium of a fluid; and we now see that one part may be considered as a mere overflow, resulting from (not determining) the other conditions. The primary assumption in the case of the market is the level of price. When we clearly distinguish rent on one side from profits and wages on the other, we see that we may also assume a level of profits. There cannot, as Ricardo constantly says, 'be two rates of profit,' that is, at the same time and in the same country. But so long as rent was lumped with other sources of revenue it was impossible to see, what Malthus and West had now made clear, that in agriculture, as in manufactures, the profits of the producer must conform to the principle. Given their theory, it follows that the power of land to yield a great revenue does not imply a varying rate of profit or a special bounty of nature bestowed upon agriculture. It means simply that, since the corn from the good and bad land sells at the same price, there is a surplus on the good. But as that surplus constitutes rent, the farmer's rate of profit will still be uniform. Thus we have got rid of one complication, and we are left with a comparatively simple issue. We have to consider the problem, What determines the distribution as between the capitalist and the labourer? That is the vital question for Ricardo.

Ricardo's theory, in the first place, is a modification of Adam Smith's. He accepts Smith's statement that wages are determined by the 'supply and demand of labourers,' and by the 'price of commodities on which their wages are expended.' [304] The appeal to 'supply and demand' implies that the rate of wages depends upon unchangeable economic conditions. He endorses [305] Malthus's statement about the absurdity of considering 'wages' as something which may be fixed by his Majesty's 'Justices of the Peace,' and infers with Malthus that wages should be left to find their 'natural level.' But what precisely is this 'natural level?' If the Justice of the Peace cannot fix the rate of wages, what does fix them? Supply and demand? What, then, is precisely meant in this case by the supply and demand? The 'supply' of labour, we may suppose, is fixed by the actual labouring population at a given time. The 'demand,' again, is in some way clearly related to 'capital.' As Smith again had said, [306] the demand for labour increases with the 'increase of revenue and "stock,"' and cannot possibly increase without it.' Ricardo agrees that 'population regulates itself by the funds which are to employ it, and therefore always increases or diminishes with the increase or diminution of capital.' [307] It was indeed a commonplace that the increase of capital was necessary to an increase of population, as it is obvious enough that population must be limited by the means of subsistence accumulated. Smith, for example, goes on to insist upon this in one of the passages which partly anticipates Malthus. [308] But this does not enable us to separate profit from wages, or solve Ricardo's problem. When we speak of supply and demand as determining the price of a commodity, we generally have in mind two distinct though related processes. One set of people is growing corn, and another working coal mines. Each industry, therefore, has a separate existence, though each may be partly dependent upon the other. But this is not true of labour and capital. They are not products of different countries or processes. They are inseparable constituents of a single process. Labour cannot be maintained without capital, nor can capital produce without labour. Capital, according to Ricardo's definition, is the 'part of the wealth of a country which is employed in production, and consists of food, clothing, raw materials, machinery, etc., necessary to give effect to labour.' [309] That part, then, of capital which is applied to the support of the labourer—his food, clothing, and so forth—is identical with wages. To say that, if it increases, his wages increase is to be simply tautologous. If, on the other hand, we include the machinery and raw materials, it becomes difficult to say in what sense 'capital' can be taken as a demand for labour. Ricardo tells Malthus that an accumulation of profit does not, as Malthus had said, necessarily raise wages [310] ; and he ultimately decided, much to the scandal of his disciple, M'Culloch, that an increase of 'fixed capital' or machinery might be actually prejudicial, under certain circumstances, to the labourer. The belief of the labouring class that machinery often injures them is not, he expressly says, 'founded on prejudice and error, but is conformable to the correct principles of political economy.' [311] The word 'capital,' indeed, was used with a vagueness which covered some of the most besetting fallacies of the whole doctrine. Ricardo himself sometimes speaks as though he had in mind merely the supply of labourers' necessaries, though he regularly uses it in a wider sense. The generalities, therefore, about supply and demand, take us little further.

From these difficulties Ricardo escapes by another method. Malthus's theory of population gives him what he requires. The 'natural price of labour' (as distinguished from its 'market price') is, as he asserts, 'that price which is necessary to enable the labourers, one with another, to subsist and perpetuate their race without either increase or diminution.' [312] This is the true 'natural price,' about which the 'market price' oscillates. An increase of capital may raise wages for a time above the natural price, but an increase of population will bring back the previous rate. Ricardo warns us, indeed, that this natural price of labour is not to be regarded as something 'absolutely fixed and constant.' [313] It varies in different times and countries, and even in the same country at different times. An English cottager now possesses what would once have been luxuries. Ricardo admits again [314] that the wages of different classes of labourers may be different, although he does not consider that this fact affects his argument. We may allow for it by considering the skilled labourer as 2 or 1-1/2 labourers rolled into one.

The assumption enables him to get out of a vicious circle. He is seeking to discover the proportions in which produce will be divided between the two classes, and which co-operate in the production. The 'demand and supply' principle may show that an increase of capital will tend to increase wages, but even that tendency, as he carefully points out, can only be admitted subject to certain important reservations. In any case, if it explains temporary fluctuations, it will not ascertain the point round which the fluctuations take place. But the two variables, wages and profit, are clearly connected, and if we can once assume that one of these variables is fixed by an independent law, we may explain in what way the other will be fixed. Having got rid of 'rent,' the remaining produce has to be divided between wages and profit. If the produce be fixed, the greater the share of the labourer the less will be the share of the capitalist, and *vice versa*. But the labourer's share again is determined by the consideration that it must be such as to enable him to keep up the population. The capitalist will get the surplus produce after allowing to the labourer the share so determined. Everything turns ultimately upon this 'natural price'—the constant which underlies all the variations.

One other point is implied. The population is limited, as we see, by the necessity of raising supplies of food from inferior soils. Moreover, this is the sole limit. A different view had been taken which greatly exercised the orthodox economists. It was generally admitted that in the progress of society the rate of profit declined. Adam Smith explained this by arguing that, as capital increased, the competition of capitalists lowered the rate. To this it was replied (as by West) that though competition equalised profits, it could not fix the rate of profit. The simple increase of capital does not prove that it will be less profitably employed. The economists had constantly to argue against the terrible possibility of a general 'glut.' The condition of things at the peace had suggested this alarm. The mischief was ascribed to 'over-production' and not to misdirected production. The best cure for our evils, as some people thought, would be to burn all the goods in stock. On this version of the argument, it would seem that an increase of wealth might be equivalent to an increase of poverty. To confute the doctrine in this form, it was only necessary to have a more intelligent conception of the true nature of exchange. As James Mill had argued in his pamphlet against Spence, every increase of supply is also an increase of demand. The more there is to sell, the more there is to buy. The error involved in the theory of a 'glut' is the confusion between a temporary dislocation of the machinery of exchange, which can and will be remedied by a new direction of industry, and the impossible case of an excess of wealth in general. [315] Malthus never quite cleared his mind of this error, and Ricardo had to argue the point with him. Abundance of capital cannot by itself, he says, 'make capital less in demand.' The 'demand for capital is infinite.' [316] The decline in the rate of profit, therefore, depends upon another cause. 'If, with every accumulation of profit, we could tack a piece of fresh fertile land to our Island, profits would never fall.' [317] Fertile land, however, is limited. We have to resort to inferior soil, and therefore to employ capital at a less advantage. In the *Principles* he enforces the same doctrine with the help of Say, who had shown 'most satisfactorily' that any amount of capital might be employed. [318] If, in short, labour and capital were always equally efficient, there would be no limit to the amount producible. If the supply of food and raw materials can be multiplied, wealth can be multiplied to any amount. The admitted tendency of profits to fall must therefore be explained simply and solely by the growing difficulty of producing the food and the raw material.

Ricardo's doctrine, then, is Malthus carried out more logically. Take a nation in a state of industrial equilibrium. The produce of the worst soil just supports the labourer, and leaves a profit to the capitalist. The labourer gets just enough to keep up his numbers to the standard; the capitalist just enough profit to induce him to keep up the capital which supports the labourer. Since there can be only one rate of wages and only one rate of profit, this fixes the shares into which the whole produce of the nation is divided, after leaving to the landlord the surplus produce of the more fertile soils. Accepting this scheme as a starting-point, we get a method for calculating the results of any changes. We can see how a tax imposed upon rents or profits or wages will affect the classes which are thus related; how improvements in cultivation or machinery, or a new demand for our manufactures, will act, assuming the conditions implied in this industrial organisation; how, in short, any disturbance of the balance will work, so as to produce a new equilibrium. Ricardo exerts all his ingenuity in working out the problem which, with the help of a few assumptions, becomes mathematical. The arithmetical illustrations which he employed for the purpose became a nuisance in the hands of his disciples. They are very useful as checks to general statements, but lend themselves so easily to the tacit introduction of erroneous assumptions as often to give a totally false air of precision to the results. Happily I need not follow him into that region, and may omit any consideration of the logical value of his deductions. I must be content to say that, so far as he is right, his system gives an economic calculus for working out the ultimate result of assigned economic changes. The pivot of the whole construction is the 'margin of cultivation'—the point at which the food for a pressing population is raised at the greatest disadvantages. 'Profits,' as he says, [319] 'depend on high and low wages; wages on the price of necessaries; and the price of necessaries chiefly on the price of food, because all other requisites may be increased almost without limit.'

Ricardo takes the actual constitution of society for granted. The threefold division into landowners, capitalists, and labourers is assumed as ultimate. For him that is as much a final fact as to a chemist it is a final fact that air and water are composed of certain elements. Each class represents certain economic categories. The landlord sits still and absorbs the overflow of wealth created by others. The labourer acts a very important but in one respect a purely passive part. His whole means of subsistence are provided by the capitalist, and advanced to him in the shape of wages. His share in the process is confined to multiplying up to a fixed standard. The capitalist is the really active agent. The labourer is simply one of the implements used in production. His wages are part of the capitalist's 'costs of production.' The capitalist virtually raises labourers, one may say, so long as raising them is profitable, just as he raises horses for his farm. Ricardo, in fact, points out that in some cases it may be for the farmer's interest to substitute horses for men. [320] If it be essential to any product that there should be a certain number of labourers or a certain number of horses, that number will be produced. But when the expense becomes excessive, and in the case of labourers that happens as worse soils have to be broken up for food, the check is provided through its effect upon the accumulation of capital. That, therefore, becomes the essential point. The whole aim of the legislator should be to give facilities for the accumulation of capital, and the way to do that is to abstain from all interference with the free play of the industrial forces. The test, for example, of the goodness of a tax—or rather of its comparative freedom from the evils of every tax—is that it should permit of accumulation by interfering as little as possible with the tendency of the capital to distribute itself in the most efficient way.

III. VALUE AND LABOUR

To solve the distribution problem, then, it is necessary to get behind the mere fluctuations of the market, and to consider what are the ultimate forces by which the market is itself governed. What effect has this upon the theory of the market itself? This leads to a famous doctrine.

According to his disciple, M'Culloch, Ricardo's great merit was that he 'laid down the fundamental theorem of the science of value.' He thus cleared up what had before been an 'impenetrable mystery,' and showed the true relations of profit, wages, and prices. [321] Ricardo's theory of value, again, was a starting-point of the chief modern Socialist theories. It marked, as has been said, [322] the point at which the doctrine of the rights of man changes from a purely political to an economical theory. Ricardo remarks in his first chapter that the vagueness of theories of value has been the most fertile source of economic errors. He admitted to the end of his life that he had not fully cleared up the difficulty. Modern economists have refuted and revised and discussed, and, let us hope, now made everything quite plain. They have certainly shown that some of Ricardo's puzzles implied confusions singular in so keen a thinker. That may serve as a warning against dogmatism. Boys in the next generation will probably be asked by examiners to expose the palpable fallacies of what to us seem to be demonstrable truths. At any rate, I must try to indicate the critical point as briefly as possible.

The word 'value,' in the first place, has varying meanings, which give an opportunity for writers of text-books to exhibit their powers of lucid exposition. The value of a thing in one sense is what it will fetch; the quantity of some other thing for which it is actually exchanged in the market. In that sense, as Ricardo incidentally observes, [323] the word becomes meaningless unless you can say what is the other thing. It is self-contradictory to speak as if a thing by itself could have a constant or any value. Value, however, may take a different sense. It is the economic equivalent of the 'utility' of Bentham's 'felicific calculus.' It means the 'lot of pleasure' which causes a thing to be desirable. If we could tell how many units of utility it contained we could infer the rate of exchange for other things. The value of anything 'in use' will correspond to the number of units of utility which it contains; and things which have the same quantity of 'utilities' will have the same 'exchangeable value.' Ricardo can thus consider the old problem of finding 'an invariable measure of value.' He points out the difficulty of finding any particular thing which will serve the purpose, inasmuch as the relations of everything to everything else are constantly varying. He therefore proposes to make use of an imaginary measure. If gold were always produced under exactly the same circumstances, with the same labour and the same capital, it would serve approximately for a standard. Accordingly he gives notice that, for the purposes of his book, he will assume this to be the case, and money to be 'invariable in value.' [324] We can thus, on the one hand, compare values at different periods. A thing has the same value at all times which at all times requires 'the same sacrifice of toil and labour to produce it.' [325] The 'sacrifice' measures the 'utility,' and we may assume that the same labour corresponds in all ages to the same psychological unit. But, on the other hand, at any given period things will exchange in proportion to the labour of producing them. This follows at once from Ricardo's postulates. Given the single rate of wages and profits, and assuming the capital employed to be in the same proportion, things must exchange in proportion to the quantity of labour employed; for if I got the same value by employing one labourer as you get by employing two, my profits would be higher. Ricardo, indeed, has to allow for many complexities arising from the fact that very different quantities of capital are required in different industries; but the general principle is given by the simplest case. Hence we have a measure of value, applicable at any given time and in comparing different times. It implies, again, what M'Culloch sums up as the 'fundamental theorem,' that the value of 'freely produced commodities' depends on the quantity of labour required for their 'production.' What is made by two men is worth twice what is made by one man. That gives what M'Culloch calls the 'clue to the labyrinth.'

The doctrine leads to a puzzle. If I can measure the 'sacrifice,' can I measure the 'utility' which it gains? The 'utility' of an ounce of gold is not something 'objective' like its physical qualities, but varies with the varying wants of the employer. Iron or coal may be used for an infinite variety of purposes and the utility will be different in each. The thing may derive part of its 'utility' from its relation to other things. The utility of my food is not really separate from the utility of my hat; for unless I eat I cannot wear hats. My desire for any object, again, is modified by all my other desires, and even if I could isolate a 'desire' as a psychological unit, it would not give me a fixed measure. Twice the article does not give twice the utility; a double stimulus may only add a small pleasure or convert it into agony. These and other difficulties imply the hopelessness of searching for this chimerical unit of 'utility' when considered as a separate thing. It shifts and escapes from our hands directly we grasp it. Ricardo discusses some of these points in his interesting chapter on 'Value and Riches.' Gold, he says, may cost two thousand times more than iron, but it is certainly not two thousand times as useful. [326] Suppose, again, that some invention enables you to make more luxuries by the same labour, you increase wealth but not value. There will be, say, twice as many hats, but each hat may have half its former value. There will be more things to enjoy, but they will only exchange for the same quantity of other things. That is, he says, the amount of 'riches' varies, while the amount of value is fixed. This, according to him, proves that value does not vary with 'utility.' 'Utility,' as he declares in his first chapter, is 'absolutely essential to value,' but it is 'not the measure of exchangeable value.' [327] A solution of these puzzles may be sought in any modern text-book. Ricardo escapes by an apparently paradoxical conclusion. He is undertaking an impossible problem when he starts from the buyers' desire of an 'utility.' Therefore he turns from the buyers to the sellers. The seller has apparently a measurable and definable motive—the desire to make so much per cent. on his capital. [328] Ricardo, unfortunately, speaks as though the two parties to the bargain somehow represented mutually exclusive processes. 'Supply and demand' determine the value of 'monopolised articles,' but the cost of other articles depends *not* 'on the state of demand and supply,' *but* 'on the increased or diminished cost of their production.' [329] Why 'not' and 'but'? If supply and demand corresponds to the whole play of motives which determines the bargain, this is like saying, according to the old illustration, that we must attribute the whole effect of a pair of scissors to one blade and not to the other. His view leads to the apparent confusion of taking for the cause of value not our desire for a thing, but the sacrifice we must make to attain it. Bentham [330] said, for example, that Ricardo confused 'cost' with 'value.' The denial that utility must in some sense or other determine value perplexes an intelligible and consistent meaning. It is clearly true, upon his postulates, that the value of goods, other than 'monopolised,' must conform to the cost of production. He speaks as if he confounded a necessary condition with an 'efficient cause,' and as if one of two correlative processes could be explained without the other. But the fact that there is a conformity, however brought about, was enough for his purpose. The demand of buyers, he would say, determines the particular direction of production: it settles whether hats should be made of silk or beaver; whether we should grow corn or spin cotton. But the ultimate force is the capitalist's desire for profit. So long as he can raise labourers' necessaries by employing part of his capital, he can employ the labour as he chooses. He can always produce wealth; all the wealth produced can be exchanged, and the demand always be equal to the supply, since the demand is merely the other side of the supply. The buyer's tastes decide how the capital shall be applied, but does not settle how much wealth there shall be, only what particular forms it shall take. Somehow or other it must always adjust itself so that the value of each particular kind shall correspond to the 'cost of production.' The cost of production includes the tools and the raw materials, which are themselves products of previous labour. All capital itself is ultimately the product of labour, and thus, as Ricardo incidentally says, may be regarded as 'accumulated labour.' [331]

This phrase sums up the doctrine which underlies his theory of value and indicates its connection with the theory of distribution. Ricardo had perceived that the supply and demand formula which would serve sufficiently in problems of exchange, or the fluctuations of market-price, could not be made to solve the more fundamental problem of distribution. We must look beneath the superficial phenomena and ask what is the nature of the structure itself: what is the driving force or the mainspring which works the whole mechanism. We seem, indeed, to be inquiring into the very origin of industrial organisation. The foundation of a sound doctrine comes from Adam Smith. Smith had said that in a primitive society the only rule would be that things should exchange in proportion to the labour of getting them. If it cost twice as much labour to kill a beaver as to kill a deer, one beaver would be worth two deer. In accepting this bit of what Smith's commentator, Dugald Stewart, [332] calls 'theoretical' or 'conjectural' history, Ricardo did not mean to state a historical fact. He was not thinking of actual Choctaws or Cherokees. The beaver was exchanged for the deer about the time when the primitive man signed the 'social contract.' He is a hypothetical person used for purposes of illustration and simplification. Ricardo is not really dealing with the question of origins; but he is not the less implying a theory of structure. It did not matter that the 'social contract' was historically a figment; it would serve equally well to explain government. It did not matter that actual savages may have exchanged beavers and deer by the help of clubs instead of competition in the market. The industrial fabric is what would have been had it been thus built up. It can be constructed from base to summit by the application of his formula. As in the imaginary state of deer and beaver, we have a number of independent persons making their bargains upon this principle of the equivalence of labour; and that principle is supposed to be carried out so that the most remote processes of the industrial machinery can be analysed into results of this principle. This gives a sufficient clue to the whole labyrinth of modern industry, and there is no need of considering the extinct forms of social structure, which we know to have existed, and under which the whole system of distribution took place under entirely different conditions. [333] A great change has taken place since the time of the deer and beaver: the capitalist has been developed, and has become the motive power. The labourer's part is passive; and the 'value' is fixed by the bargaining between the proprietors of 'accumulated labour,' forced by competition to make equal profits, instead of being fixed by the equitable bargain between the two hunters exchanging the products of their individual labour. Essentially, however, the principle is the same. In the last as in the first stage of society, things are exchanged in proportion to the labour necessary to produce them. Now it is plain enough that such a doctrine cannot lead to a complete solution of the problem of distribution. It would be a palpably inadequate account of historical processes which have determined the actual relation of classes. The industrial mechanism has been developed as a part of the whole social evolution; and, however important the economic forces, they have been inextricably blended with all the other forces by which a society is built up. For the same reason, Ricardo's theorem would be inadequate 'sociologically,' or as a formula which would enable us to predict the future distribution of wealth. It omits essential factors in the process, and therefore supposes forces to act automatically and invariably which will in fact be profoundly modified in societies differently organised and composed of individuals differing in character. The very fundamental assumptions as to the elasticity of population, and the accumulation of capital as wages and profits fluctuate, are clearly not absolute truths. An increase of the capitalist's share, for example, at the expense of wages, may lead to the lowered efficiency of the labourer; and, instead of the compensating process supposed to result from the stimulus to accumulation, the actual result may be a general degeneration of the industry. Or, again, the capacity of labourers to combine both depends and reacts upon their intelligence and moral character, and will profoundly modify the results of the general competition. [334] Such remarks, now familiar enough, are enough to suggest that a full explanation of the economic phenomena would require reference to considerations which lie beyond the proper sphere of the economist. Yet the economist may urge that he is making a fair and perhaps necessary abstraction. He may consider the forces to be constant, although he may be fully aware that the assumption requires to be corrected when his formulæ are applied to facts. He may consider what is the play at any given time of the operations of the market, though the market organisation is itself dependent upon the larger organisation of which it is a product. He does not profess to deal in 'sociology,' but 'pure political economy.' In that more limited sphere he may accept Ricardo's postulates. The rate of wages is fixed at any given moment by the 'labour market.' That is the immediate organ through which the adjustment is effected. Wages rise and fall like the price of commodities, when for any reason the number of hirers or the number of purchasers varies. The 'supply and demand' formula, however, could not, as Ricardo saw, be summarily identified with labour and capital. We must go behind the immediate phenomena to consider how they are regulated by the ultimate moving power. Then, with the help of the theories of population and rent, we find that the wages are one product of the whole industrial process. We must look beyond the immediate market fluctuation to the effect upon the capitalists who constitute the market. The world is conceived as one great market, in which the motives of the capitalist supply the motive power; and the share which goes to the labourer is an incidental or collateral result of the working of the whole machinery. Now, though the sociologist would say that this is quite inadequate for his purpose, and that we must consider the whole social structure, he may also admit that the scheme has a validity in its own sphere. It describes the actual working of the mechanism at any given time; and it may be that in Ricardo's time it gave an approximate account of the facts. To make it complete, it requires to be set, so to speak, in a more general framework of theory; and we may then see that it cannot give a complete solution. Still, as a consistent scheme which corresponds to the immediate phenomena, it helps us to understand the play of the industrial forces which immediately regulate the market.

Ricardo's position suggested a different line of reply. The doctrines that capital is 'accumulated labour' and that all value is in proportion to the labour fell in with the Socialist theory. If value is created by labour, ought not 'labour' to possess what it makes? The right to the whole produce of labour seemed to be a natural conclusion. Ricardo might answer that when I buy your labour, it becomes mine. I may consider myself to have acquired the rights of the real creator of the wealth, and to embody all the labourers, whose 'accumulated labour' is capital. Still, there is a difficulty. The beaver and deer case has an awkward ethical aspect. To say that they are exchanged at such a rate seems to mean that they ought to be exchanged at the rate. This again implies the principle that a man has a right to what he has caught; that is, to the whole fruits of his labour. James Mill, as we have seen, starts his political treatise by assuming this as obvious. [335] He did not consider the possible inferences; for it is certainly a daring assumption that the principle is carried out by the economic system. According to Ricardo rent is paid to men who don't labour at all. The fundholder was a weight upon all industry, and as dead a weight as the landlord. The capitalist, Ricardo's social mainspring, required at least cross-examination. He represents 'accumulated labour' in some fashion, but it is not plain that the slice which he takes out of the whole cake is proportioned accurately to his personal labour. The right and the fact which coincided in the deer and beaver period have somehow come to diverge.

Here, then, we are at a point common to the two opposing schools. Both are absolute 'individualists' in different senses. Society is built up, and all industrial relations determined, by the competition of a multitude of independent atoms, each aiming at self-preservation. Malthus's principle applies this to the great mass of mankind. Systematically worked out, it has led to Ricardo's identification of value with quantities of labour. Keeping simply to the matter of fact, it shows how a small minority have managed to get advantages in the struggle, and to raise themselves upon the shoulders of the struggling mass. Malthus shows that the resulting inequality prevents the struggle from lowering every one to starvation point. But the advantage was not obvious to the struggling mass which exemplified the struggle for existence. If equality meant not the initial facts but the permanent right, society was built upon injustice. Apply the political doctrine of rights of man to the economic right to wealth, and you have the Socialist doctrine of right to the whole produce of labour. It is true that it is exceedingly difficult to say what each man has created when he is really part of a complex machinery; but that is a problem to which Socialists could apply their ingenuity. The real answer of the political economists was that although the existing order implied great inequalities of wealth it was yet essential to industrial progress, and therefore to an improvement in the general standard of comfort. This, however, was the less evident the more they insisted upon the individual interest. The net result seemed to be that by accident or inheritance, possibly by fraud or force, a small number of persons have got a much larger share of wealth than their rivals. Ricardo may expound the science accurately; and, if so, we have to ask, What are the right ethical conclusions?

For the present, the Utilitarians seem to have considered this question as superfluous. They were content to take the existing order for granted; and the question remains how far their conclusions upon that assumption could be really satisfactory.

IV. THE CLASSICAL POLITICAL ECONOMY.

Ricardo had worked out the main outlines of the 'Classical Political Economy': the system which to his disciples appeared to be as clear, consistent, and demonstrable as Euclid; and which was denounced by their opponents as mechanical, materialistic, fatalistic, and degrading. After triumphing for a season, it has been of late years often treated with contempt, and sometimes banished to the limbo of extinct logomachies. It is condemned as 'abstract.' Of all delusions on the subject, replies a very able and severe critic, [336] there is none greater than the belief that it was 'wholly abstract and unpractical.' Its merits lay in its treatment of certain special questions of the day; while in the purely scientific questions it was hopelessly confused and inconsistent. Undoubtedly, as I have tried to point out, Malthus and Ricardo were reasoning upon the contemporary state of things. The doctrine started from observation of facts; it was too 'abstract' so far as it neglected elements in the concrete realities which were really relevant to the conclusions. One cause of confusion was the necessity of starting from the classification implied in ordinary phrases. It is exemplified by the vague use of such words as 'capital,' 'value,' 'supply and demand.' Definitions, as is often remarked, [337] come at the end of an investigation, though they are placed at the beginning of an exposition. When the primary conceptions to be used were still so shifting and contradictory as is implied in the controversies of the day, it is no wonder that the formulæ should be wanting in scientific precision. Until we have determined what is meant by 'force' we cannot have a complete science of dynamics. The economists imagined that they had reached the goal before they had got rid of ambiguities hidden in the accepted terminology. Meanwhile it will be enough if I try to consider broadly what was the nature of the body of statements which thus claimed to be an elaborated science.

Ricardo's purpose was to frame a calculus, to give a method of reasoning which will enable us to clinch our economic reasoning. We are to be sure that we have followed out the whole cycle of cause and effect. Capitalists, landowners, labourers form parts of a rounded system, implying reciprocal actions and reactions. The imposition of a tax or a tariff implies certain changes in existing relations: that change involves other changes; and to trace out the total effect, we must understand what are the ultimate conditions of equilibrium, or what are the processes by which the system will adjust itself to the new conditions. To describe, again, the play of a number of reciprocal forces, we have to find what mathematicians call an 'independent variable': some one element in the changes on which all other changes will depend. That element, roughly speaking, ultimately comes out to be 'labour.' The simplicity of the system gave an impression both of clearness and certainty, which was transferred from the reasoning to the premises. The facts seemed to be established, because they were necessary to the system. The first step to an estimate of the value of the doctrine would be to draw up a statement of the 'postulates' implied. Among them, we should have such formulæ as the single rate of profits and wages; which imply the 'transferability' of labour and capital, or the flow of either element to the best-paid employment. We should have again the Malthusian doctrine of the multiplication of labour up to a certain standard; and the fact that scarcity means dearness and plenty cheapness. These doctrines at least are taken for granted; and it may perhaps be said that they are approximations which only require qualifications, though sometimes very important qualifications, to hold good of the society actually contemplated.

They were true enough to give the really conclusive answer to many popular fallacies. The type of sophistry which Ricardo specially assailed was that which results from neglecting the necessary implications of certain changes. The arguments for the old 'mercantile theory' — for 'protection' of industry, for the poor-law, for resisting the introduction of machinery, the fear of 'gluts' and all manner of doctrines about the currency — were really exposed by the economists upon the right grounds. It was absurd to suppose that by simply expanding the currency, or by making industry less efficient, or forcing it to the least profitable employments, you were increasing the national wealth; or to overlook the demoralising effects of a right to support because you resolved only to see the immediate benefits of charity to individuals. It is true, no doubt, that in some cases there might be other arguments, and that the economists were apt to take a narrow view of the facts. Yet they decisively exploded many bad arguments, and by the right method of enforcing the necessity of tracing out the whole series of results. It was partly to their success in confuting absurd doctrines that their confidence was due; though the confidence was excessive when it was transferred to the axioms from which they professed to start. A doctrine may be true enough to expose an error, and yet not capable of yielding definite and precise conclusions. If I know that nothing can come out of nothing, I am on the way to a great scientific principle and able to confute some palpable fallacies; but I am still a very long way from understanding the principle of the 'conservation of energy.' The truth that scarcity meant dearness was apparently well known to Joseph in Egypt, and applied very skilfully for his purpose. Economists have framed a 'theory of value' which explains more precisely the way in which this is brought about. A clear statement may be valuable to psychologists; but for most purposes of political economy Joseph's knowledge is quite sufficient. It is the doctrine which is really used in practice whatever may be its ultimate justification.

The postulates, however, were taken by the economists to represent something more than approximate statements of the fact. They imply certain propositions which might be regarded as axioms. Men desire wealth and prefer their own interests. The whole theory might then be regarded as a direct deduction from the axioms. It thus seemed to have a kind of mathematical certainty. When facts failed to conform to the theory the difficulty could be met by speaking, as Malthus spoke, of 'tendencies,' or by appealing to the analogy of 'friction' in mechanics. The excuse might be perfectly valid in some cases, but it often sanctioned a serious error. It was assumed that the formula was still absolutely true of something, and that the check or friction was a really separable and accidental interference. Thus it became easy to discard, as irrelevant, objections which really applied to the principle itself, and to exaggerate the conformity between fact and theory. The economic categories are supposed to state the essential facts, and the qualifications necessary to make them accurate were apt to slip out of sight. Ricardo, [338] to mention a familiar instance, carefully points out that the 'economic rent,' which clearly represents an important economic category, is not to be confounded, as in 'popular' use, with the payments actually made, which often include much that is really profit. The distinction, however, was constantly forgotten, and the abstract formula summarily applied to the concrete fact.

The economists had constructed a kind of automaton which fairly represented the actual working of the machinery. But then, each element of their construction came to represent a particular formula, and to represent nothing else. The landlord is simply the receiver of surplus value; the capitalist the one man who saves, and who saves in proportion to profit; and the labourer simply the embodiment of Malthus's multiplying tendency. Then the postulates as to the ebb and flow of capital and labour are supposed to work automatically and instantaneously. Ricardo argues that a tax upon wages will fall, not, as Buchanan thought, upon the labourer, nor, as Adam Smith thought, upon rent, but upon profits; and his reason is apparently that if wages were 'lowered the requisite population would not be kept up.' [339] The labourer is able to multiply or diminish so rapidly that he always conforms at once to the required standard. This would seem to neglect the consideration that, after all, some time is required to alter the numbers of a population, and that other changes of a totally different character may be meanwhile set up by rises and falls of wages. Ricardo, as his letters show, [340] was well aware of the necessity of making allowance for such considerations in applying his theorems. He simplified the exposition by laying them down too absolutely; and the doctrine, taken without qualification, gives the 'economic man,' who must be postulated to make the doctrine work smoothly. The labourer is a kind of constant unit— absolutely fixed in his efficiency, his wants, and so forth; and the same at one period as at another, except so far as he may become more prudent, and therefore fix his 'natural price' a little higher. An 'iron law' must follow when you have invented an iron unit. In short, when society is represented by this hypothetical mechanism, where each man is an embodiment of the required formula, the theory becomes imperfect so far as society is made up of living beings, varying, though gradually, in their whole character and attributes, and forming part of an organised society incomparably too complex in its structure to be adequately represented by the three distinct classes, each of which is merely a formula embodied in an individual man. The general rules may be very nearly true in a great many cases, especially on the stock-exchange; but before applying them to give either a history or a true account of the actual working of concrete institutions, a much closer approximation must be made to the actual data.

I need not enlarge, however, upon a topic which has been so often expounded. I think that at present the tendency is rather to do injustice to the common-sense embodied in this system, to the soundness of its aims, and to its value in many practical and immediate questions, than to overestimate its claim to scientific accuracy. That claim may be said to have become obsolete.

One point, however, remains. The holders of such a doctrine must, it is said, have been without the bowels of compassion. Ricardo, as critics observe with undeniable truth, was a Jew and a member of the stock-exchange. Now Jews, in spite of Shylock's assertions, and certainly Jewish stockbrokers, are naturally without human feeling. If you prick them, they only bleed banknotes. They are fitted to be capitalists, who think of wages as an item in an account, and of the labourer as part of the tools used in business. Ricardo, however, was not a mere money-dealer, nor even a walking treatise. He was a kindly, liberal man, desirous to be, as he no doubt believed himself to be, in sympathy with the leaders of political and scientific thought, and fully sharing their aspirations. No doubt he, like his friends, was more conspicuous for coolness of head than for impulsive philanthropy. Like them, he was on his guard against 'sentimentalism' and 'vague generalities,' and thought that a hasty benevolence was apt to aggravate the evils which it attacked. The Utilitarians naturally translated all aspirations into logical dogmas; but some people who despised them as hard-hearted really took much less pains to give effect to their own benevolent impulses. Now Ricardo, in this matter, was at one with James Mill and Bentham, and especially Malthus. [341] The essential doctrine of Malthus was that the poor could be made less poor by an improved standard of prudence. In writing to Malthus, Ricardo incidentally remarks upon the possibility of raising the condition of the poor by 'good education' and the inculcation of foresight in the great matter of marriage. [342] Incidental references in the *Principles* are in the same strain. He accepts Malthus's view of the poor-laws, and hopes that, by encouraging foresight, we may by degrees approach 'a sounder and more healthful state.' [343] He repudiates emphatically a suggestion of Say that one of his arguments implies 'indifference to the happiness' of the masses, [344] and holds that 'the friends of humanity' should encourage the poor to raise their standard of comfort and enjoyment. The labourers, as he elsewhere incidentally observes, are 'by far the most important class in society.' [345] How should they not be if the greatest happiness of the greatest number be the legitimate aim of all legislation?

It is true that in his argument Ricardo constantly assumes that his 'natural price' will also be the real price of labour. The assumption that the labourers' wages tend to a minimum is a base for his general arguments. The inconsistency, if there be one, is easily intelligible. Ricardo agreed with Malthus that, though the standard might be raised, and though a rise was the only way to improvement, the chances of such a rise were not encouraging. Improved wages, as he says, [346] might enable the labourer to live more comfortably if only he would not multiply. But 'so great are the delights of domestic society, that in practice it is invariably found that an increase of population follows an amended condition of the labourer,' and thus the advantage is lost as soon as gained.

I have tried to show what was the logical convenience of the assumption. Ricardo, who has always to state an argument at the cost of an intellectual contortion, is content to lay down a rule without introducing troublesome qualifications and reserves. Yet he probably held that his postulate was a close approximation to the facts. Looking at the actual state of things at the worst time of the poor-law, and seeing how small were the prospects of stirring the languid mind of the pauper to greater forethought, he thought that he might assume the constancy of an element which varied so slowly. The indifference of the Ricardo school generally to historical inquiry had led them no doubt to assume such constancy too easily. Malthus, who had more leaning to history, had himself called attention to many cases in which the 'prudential check' operated more strongly than it did among the English poor. Probably Ricardo was in this, as in other cases, too hasty in assuming facts convenient for his argument. The poor man's character can, it is clear, be only known empirically; and, in fact, Ricardo simply appeals to experience. He thinks that, as a fact, men always do multiply in excess. But he does not deny that better education might change their character in this respect. Indeed, as I have said, an even excessive faith in the possible modification of character by education was one of the Utilitarian tenets. If Ricardo had said broadly that a necessary condition of the improvement of the poor was a change of the average character, I think that he would have been saying what was perfectly true and very much to the purpose both then and now. The objection to his version of a most salutary doctrine is that it is stated in too narrow terms. The ultimate unit, the human being, is indeed supposed to be capable of great modification, but it is solely through increasing his foresight as to the effects of multiplication that the change is supposed to be attainable. The moral thus drawn implied a very limited view of the true nature and influence of great social processes, and in practice came too often to limiting possible improvement to the one condition of letting things alone. Let a man starve if he will not work, and he will work. That, as a sole remedy, may be insufficient; though, even in that shape, it is a doctrine more likely to be overlooked than overvalued. And meanwhile the acquiescence in the painful doctrine that, as a matter of fact, labourers would always multiply to starvation point, was calculated to produce revolt against the whole system. Macaulay's doctrine that the Utilitarians had made political economy unpopular was so far true that the average person resented the unpleasant doctrines thus obtruded upon him in their most unpleasant shape; and, if he was told that they were embodied logic, revolted against logic itself.

V. THE RICARDIANS

It will be quite sufficient to speak briefly of the minor prophets who expounded the classical doctrine; sometimes falling into fallacies, against which Ricardo's logical instinct had warned him; and sometimes perhaps unconsciously revealing errors which really lurked in his premises. When Ricardo died, James Mill told M'Culloch that they were 'the two and only genuine disciples' of their common friend. [347] Mill wrote what he intended for a Schoolbook of Political Economy. [348] Brief, pithy, and vigorous, it purports to give the essential principles in their logical order; but, as his son remarks, [349] had only a passing importance. M'Culloch took a more important place by his writings in the *Edinburgh Review* and elsewhere, and by his lectures at Edinburgh and at London. He was one of the first professors of the new university. His *Principles of Political Economy* [350] became a text-book, to be finally superseded by John Stuart Mill. Other works statistical and bibliographical showed great industry, and have still their value. He was so much the typical economist of the day that he has been identified with Carlyle's *M'Crowdy*, the apostle of the dismal science. [351] He writes, however, with enough vivacity and fervour of belief in his creed to redeem him from the charge of absolute dulness. An abler thinker was Colonel (Robert) Torrens (1780-1864). [352] He had served with distinction in the war; but retired on half-pay, and was drawn by some natural idiosyncrasy into the dry paths of economic discussion. He was already confuting the French economists in 1808; and was writing upon the Bank-charter Act and the Ten Hours' Bill in 1844. Torrens held himself, apparently with justice, to be rather an independent ally than a disciple of Ricardo. His chief works were an essay upon the 'External Corn-trade' (1815) [353] and an 'Essay on the Production of Wealth' (1821). Ricardo pronounced his arguments upon the Corn-trade to be 'unanswered and unanswerable,' [354] and he himself claimed to be an independent discoverer of the true theory of rent. [355] He was certainly a man of considerable acuteness and originality. In these writings we find the most sanguine expressions of the belief that political economy was not only a potential, but on the verge of becoming an actual, science. Torrens observes that all sciences have to pass through a period of controversy; but thinks that economists are emerging from this stage, and rapidly approaching unanimity. In twenty years, says this hopeful prophet, there will scarcely exist a 'doubt of its' (Political Economy's) 'fundamental principles.' [356] Torrens thinks that Ricardo has generalised too much, and Malthus too little; but proposes, with proper professions of modesty, to take the true *via media*, and weld the sound principles into a harmonious whole by a due combination of observation and theory. The science, he thinks, is 'analogous to the mixed mathematics.' [357] As from the laws of motion we can deduce the theory of dynamics, so from certain simple axioms about human nature we can deduce the science of Political Economy. M'Culloch, at starting, insists in edifying terms upon the necessity of a careful and comprehensive induction, and of the study of industrial phenomena in different times and places, and under varying institutions. [358] This, however, does not prevent him from adopting the same methods of reasoning. 'Induction' soon does its office, and supplies a few simple principles, from which we may make a leap to our conclusions by a rapid, deductive process.

The problems appear to be too simple to require long preliminary investigations of fact. Torrens speaks of proving by 'strictly demonstrative evidence' or of 'proceeding to demonstrate' by strict analysis. [359] This is generally the preface to one of those characteristic arithmetical illustrations to which Ricardo's practice gave a sanction. We are always starting an imaginary capitalist with so many quarters of corn and suits of clothes, which he can transmute into any kind of product, and taking for granted that he represents a typical case. This gives a certain mathematical air to the reasoning, and too often hides from the reasoner that he may be begging the question in more ways than one by the arrangement of his imaginary case. One of the offenders in this kind was Nassau Senior (1790-1864), a man of remarkable good sense, and fully aware of the necessity of caution in applying his theories to facts. He was the first professor of Political Economy at Oxford (1825-1830), and his treatise [360] lays down the general assumption of his orthodox contemporaries clearly and briefly. The science, he tells us, is deducible from four elementary propositions: the first of which asserts that every 'man desires to obtain additional wealth with as little sacrifice as possible'; while the others state the first principles embodied in Malthus's theory of population, and in the laws corresponding to the increasing facility of manufacturing and the decreasing facility of agricultural industry. [361] As these propositions include no reference to the particular institutions or historical development of the social structure, they virtually imply that a science might be constructed equally applicable in all times and places; and that, having obtained them, we need not trouble ourselves any further with inductions. Hence it follows that we can at once get from the abstract 'man' to the industrial order. We may, it would seem, abstract from history in general. This corresponds to the postulate explicitly stated by M'Culloch. 'A state,' he tells us, 'is nothing more than an aggregate of individuals': men, that is, who 'inhabit a certain tract of country.' [362] He infers that 'whatever is most advantageous to them' (the individuals) 'is most advantageous to the state.' Self-interest, therefore, the individual's desire of adding to his 'fortune,' is the mainspring or *causa causans* of all improvement. [363] This is, of course, part of the familiar system, which applies equally in ethics and politics. M'Culloch is simply generalising Adam Smith's congenial doctrine that statesmen are guilty of absurd presumption when they try to interfere with a man's management of his own property. [364] This theory, again, is expressed by the familiar maxim *pas trop gouverner*, which is common to the whole school, and often accepted explicitly. [365]

It will be quite enough to notice one or two characteristic results. The most important concern the relation between the labourer and the capitalist. Malthus gives the starting-point. Torrens, for example, says that the 'real wages of labour have a constant tendency to settle down' to the amount rendered necessary by 'custom and climate' in order to keep up his numbers. [366] Mill observes in his terse way that the capitalist in the present state of society 'is as much the owner of the labour' as the manufacturer who operates with slaves. The only 'difference is in the mode of purchasing.' [367] One buys a man's whole labour; the other his labour for a day. The rate of wages can therefore be raised, like the price of slaves, only by limiting the supply. Hence the 'grand practical problem is to find the means of limiting the number of births.' [368] M'Culloch is equally clear, and infers that every scheme 'not bottomed on' the principle of proportioning labour to capital must be 'completely nugatory and ineffectual.' [369]

The doctrine common to the whole school led M'Culloch to conclusions which became afterwards notorious enough to require a word of notice. Torrens, like Ricardo, speaks of capital as 'accumulated labour,' but makes a great point of observing that, although this is true, the case is radically changed in a developed state of society. The value of things no longer depends upon the labour, but upon the amount of capital employed in their production. [370] This, indeed, may seem to be the most natural way of stating the accepted principle. M'Culloch replies that the change makes no difference in the principle, [371] inasmuch as capital being 'accumulated labour,' value is still proportioned to labour, though in a transubstantiated shape. M'Culloch supposed that by carrying out this principle systematically he was simplifying Ricardo and bringing the whole science into unity. All questions, whether of value in exchange, or of the rate of wages, can then be reduced to comparing the simple unit called labour. Both Mill and M'Culloch regard capital as a kind of labour, so that things may be produced by capital alone, 'without the co-operation of any immediate labour' [372] —a result which can hardly be realised with the discovery of a perpetual motion. So, again, the value of a joint product is the 'sum' of these two values. [373] All value, therefore, can be regarded as proportioned to labour in one of its two states. M'Culloch advanced to an unfortunate conclusion, which excited some ridicule. Though Ricardo and Torrens [374] rejected it, it was accepted by Mill in his second edition. [375] Wine kept in a cask might increase in value. Could that value be ascribed to 'additional labour actually laid out'? M'Culloch gallantly asserted that it could, though 'labour' certainly has to be interpreted in a non-natural sense. [376] Not only is capital labour, but fermentation is labour, or how can we say that all value is proportioned to labour? This is only worth notice as a pathetic illustration of the misfortunes of a theorist ridden by a dogma of his own creation. Another conclusion is more important. The 'real value' of anything is measured by the labour required to produce it. Nothing 'again is more obvious' than that equal labour implies the 'same sacrifice' in all states of society. [377] It might seem to follow that the value of anything was measured by the labour which it would command. This doctrine, however, though maintained by Malthus, was, according to M'Culloch, a pestilent heresy, first exploded by Ricardo's sagacity. [378] Things exchange, as he explains, in proportion to the labour which produces them, but the share given to the labourer may vary widely. The labourer, he says, 'gives a constant, but receives a variable quantity in its stead.' He makes the same sacrifice when he works for a day, but may get for it what he produces in ten hours, or only in one. In every case, however, he gets less than he produces, for the excess 'constitutes profits.' [379] The capitalist must get his interest, that is, the wages of the accumulated labour. Here we come again to the Socialist position, only that the Socialist infers that the labourer is always cheated by the capitalist, and does not consider that the machine can ask for 'wages' on the pretext that it is accumulated labour. What, however, determines the share actually received? After all, as a machine is not actually a labourer, and its work not a separable product, we cannot easily see how much wages it is entitled to receive. M'Culloch follows the accepted argument. 'No proposition,' he says, 'can be better established than that the market rate of wages ... is exclusively determined by the proportion between capital and population.' [380] We have ultimately here, as elsewhere, 'the grand principle to which we must always come at last,' namely, 'the cost of production.' [381] Wages must correspond to the cost of raising the labourer. This leads to a formula, which afterwards became famous. In a pamphlet [382] devoted to the question, he repeats the statement that wages depend upon the proportion between population and capital; and then, as if the phrase were identical, substitutes that portion of capital which is required for the labourer's consumption. This is generally cited as the first statement of the 'wage-fund' theory, to which I shall have to return.

I need not pursue these illustrations of the awkward results of excessive zeal in a disciple. It is worth noticing, however, that M'Culloch's practical conclusions are not so rigid as might be inferred. His abstract doctrines do not give his true theory, so much as what he erroneously took to be his theory. The rules with which he works are approximately true under certain conditions, and he unconsciously assumes the conditions to be negligible, and the rules therefore absolute. It must be added that he does not apply his conclusions so rigidly as might be expected. By the help of 'friction,' or the admission that the ride is only true in nineteen cases out of twenty, he can make allowance for many deviations from rigid orthodoxy. He holds, for example, that government interference is often necessary. He wishes in particular for the establishment of a 'good system of public education.' [383]

He seems to have become more sentimental in later years. In the edition of 1843 he approves the Factory Acts, remarking that the last then passed 'may not, in some respects, have gone far enough.' [384] He approves a provision for the 'impotent poor,' on the principle of the Elizabethan act, though he disapproves the centralising tendency of the new poor-law. Though he is a good Malthusian, [385] and holds the instinct of population to be a 'constant quantity,' [386] he does not believe in the impossibility of improvement. The 'necessary' rate of wages fixes only a minimum: an increase of population has been accompanied by an increase of comfort. [387] Wages rise if the standard of life be raised, and a rise of wages tends to raise the standard. He cordially denounces the benevolent persons who held that better wages only meant more dissipation. Better wages are really the great spur to industry and improvement. [388] Extreme poverty causes apathy; and the worst of evils is the sluggishness which induces men to submit to reductions of wages. A sense of comfort will raise foresight; and the *vis medicatrix* should be allowed to act upon every rank of society. He is no doubt an individualist, as looking to the removal of restrictions, such as the Conspiracy Laws, [389] rather than to a positive action of the government; but it is worth notice that this typical economist is far from accepting some of the doctrines attributed to the school in general.

The classical school blundered when it supposed that the rules which it formulated could be made absolute. To give them that character, it was necessary to make false assumptions as to the ultimate constitution of society; and the fallacy became clear when the formulæ were supposed to give a real history or to give first principles, from which all industrial relations could be deduced. Meanwhile, the formulæ, as they really expressed conditional truths, might be very useful so long as, in point of fact, the conditions existed, and were very effective in disposing of many fallacies. The best illustration would probably be given by the writings of Thomas Tooke (1774-1858), [390] one of the founders of the Political Economy Club. The *History of Prices* is an admirable explanation of phenomena which had given rise to the wildest theories. The many oscillations of trade and finance during the great struggle, the distress which had followed the peace, had bewildered hasty reasoners. Some people, of course, found consolation in attributing everything to the mysterious action of the currency; others declared that the war-expenditure had supplied manufacturers and agriculturists with a demand for their wares, apparently not the less advantageous because the payment came out of their own pockets. [391] Tooke very patiently and thoroughly explodes these explanations, and traces the fluctuations of price to such causes as the effect of the seasons and the varying events of the war which opened or closed the channels of commerce. The explanation in general seems to be thoroughly sound and conclusive, and falls in, as far as it goes, with the principles of his allies. He shows, for example, very clearly what were the conditions under which the orthodox theory of rent was really applicable; how bad seasons brought gain instead of loss to the 'agricultural interest,' that is, as Tooke explains, to the landlord and farmer; how by a rise of price out of proportion to the diminution of supply, the farmer made large profits; how rents rose, enclosure bills increased, and inferior land was brought under the plough. The landlord's interest was for the time clearly opposed to that of all other classes, however inadequate the doctrine might become when made absolute by a hasty generalisation. I need not dwell upon the free-trade argument which made the popular reputation of the economists. It is enough to note briefly that the error as to the sphere of applicability of the doctrine did not prevent many of the practical conclusions from being of the highest value.

FOOTNOTES:

[294] A life of Ricardo by M'Culloch is prefixed to his *Works*. I cite the edition of 1880. Ricardo's letters to Malthus were published by Mr. Bonar in 1887; his letters to M'Culloch, edited by Mr. Hollander for the American Economic Association, in 1895; and his letters to H. Trower, edited by Mr. Bonar and Mr. Hollander, have just appeared (1900).

[295] He remarks upon this difficulty in the case of Smith's treatment of rent, and gives a definition to which he scarcely adheres.—*Works*, p. 34 ('Principles,' ch. ii., 1888).

[296] *Works*, p. 378. Ricardo, it should be said, complained when Malthus interpreted him to mean that this opposition of interests was permanent and absolute.

[297] Malthus admits the general principle of free trade, but supports some degree of protection to corn, mainly upon political grounds. He holds, however, with Adam Smith, that 'no equal quantity of productive labour employed in manufactures could ever occasion so great a reproduction as in agriculture' (*Grounds of an Opinion, etc.*, p. 35)—a relic of the 'physiocrat' doctrine.

[298] *Works*, p. 385.

[299] *Ibid*.

[300] See also *Letters to Malthus*, p. 175.

[301] 'Your modern political economists say that it is a principle in their science that all things find their level; which I deny, and say, on the contrary, that it is the true principle that all things are finding their level, like water in a storm.'—Coleridge's *Table-Talk*, 17th May 1833.

[302] *Letters to Malthus*, p. 96; and see the frequently quoted passage where he complains that Malthus has taken his book as more 'practical' than he had intended it to be, and speaks of his method of imagining 'strong cases.'—*Ibid.* p. 167.

[303] *Works*, p. 40 *n.* (ch. ii.).

[304] *Works*, p. 53 (ch. v.), and p. 124 (ch. xvi.), where he quotes from the *Wealth of Nations* (M'Culloch), p. 390 (bk. v. ch. ii. art. 3).

[305] *Works*, p. 131.

[306] *Wealth of Nations* (M'Culloch), p. 31 (bk. i. ch. viii.).

[307] *Works*, p. 41 (ch. ii.).

[308] *Wealth of Nations* (M'Culloch), p. 36.

[309] *Works*, p. 51 (ch. v.).

[310] *Letters to Malthus*, p. 98.

[311] *Works*, p. 239 (ch. xxxi., added in third edition, 1821).

[312] *Ibid.* p. 50 (ch. v.).

[313] *Ibid.*

[314] *Ibid.* ch. i. sec. ii.).

[315] There is, indeed, a difficulty which I happily need not discuss. Undoubtedly the doctrine of gluts was absurd. There is, of course, no limit to the amount of wealth which can be used or exchanged. But there certainly seems to be a great difficulty in effecting such a readjustment of the industrial system as is implied in increased production of wealth; and the disposition to save may at a given time be greater than the power of finding profitable channels for employing wealth. This involves economical questions beyond my ability to answer, and happily not here relevant.

[316] *Letters to Malthus*, p. 101.

[317] *Ibid.*

[318] *Works*, p. 174 (ch. xxi.).

[319] *Works*, p. 66 (ch. vi.).

[320] *Works*, p. 240 (ch. xxxi.).

[321] Ricardo, *Works*, p. xxiv.

[322] Menger's *Das Recht auf den vollen Arbeitsertrag* (1891), p. 38.

[323] *Works*, p. 228 (ch. xxviii.).

[324] *Works*, pp. 29, 60.

[325] *Ibid.*

[326] *Works*, p. 170 (ch. xx.).

[327] *Ibid.*

[328] So he tells Malthus (*Letters*, pp. 173, 174) that the buyer has 'the least to do in the world' with the regulation of prices. It is all the competition of the sellers. 'Demand' influences price for the moment, but 'supply follows close upon its heels, and takes up the regulation of price.'

[329] *Works*, p. 234.

[330] Bentham's *Works*, x. 498.

[331] *Works*, p. 250 (ch. xxxii.).

[332] Stewart's *Works*, x. 34.

[333] See Bagehot's remarks upon J. S. Mill's version of this doctrine in *Economic Studies*: chapter on 'Cost of Production.'

[334] Another illustration of the need of such considerations is given, as has been pointed out, in Adam Smith's famous chapter upon the variation in the rate of wages. He assumes that the highest wages will be paid for the least agreeable employments, whereas, in fact, the least agreeable are generally the worst paid. His doctrine, that is, is only true upon a tacit assumption as to the character and position of the labourer, which must be revised before the rule can be applied.

[335] J. S. Mill, too, in his *Political Economy* makes the foundation of private property 'the right of producers to what they themselves have produced.' (Bk. ii. ch. ii. § 1.)

[336] Mr. Edwin Cannan, in *Production and Distribution* (1894), p. 383.

[337] A definition, says Burke in his essay on the 'Sublime and Beautiful' (introduction) 'seems rather to follow than to precede our inquiry, of which it ought to be considered as the result.'

[338] *Works*, p. 34 (chap. ii.). Rent is there defined as the sum paid for the original and indestructible powers of the soil.

[339] *Works*, p. 132 (chap. xvii.). He admits (*Ibid.* p. 210 *n.*) that the labourer may have a little more than what is absolutely necessary, and that his inference is therefore 'expressed too strongly.'

[340] See *Letters to M'Culloch*, p. xxi.

[341] 'The assaults upon Malthus's "great work,"' he says (*Works*, p. 243, ch. xxxii.), 'have only served to prove its strength.'

[342] *Letters to Malthus*, p. 226.

[343] *Works*, p. 58 (ch. v.).

[344] *Ibid.* p. 211 *n.* (ch. xxvi.).

[345] *Ibid.* p. 258 (ch. xxxii.).

[346] *Works*, p. 248 (ch. xxii.).

[347] Bain's *James Mill*, p. 211.

[348] Editions in 1821, 1824, and 1826.

[349] *Autobiography*, p. 204.

[350] The first edition, an expanded version of an article in the *Encyclopædia Britannica*, appeared in 1825.

[351] *Latter-day Pamphlets* (New Downing Street). M'Crowdy is obviously a type, not an individual.

[352] See Mr. Hewin's life of him in *Dictionary of National Biography*.

[353] Fourth edition in 1827.

[354] Ricardo's *Works*, p. 164 *n*.

[355] *External Corn-trade*, preface to fourth edition. J. S. Mill observes in his chapter upon 'International Trade' that Torrens was the earliest expounder of the doctrine afterwards worked out by Ricardo and Mill himself. For Ricardo's opinion of Torrens, see *Letters to Trower*, p. 39.

[356] *Production of Wealth* (Preface).

[357] *Production of Wealth* (Preface).

[358] *Political Economy* (1825), p. 21.

[359] *External Corn-trade*, pp. xviii, 109, 139; *Production of Wealth*, p. 375.

[360] Originally in the *Encyclopædia Metropolitana*, 1836.

[361] Senior's *Political Economy* (1850), p. 26.

[362] *Ibid.* (1825), pp. 55, 129-131.

[363] Senior's *Political Economy* (150), p. 125.

[364] *Ibid.* p. 135. M'Culloch admits the possibility that a man may judge his own interests wrongly, but thinks that this will not happen in one case out of twenty (*Ibid.* p. 15).

[365] See Torrens's *Production of Wealth*, p. 208; and M'Culloch's *Political Economy* (1843), p. 294, where he admits some exceptions.

[366] *External Corn-trade*, p. 87, etc.

[367] *Political Economy* (second edition), pp. 21, 22.

[368] *Ibid.*

[369] *Political Economy* (1825), p. 329.

[370] *Production of Wealth*, p. 34, etc.

[371] *Political Economy* (1825), p. 318.

[372] Mill's *Political Economy* (second edition), p. 102; M'Culloch's *Political Economy* (1825), pp. 289-291.

[373] M'Culloch's *Political Economy*, p. 290.

[374] Preface to *External Corn-trade*.

[375] *Ibid.*

[376] *Political Economy* (1825), pp. 313-18. This argument disappears in later editions.

[377] *Ibid.*

[378] *Political Economy*, p. 221. De Quincey makes a great point of this doctrine, of which it is not worth while to examine the meaning.

[379] *Political Economy*, p. 221 *n.*

[380] *Ibid.*

[381] *Ibid.*

[382] 'Essay upon the Circumstances which determine the Rate of Wages' (1826), p. 113. This was written for Constable's *Miscellany*, and is mainly repetition from the *Political Economy*. It was republished, with alterations, in 1851.

[383] *Political Economy*, pp. 359-61.

[384] *Ibid.* (1843), p. 178. And see his remarks on the unfavourable side of the Factory System, p. 186 *seq.*

[385] 'Wherever two persons have the means of subsisting,' as he quaintly observes, 'a marriage invariably takes place' (*Political Economy*, p. 154).

[386] *Political Economy*, p. 206.

[387] *Political Economy*, p. 344.

[388] *Ibid.*

[389] See pamphlet on the rate of wages, pp. 178-204.

[390] Tooke's *Thoughts and Details on the High and Low Prices of the last Thirty Years* appeared in 1823 (second edition 1824). This was rewritten and embodied in the *History of Prices*, the first two volumes of which appeared in 1838. Four later volumes appeared in 1839, 1848, and 1857.

[391] The popular view is given by Southey. The Radicals, he says in 1823, desire war because they expect it to lead to revolution. 'In this they are greatly deceived, for it would restore agricultural prosperity, and give a new spur to our manufactures' (*Selections from Southey's Letters*, iii. 382. See also *Life and Correspondence*, iv. 228, 386).

CHAPTER VI
ECONOMIC HERETICS

I. THE MALTHUSIAN CONTROVERSY

The Economic theory became triumphant. Expounded from new university chairs, summarised in text-books for schools, advocated in the press, and applied by an energetic party to some of the most important political discussions of the day, it claimed the adhesion of all enlightened persons. It enjoyed the prestige of a scientific doctrine, and the most popular retort seemed to be an involuntary concession of its claims. When opponents appealed from 'theorists' to practical men, the Utilitarians scornfully set them down as virtually appealing from reason to prejudice. No rival theory held the field. If Malthus and Ricardo differed, it was a difference between men who accepted the same first principles. They both professed to interpret Adam Smith as the true prophet, and represented different shades of opinion rather than diverging sects. There were, however, symptoms of opposition, which, at the time, might be set down as simple reluctance to listen to disagreeable truths. In reality, they were indications of a dissatisfaction which was to become of more importance and to lead in time to a more decided revolt. I must indicate some of them, though the expressions of dissent were so various and confused that it is not very easy to reduce them to order.

Malthus's doctrine was really at the base of the whole theory, though it must be admitted that neither Malthus himself nor his opponents were clear as to what his doctrine really was. His assailants often attacked theories which he disavowed, or asserted principles which he claimed as his own. [392] I mention only to set aside some respectable and wearisome gentlemen such as Ingram, Jarrold, Weyland, and Grahame, who considered Malthus chiefly as impugning the wisdom of Providence. They quote the divine law, 'Increase and multiply'; think that Malthus regards vice and misery as blessings, and prove that population does not 'tend' to increase too rapidly. Jarrold apparently accepts the doctrine which Malthus attributes to Süssmilch, that lives have been shortened since the days of the patriarchs, and the reproductive forces diminished as the world has grown fuller. Grahame believes in a providential 'ordeal,' constituted by infant mortality, which is not, like war and vice, due to human corruption, but a beneficent regulating force which correlates fertility with the state of society. This might be taken by Malthus as merely amounting to another version of his checks. Such books, in fact, simply show, what does not require to be further emphasised, that Malthus had put his version of the struggle for existence into a form which seemed scandalous to the average orthodox person. The vagueness of Malthus himself and the confused argument of such opponents makes it doubtful whether they are really answering his theories or reducing them to a less repulsive form of statement.

In other directions, the Malthusian doctrine roused keen feeling on both sides, and the line taken by different parties is significant. Malthus had appeared as an antagonist of the revolutionary party. He had laid down what he took to be an insuperable obstacle to the realisation of their dreams. Yet his views were adopted and extended by those who called themselves thorough Radicals. As, in our days, Darwinism has been claimed as supporting both individualist and socialistic conclusions, the theory of his predecessor, Malthus, might be applied in a Radical or a Conservative sense. In point of fact, Malthus was at once adopted by the Whigs, as represented by the *Edinburgh Review*. They were followers of Adam Smith and Dugald Stewart; they piqued themselves, and, as even James Mill admitted, with justice, upon economic orthodoxy. They were at the same time predisposed to a theory which condemned the revolutionary Utopias. It provided them with an effective weapon against the agitators whom they especially dreaded. The Tories might be a little restrained by orthodox qualms. In 1812 Southey was permitted to make an onslaught upon Malthus in the *Quarterly*; [393] but more complimentary allusions followed, and five years later the essay was elaborately defended in an able article. [394] An apology was even insinuated for the previous assault, though the blame was thrown upon Malthus for putting his doctrines in an offensive shape. A reference to Owen suggests that the alarm excited by Socialism had suggested the need of some sound political economy.

Another controversy which was being carried on at intervals indicates the line of cleavage between the capitalist and the landed interest. James Mill's early pamphlet, *Commerce Defended* (1808), and Torrens's pamphlet, *Economists Refuted*, were suggested by this discussion. Although the war was partly in defence of British trade, its vicissitudes produced various commercial crises; and the patriotic Tories were anxious to show that we could thrive even if our trade was shut out from the Continent. The trading classes maintained that they really supplied the sinews of war, and had a right to some control of the policy. The controversy about the orders in council and Berlin decrees emphasised these disputes, and called some attention to the questions involved in the old controversy between the 'mercantile' and the 'agricultural' systems. A grotesque exaggeration of one theory was given by Mill's opponent, William Spence [395] (1783-1860), in his *Britain independent of Commerce*, which went through several editions in 1808, and refurbished or perverted the doctrine of the French economists. The argument, at least, shows what fallacies then needed confutation by the orthodox. In the preface to his collected tracts, Spence observes that the high price of corn was the cause of 'all our wealth and prosperity during the war.' The causes of the high price ('assisted,' he admits, 'by occasional bad seasons') were the 'national debt, in other words, taxation,' which raised the price, first, of necessaries, and then of luxuries (thus, he says, 'neutralising its otherwise injurious effects'), and the virtual monopoly by the agriculturist of the home market. [396] All our wealth, that is, was produced by taxation aided by famine, or, in brief, by the landowner's power of squeezing more out of the poor. Foreign trade, according to Spence, is altogether superfluous. Its effect is summed up by the statement that we give hardware to America, and, in return, get only 'the vile weed, tobacco.' [397] Spence's writings only show the effect of strong prejudices on a weak brain. A similar sentiment dictated a more noteworthy argument to a much abler writer, whose relation to Malthus is significant—Thomas Chalmers (1780-1847), [398] probably best remembered at present for his leadership of the great disruption of 1843. He had a reputation for eloquence and philosophic ability not fully intelligible at the present day. His appearance was uncouth, and his written style is often clumsy. He gave an impression at times of indolence and of timidity. Yet his superficial qualities concealed an ardent temperament and cordial affections. Under a sufficient stimulus he could blaze out in stirring speech and vigorous action. His intellectual training was limited. He had, we are told, been much influenced in his youth by the French philosophers of the time, and had appeared on the side of the more freethinking party in the famous Leslie controversy. Soon afterwards, however, he was converted to 'evangelical' views. He still accepted Thomas Brown as a great metaphysician, [399] but thought that in moral questions Brown's deistical optimism required to be corrected by an infusion of Butler's theory of conscience. He could adapt Butler's *Analogy*, and write an edifying Bridgewater Treatise. I need only say, however, that, though his philosophy was not very profound, he had an enthusiasm which enables him at times to write forcibly and impressively.

Chalmers was from 1803 to 1815 minister of Kilmany, Fifeshire, and his attention had already been drawn to the question of pauperism. He took part in the Spence controversy, by an essay upon the *Extent and Stability of National Resources.* [400] In this he expounds a doctrine which is afterwards given in his *Political Economy in Connection with the Moral State and Moral Aspects of Society*. [401] The main purpose of his early book is the patriotic. It is meant, like Spence's pamphlet, to prove that Napoleon could do us no vital injury. Should he succeed, he would only lop off superfluous branches, not hew down the main trunk. Chalmers's argument to show the ease with which a country may recover the effects of a disastrous war is highly praised by J. S. Mill [402] as the first sound explanation of the facts. Chalmers's position, however, is radically different from the position of either James or J. S. Mill. Essentially it is the development of the French economists' theory, though Chalmers is rather unwilling to admit his affinity to a discredited school. [403] He has reached some of their conclusions, he admits, but by a different path. [404] He coincides, in this respect, with Malthus, who was equally impressed by the importance of 'subsistence,' or of the food-supply of the labourer. The great bulk of the food required must be raised within our own borders. As Chalmers says, in 1832, the total importation of corn, even in the two famine years, 1800 and 1801, taken together, had only provided food for five weeks, [405] and could normally represent a mere fringe or superfluous addition to our resources. His main argument is simple. The economists have fallen into a fatal error. A manufacturer, he observes, only makes his own article. [406] The economists somehow imagine that he also supports himself. You see a prosperous 'shawl-making village.' You infer that its ruin would cause the destitution of so many families. It would only mean the loss of so many shawls. The food which supports the shawl-makers would still be produced, and would be only diverted to support makers of some other luxury. [407] There would be a temporary injury to individuals, but no permanent weakening of national resources. Hence we have his division of the population. The agriculturists, and those who make the 'second necessaries' (the cottages, ploughs, and so forth, required by the agriculturist), create the great wealth of the country. Besides these we have the 'disposable' population, which is employed in making luxuries for the landowners, and, finally, the 'redundant' or what he calls in his later book the 'excrescent' or 'superinduced' population, [408] which is really supported by foreign trade. Commerce, then, is merely 'the efflorescence of our agriculture.' [409] Were it annihilated this instant, we should still retain our whole disposable population. The effect of war is simply to find a different employment for this part of the nation. Napoleon, he says, is 'emptying our shops and filling our battalions.' [410] All the 'redundant' population might be supported by simply diminishing the number of our cart-horses. [411] Similarly, the destruction of the commerce of France 'created her armies.' It only transferred men from trade to war, and 'millions of artisans' were 'transformed into soldiers.' [412] Pitt was really strengthening when he supposed himself to be ruining his enemy. 'Excrescence' and 'efflorescence' are Chalmers's equivalent for the 'sterility' of the French economists. The backbone of all industry is agriculture, and the manufacturers simply employed by the landowner for such purposes as he pleases. Whether he uses them to make his luxuries or to fight his battles, the real resources of the nation remain untouched. The Ricardians insist upon the vital importance of 'capital.' The one economic end of the statesmen, as the capitalist class naturally thinks, should be to give every facility for its accumulation, and consequently for allowing it to distribute itself in the most efficient way. Chalmers, on the contrary, argues that we may easily have too much capital. He was a firm believer in gluts. He admits that the extension of commerce was of great good at the end of the feudal period, but not as the 'efficient cause' of wealth, only as 'unlocking the capabilities of the soil.' [413] This change produced the illusion that commerce has a 'creative virtue,' whereas its absolute dependence upon agriculture is a truth of capital importance in political economy. More Malthusian than Malthus, Chalmers argues that the case of capital is strictly parallel to the case of population. [414] Money may be redundant as much as men, and the real causes of every economic calamity are the 'over-speculation of capitalists,' and the 'over-population of the community at large.' [415] In this question, however, Chalmers gets into difficulties, which show so hopeless a confusion between 'capital,' income, and money, that I need not attempt to unravel his meaning. [416] Anyhow, he is led to approve the French doctrine of the single tax. Ultimately, he thinks, all taxes fall upon rent. [417] Agriculture fills the great reservoir from which all the subsidiary channels are filled. Whether the stream be tapped at the source or further down makes no difference. Hence he infers that, as the landlords necessarily pay the taxes, they should pay them openly. By an odd coincidence, he would tax rents like Mill, though upon opposite grounds. He holds that the interest of the landowners is not opposed to, but identical with, the interest of all classes. Politically, as well as economically, they should be supreme. They are, 'naturally and properly, the lords of the ascendant,' and, as he oddly complains in the year of the Reform Bill, not 'sufficiently represented in parliament.' [418] A 'splendid aristocracy' is, he thinks, a necessary part of the social edifice; [419] the law of primogeniture is necessary to support them; and the division of land will cause the decay of France. The aristocracy are wanted to keep up a high standard of civilisation and promote philosophy, science, and art. [420] The British aristocracy in the reign of George iv. scarcely realised this ideal, and would hardly have perceived that to place all the taxes upon their shoulders would be to give them a blessing in disguise. According to Chalmers, however, an established church represents an essential part of the upper classes, and is required to promote a high standard of life among the poor. [421] In connection with this, he writes a really forcible chapter criticising the economical distinction of productive and unproductive labour, and shows at least that the direct creation of material wealth is not a sufficient criterion of the utility of a class.

Chalmers's arguments are of interest mainly from their bearing upon his practical application of the Malthusian problem. His interest in the problem of pauperism had been stimulated by his residence in Glasgow, where from 1815 to 1823 he had been actively engaged in parochial duties. In 1819 he had set up an organised system of charity in a poor district, which both reduced the expenditure and improved the condition of the poor. The experiment, though dropped some years later, became famous, and in later years Chalmers successfully started a similar plan in Edinburgh. It was this experience which gave shape to his Malthusian theories. He was, that is, a Malthusian in the sense of believing that the great problem was essentially the problem of raising the self-respect and spirit of independence of the poor. The great evil which confronted him in Glasgow was the mischief connected with the growth of the factory system. He saw, as he thought, the development of wealth leading to the degradation of the labourer. The great social phenomenon was the tendency to degeneration, the gradual dissolution of an organism, and corruption destroying the vital forces. On the one hand, this spectacle led him, as it led others, to look back fondly to the good old times of homely food and primitive habits, to the peasantry as represented in Burns's *Cotter's Saturday Night* or Scott's *Heart of Midlothian*, when the poor man was part of a social, political, and ecclesiastical order, disciplined, trained, and self-respecting, not a loose waif and stray in a chaotic welter of separate atoms. These were the facts which really suggested his theory of the 'excrescent' population, produced by the over-speculation of capitalists. The paupers of Glasgow were 'excrescent,' and the 'gluts' were visible in the commercial crises which had thrown numbers of poor weavers out of employment and degraded them into permanent paupers. The facts were before his eyes, if the generalisation was hasty and crude. He held, on the other hand, that indiscriminate charity, and still more the establishment by poor-laws of a legal right to support, was stimulating the evil. The poor-law had worked incalculable mischiefs in England, [422] and he struggled vigorously, though unavailingly, to resist its introduction into Scotland. Chalmers, however, did not accept the theory ascribed to the Utilitarians, that the remedy for the evils was simply to leave things alone. He gives his theory in an article upon the connection between the extension of the church and the extinction of pauperism. He defends Malthus against the 'execrations' of sentimentalism. Malthus, he thinks, would not suppress but change the direction of beneficence. A vast expenditure has only stimulated pauperism. The true course is not to diminish the rates but to make them 'flow into the wholesome channel of maintaining an extended system of moral and religious instruction.' [423] In other words, suppress workhouses but build schools and churches; organise charity and substitute a systematic individual inspection for reckless and indiscriminate almsgiving. Then you will get to the root of the mischief. The church, supported from the land, is to become the great civilising agent. Chalmers, accordingly, was an ardent advocate of a church establishment. He became the leader of the Free Church movement not as objecting to an establishment on principle, but because he thought that the actual legal fetters of the Scottish establishment made it impossible to carry out an effective reorganisation and therefore unable to discharge its true functions.

Here Chalmers's economical theories are crossed by various political and ecclesiastical questions with which I am not concerned. His peculiarities as an economist bring out, I think, an important point. He shows how Malthus's views might be interpreted by a man who, instead of sharing, was entirely opposed to the ordinary capitalist prejudices. It would be idle to ask which was the more logical development of Malthus. When two systems are full of doubtful assumptions of fact and questionable logic and vague primary conceptions, that question becomes hardly intelligible. We can only note the various turns given to the argument by the preconceived prejudices of the disputants. By most of them the Malthusian view was interpreted as implying the capitalist as distinguished from the landowning point of view.

To Southey as to Chalmers the great evil of the day was the growth of the disorganised populace under the factory system. The difference is that while Chalmers enthusiastically adopted Malthus's theory as indicating the true remedy for the evil, Southey regards it with horror as declaring the evil to be irremediable. Chalmers, a shrewd Scot actively engaged in parochial work, had his attention fixed upon the reckless improvidence of the 'excrescent' population, and welcomed a doctrine which laid stress upon the necessity of raising the standard of prudence and morality. He recognised and pointed out with great force the inadequacy of such palliatives as emigration, home-colonisation, and so forth. [424] Southey, an ardent and impulsive man of letters, with no practical experience of the difficulties of social reform, has no patience for such inquiries. His remedy, in all cases, was a 'paternal government' vigorously regulating society; and Malthus appears to him to be simply an opponent of all such action. Southey had begun the attack in 1803 by an article in the *Annual Review* (edited by A. Aikin) for which the leading hints were given by Coleridge, then with Southey at Keswick. [425] In his letters and his later articles he never mentions Malthus without abhorrence. [426] Malthus, according to his article in the *Annual Review*, regards 'vice' and 'misery' as desirable; thinks that the 'gratification of lust' is a 'physical necessity'; and attributes to the 'physical constitution of our nature' what should be ascribed to the 'existing system of society.' Malthus, that is, is a fatalist, a materialist, and an anarchist. His only remedy is to abolish the poor-rates, and starve the poor into celibacy. The folly and wickedness of the book have provoked him, he admits, to contemptuous indignation; and Malthus may be a good man personally. Still, the 'farthing candle' of Malthus's fame as a political philosopher must soon go out. So in the *Quarterly Review* Southey attributes the social evils to the disintegrating effect of the manufacturing system, of which Adam Smith was the 'tedious and hard-hearted' prophet. The excellent Malthus indeed becomes the 'hard-hearted' almost as Hooker was the 'judicious.' This sufficiently represents the view of the sentimental Tory. Malthus, transformed into a monster, deserves the 'execrations' noticed by Chalmers. There is a thorough coincidence between this view and that of the sentimental Radicals. Southey observes that Malthus (as interpreted by him) does not really answer Godwin. Malthus argues that 'perfectibility' gives an impossible end because equality would lead to vice and misery. But why should we not suppose with Godwin a change of character which would imply prudence and chastity? Men as they are may be incapable of equality because they have brutal passions. But men as they are to be may cease to be brutal and become capable of equality. This, indeed, represents a serious criticism. What Malthus was really concerned to prove was that the social state and the corresponding character suppose each other; and that real improvement supposes that the individual must somehow acquire the instincts appropriate to an improved state. The difference between him and his opponents was that he emphasised the mischief of legislation, such as that embodied in the poor-law, which contemplated a forcible change, destroying poverty without raising the poor man's character. Such a rise required a long and difficult elaboration, and he therefore dwells mainly upon the folly of the legislative, unsupported by the moral, remedy. To Godwin, on the other hand, who professed an unlimited faith in the power of reason, this difficulty was comparatively unimportant. Remove political inequalities and men will spontaneously become virtuous and prudent.

Godwin accordingly, when answering Dr. Parr and Mackintosh, [427] in 1801, welcomed Malthus's first version of the essay. He declares it to be as 'unquestionable an addition to the theory of political economy' as has been made by any writer for a century past; and 'admits the ratios to their full extent.' [428] In this philosophical spirit he proceeds to draw some rather startling conclusions. He hopes that, as mankind improves, such practices as infanticide will not be necessary; but he remarks that it would be happier for a child to perish in infancy than to spend seventy years in vice and misery. [429] He refers to the inhabitants of Ceylon as a precedent for encouraging other practices restrictive of population. In short, though he hopes that such measures may be needless, he does not shrink from admitting their possible necessity. So far, then, Godwin and Malthus might form an alliance. Equality might be the goal of both; and both might admit the necessity of change in character as well as in the political framework; only that Malthus would lay more stress upon the evil of legislative changes outrunning or independent of moral change. Here, however, arose the real offence. Malthus had insisted upon the necessity of self-help. He had ridiculed the pretensions of government to fix the rate of wages; and had shown how the poor-laws defeated their own objects. This was the really offensive ground to the political Radicals. They had been in the habit of tracing all evils to the selfishness and rapacity of the rulers; pensions, sinecures, public debts, huge armies, profligate luxuries of all kinds, were the fruits of bad government and the true causes of poverty. Kings and priests were the harpies who had settled upon mankind, and were ruining their happiness. Malthus, they thought, was insinuating a base apology for rulers when he attributed the evil to the character of the subjects instead of attributing it to the wickedness of their rulers. He was as bad as the old Tory, Johnson, [430] exclaiming:—

> 'How small of all that human hearts endure That part
> which kings and laws can cause or cure!'

He was, they held, telling the tyrants that it was not their fault if the poor were miserable. The essay was thus an apology for the heartlessness of the rich. This view was set forth by Hazlitt in an attack upon Malthus in 1807. [431] It appears again in the *Enquiry* by G. Ensor (1769-1843)—a vivacious though rather long-winded Irishman, who was known both to O'Connell and to Bentham. [432] Godwin himself was roused by the appearance of the fifth edition of Malthus's *Essay* to write a reply, which appeared in 1820. He was helped by David Booth (1766-1846), [433] a man of some mathematical and statistical knowledge. Hazlitt's performance is sufficiently significant of the general tendency. Hazlitt had been an enthusiastic admirer of Godwin, and retained as much of the enthusiasm as his wayward prejudices would allow. He was through life what may be called a sentimental Radical, so far as Radicalism was compatible with an ardent worship of Napoleon. To him Napoleon meant the enemy of Pitt and Liverpool and Castlereagh and the Holy Alliance. Hazlitt could forgive any policy which meant the humiliation of the men whom he most heartily hated. His attack upon Malthus was such as might satisfy even Cobbett, whose capacity for hatred, and especially for this particular object of hatred, was equal to Hazlitt's. The personal rancour of which Hazlitt was unfortunately capable leads to monstrous imputations. Not only does Malthus's essay show the 'little low rankling malice of a parish beadle ... disguised in the garb of philosophy,' and bury 'false logic' under 'a heap of garbled calculations,' [434] and so forth; but he founds insinuations upon Malthus's argument as to the constancy of the sexual passion. Malthus, he fully believes, has none of the ordinary passions, anger, pride, avarice, or the like, but declares that he must be a slave to an 'amorous complexion,' and believe all other men to be made 'of the same combustible materials.' [435] This foul blow is too characteristic of Hazlitt's usual method; but indicates also the tone which could be taken by contemporary journalism.

The more serious argument is really that the second version of Malthus is an answer to his first. Briefly, the 'moral check' which came in only as a kind of afterthought is a normal part of the process by which population is kept within limits, and prevents the monstrous results of the 'geometrical ratio.' Hazlitt, after insisting upon this, admits that there is nothing in 'the general principles here stated that Mr. Malthus is at present disposed to deny, or that he has not himself expressly insisted upon in some part or other of his various works.' [436] He only argues that Malthus's concessions are made at the cost of self-contradiction. Why then, it may be asked, should not Hazlitt take the position of an improver and harmoniser of the doctrine rather than of a fierce opponent? The answer has been already implied. He regards Malthus as an apologist for an unjust inequality. Malthus, he says, in classifying the evils of life, has 'allotted to the poor all the misery, and to the rich as much vice as they please.' [437] The check of starvation will keep down the numbers of the poor; and the check of luxury and profligacy will restrain the multiplication of the rich. 'The poor are to make a formal surrender of their right to provoke charity or parish assistance that the rich may be able to lay out all their money on their vices.' [438] The misery of the lower orders is the result of the power of the upper. A man born into a world where he is not wanted has no right, said Malthus, to a share of the food. That might be true if the poor were a set of lazy supernumeraries living on the industrious. But the truth is that the poor man does the work, and is forced to put up in return with a part of the produce of his labour. [439] The poor-laws recognise the principle that those who get all from the labour of others should provide from their superfluities for the necessities of those in want. [440] The 'grinding necessity' of which Malthus had spoken does not raise but lower the standard; and a system of equality would lessen instead of increasing the pressure. Malthus, again, has proposed that parents should be responsible for their children. That is, says Hazlitt, Malthus would leave children to starvation, though he professes to disapprove infanticide. He would 'extinguish every spark of humanity ... towards the children of others' on pretence of preserving the 'ties of parental affection.' Malthus tries to argue that the 'iniquity of government' is not the cause of poverty. That belief, he says, has generated discontent and revolution. That is, says Hazlitt, the way to prevent revolutions and produce reforms is to persuade people that all the evils which government may inflict are their own fault. Government is to do as much mischief as it pleases, without being answerable for it. [441] The poor-laws, as Hazlitt admits, are bad, but do not show the root of the evil. The evils are really due to increasing tyranny, dependence, indolence, and unhappiness due to other causes. Pauperism has increased because the government and the rich have had their way in everything. They have squandered our revenues, multiplied sinecures and pensions, doubled salaries, given monopolies and encouraged jobs, and depressed the poor and industrious. The 'poor create their own fund,' and the necessity for it has arisen from the exorbitant demands made by the rich. [442] Malthus is a Blifil, [443] hypocritically insinuating arguments in favour of tyranny under pretence of benevolence.

Hazlitt's writing, although showing the passions of a bitter partisan, hits some of Malthus's rather cloudy argumentation. His successor, Ensor, representing the same view, finds an appropriate topic in the wrongs of Ireland. Irish poverty, he holds, is plainly due not to over-population but to under-government, [444] meaning, we must suppose, misgovernment. But the same cause explains other cases. The 'people are poor and are growing poorer,' [445] and there is no mystery about it. The expense of a court, the waste of the profits and money in the House of Commons, facts which are in striking contrast to the republican virtues of the United States, are enough to account for everything; and Malthus's whole aim is to 'calumniate the people.' Godwin in 1820 takes up the same taunts. Malthus ought, he thinks, to welcome war, famine, pestilence, and the gallows. [446] He has taught the poor that they have no claim to relief, and the rich that, by indulging in vice, they are conferring a benefit upon the country. The poor-laws admit a right, and he taunts Malthus for proposing to abolish it, and refusing food to a poor man on the ground that he had notice not to come into the world two years before he was born. [447]

Godwin, whose earlier atheism had been superseded by a vague deism, now thinks with Cobbett that the poor were supported by the piety of the mediæval clergy, who fed the hungry and clothed the naked from their vast revenues, while dooming themselves to spare living. [448] He appeals to the authority of the Christian religion, which indeed might be a fair *argumentum ad hominem* against 'Parson Malthus.' He declares that Nature takes more care of her work than such irreverent authors suppose, and 'does not ask our aid to keep down the excess of population.' [449] In fact, he doubts whether population increases at all. Malthus's whole theory, he says, rests upon the case of America; and with the help of Mr. Booth and some very unsatisfactory statistics, he tries to prove that the increase shown in the American census has been entirely due to immigration. Malthus safely declined to take any notice of a production which in fact shows that Godwin had lost his early vigour. The sound Utilitarian, Francis Place, took up the challenge, and exploded some of Godwin's statistics. He shows his Radicalism by admitting that Malthus, to whose general benevolence he does justice, had not spoken of the poor as one sprung like himself from the poor would naturally do; and he accepts modes of limiting the population from which Malthus himself had shrunk. For improvement, he looks chiefly to the abolition of restrictive laws.

II. SOCIALISM

The arguments of Hazlitt and his allies bring us back to the Socialist position. Although it was represented by no writer of much literary position, Owen was becoming conspicuous, and some of his sympathisers were already laying down principles more familiar to-day. Already, in the days of the Six Acts, the government was alarmed by certain 'Spencean Philanthropists.' According to Place they were a very feeble sect, numbering only about fifty, and perfectly harmless. Their prophet was a poor man called Thomas Spence (1750-1815), [450] who had started as a schoolmaster, and in 1775 read a paper at Newcastle before a 'Philosophical Society.' [451] He proposed that the land in every village should belong to all the inhabitants—a proposal which Mr. Hyndman regards as a prophecy of more thoroughgoing schemes of Land Nationalisation. Spence drifted to London, picked up a precarious living, partly by selling books of a revolutionary kind, and died in 1815, leaving, it seems, a few proselytes. A writer of higher literary capacity was Charles Hall, a physician at Tavistock, who in 1805 published a book on *The Effects of Civilisation*. [452] The effects of civilisation, he holds, are simply pernicious. Landed property originated in violence, and has caused all social evils. A great landlord consumes unproductively as much as would keep eight thousand people. [453] He gets everything from the labour of the poor; while they are forced to starvation wages by the raising of rents. Trade and manufactures are equally mischievous. India gets nothing but jewellery from Europe, and Europe nothing but muslin from India, while so much less food is produced in either country. [454] Manufactures generally are a cause and sign of the poverty of nations. [455]

Such sporadic protests against the inequalities of wealth may be taken as parts of that 'ancient tale of wrong' which has in all ages been steaming up from the suffering world, and provoking a smile from epicurean deities. As Owenism advanced, the argument took a more distinct form. Mill [456] mentions William Thompson of Cork as a 'very estimable man,' who was the 'principal champion' of the Owenites in their debates with the Benthamites. He published in 1824 a book upon the distribution of wealth. [457] It is wordy, and is apt to remain in the region of 'vague generalities' just at the points where specific statements would be welcome. But besides the merit of obvious sincerity and good feeling, it has the interest of showing very clearly the relation between the opposing schools. Thompson had a common ground with the Utilitarians, though they undoubtedly would consider his logic to be loose and overridden by sentimentalism. In the first place, he heartily admired Bentham: 'the most profound and celebrated writer on legislation in this or any other country.' [458] He accepts the 'greatest happiness principle' as applicable to the social problem. He argues for equality upon Bentham's ground. Take a penny from a poor man to give it to the rich man, and the poor man clearly loses far more happiness than the rich man gains. With Bentham, too, he admits the importance of 'security,' and agrees that it is not always compatible with equality. A man should have the fruits of his labour; and therefore the man who labours most should have most. But, unlike Bentham, he regards equality as more important than security. To him the main consideration is the monstrous mass of evil resulting from vast accumulations of wealth in a few hands. In the next place, he adapts to his own purpose the Ricardian theory of value. All value whatever, he argues, is created by labour. The labourer, he infers, should have the value which he creates. As things are, the labourer parts with most of it to the capitalist or the owner of rents. The capitalist claims a right to the whole additional production due to the employment of capital. The labourer, on the other hand, may claim a right to the whole additional production, after replacing the wear and tear and allowing to the capitalist enough to support him in equal comfort with the productive labourers. [459] Thompson holds that while either system would be compatible with 'security,' the labourer's demand is sanctioned by 'equality.' In point of fact, neither system has been fully carried out; but the labourer's view would tend to prevail with the spread of knowledge and justice. While thus anticipating later Socialism, he differs on a significant point. Thompson insists upon the importance of 'voluntary exchange' as one of his first principles. No one is to be forced to take what he does not himself think a fair equivalent for his labour. Here, again, he would coincide with the Utilitarians. They, not less than he, were for free trade and the abolition of every kind of monopoly. But that view may lead by itself to the simple adoption of the do-nothing principle, or, as modern Socialists would say, to the more effectual plunder of the poor. The modern Socialist infers that the means of production must be in some way nationalised. Thompson does not contemplate such a consummation. He denounces, like all the Radicals of the day, monopolies and conspiracy laws. Sinecures and standing armies and State churches are the strongholds of tyranny and superstition. The 'hereditary possession of wealth' is one of the master-evils, and with sinecures will disappear the systems of entails and unequal distribution of inheritance. [460] Such institutions have encouraged the use of fraud and force, and indirectly degraded the labourer into a helpless position. He would sweep them all away, and with them all disqualifications imposed upon women. [461] This once done, it will be necessary to establish a universal and thoroughgoing system of education. Then the poor man, freed from the shackles of superstition and despotism, will be able to obtain his rights as knowledge and justice spread through the whole community. The desire to accumulate for selfish purposes will itself disappear. The labourer will get all that he creates; the aggregate wealth will be enormously multiplied, though universally diffused; and the form taken by the new society will, as he argues at great length, be that of voluntary co-operative associations upon Owen's principles.

The economists would, of course, reject the theory that the capitalists should have no profits; but, in spite of this, they might agree to a great extent with Thompson's aspirations. Thompson, however, holds the true Socialist sentiment of aversion to Malthus. He denies energetically what he takes to be the Malthusian doctrine: that increased comfort will always produce increased numbers. [462] This has been the 'grand scarecrow to frighten away all attempts at social improvement.' Thompson accordingly asserts that increased comfort always causes increased prudence ultimately; and looks forward to a stationary state in which the births will just balance the deaths. I need not inquire here which theory puts the cart before the horse. The opposition possibly admits of reconciliation; but here I only remark once more how Malthus stood for the appeal to hard facts which always provoked the Utopians as much as it corresponded to the stern Utilitarian view.

Another writer, Thomas Hodgskin, honorary secretary of the Birkbeck Institution, who published a tract called *Labour defended against the Claims of Capital, or the Unproductiveness of Capital proved* (1825), and afterwards gave some popular lectures on political economy, has been noticed as anticipating Socialist ideas. He can see, he says, why something should go to the maker of a road and something be paid by the person who gets the benefit of it. But he does not see why the road itself should have anything. [463] Hodgskin writes without bitterness, if without much logic. It is not for me to say whether modern Socialists are well advised in admitting that these crude suggestions were anticipations of their own ideas. The most natural inference would be that vague guesses about the wickedness of the rich have been in all ages current among the poor, and now and then take more pretentious form. Most men want very naturally to get as much and to work as little as they can, and call their desire a first principle of justice.

Perhaps, however, it is fairer to notice in how many points there was unconscious agreement; and how by converting very excellent maxims into absolute dogmas, from which a whole system was deducible, the theories appeared to be mutually contradictory, and, taken separately, became absurd. The palpable and admitted evil was the growth of pauperism and demoralisation of the labourer. The remedy, according to the Utilitarians, is to raise the sense of individual responsibility, to make a man dependent upon his own exertions, and to give him security that he will enjoy their fruit. Let government give education on one hand and security on the other, and equality will follow in due time. The sentimental Radical naturally replies that leaving a man to starve does not necessarily make him industrious; that, in point of fact, great and growing inequality of wealth has resulted; and that the rights of man should be applied not only to political privilege, but to the possession of property. The Utilitarians have left out justice by putting equality in the background. Justice, as Bentham replied, has no meaning till you have settled by experience what laws will produce happiness; and your absolute equality would destroy the very mainspring of social improvement. Meanwhile the Conservative thinks that both parties are really fostering the evils by making individualism supreme, and that organisation is necessary to improvement; while one set of Radicals would perpetuate a mere blind struggle for existence, and the other enable the lowest class to enforce a dead level of ignorance and stupidity. They therefore call upon government to become paternal and active, and to teach not only morality but religion; and upon the aristocracy to discharge its functions worthily, in order to stamp out social evils and prevent a servile insurrection. But how was the actual government of George IV. and Sidmouth and Eldon to be converted to a sense of its duties? On each side appeal is made to a sweeping and absolute principle, and amazingly complex and difficult questions of fact are taken for granted. The Utilitarians were so far right that they appealed to experience, as, in fact, such questions have to be settled by the slow co-operation of many minds in many generations. Unfortunately the Utilitarians had, as we have seen, a very inadequate conception of what experience really meant, and were fully as rash and dogmatic as their opponents. I must now try to consider what were the intellectual conceptions implied by their mode of treating these problems.

FOOTNOTES:

[392] The discussions of population most frequently mentioned are:—W. Godwin, *Thoughts occasioned by Dr. Parr's Spital Sermon*, etc., 1801; R. Southey, in (Aikin's) *Annual Review for 1803*, pp. 292-301; Thomas Jarrold, *Dissertations on Man*, etc., 1806; W. Hazlitt, *Reply to the Essay on Population*, 1807; A. Ingram, *Disquisitions on Population*, 1808; John Weyland, *Principles of Population*, etc., 1806; James Grahame, *Inquiry into the Principle of Population*, 1816; George Ensor, *Inquiry concerning the Population of Nations*, 1818; W. Godwin, *On Population*, 1820; Francis Place, *Principles of Population*, 1822; David Booth, *Letter to the Rev. T. R. Malthus*, 1823; M. T. Sadler, *Law of Population*, 1830; A. Alison, *Principles of Population*, 1840; T. Doubleday, *True Law of Population*, 1842.

[393] *Quarterly Review*, Dec. 1812 (reprinted in Southey's *Moral and Political Essays*, 1832).

[394] *Quarterly Review*, July 1817, by (Archbishop) Sumner, Malthus's commentator in the *Records of Creation*. Ricardo's *Letters to Trower*, p. 47.

[395] *Spence's Tracts on Political Economy* were collected with a preface in 1822. Spence is better known as an entomologist, and collaborated with William Kirby.

[396] *Tracts* (1822), p. xiii.

[397] *Ibid.*

[398] Chalmers's *Works* were published in twenty-five volumes in 1841-42.

[399] Chalmers's *Works*, i. 237.

[400] This essay is not in his collected *Works*, though in vol. xxi. it is promised for the next volume.

[401] *Works*, xix. and xx.

[402] Mill's *Political Economy*, bk. i. ch. v. § 7 and 8. See Chalmers, xix. 140.

[403] *National Resources* (Appendix).

[404] *Works*, xix. 306.

[405] *Ibid.* xix. 226, 233.

[406] *National Resources*, p. 48.

[407] *Works*, xix. 64.

[408] *Works*, xix. 226.

[409] *Ibid.* xix. 235.

[410] *National Resources*, p. 158.

[411] *Ibid.*

[412] *Works*, xix. 262.

[413] *Works*, xix. 75.

[414] *Ibid.* xix. 118-47.

[415] *Ibid.* xix. 343.

[416] See *Ibid.* xix. 171. J. S. Mill speaks of Chalmers's speculations with a respect which it is difficult to understand.

[417] Chalmers holds that the Ricardian doctrine of rent inverts the true order. Fertile lands do not pay rent because poor lands are brought into cultivation, but poor lands are cultivated because fertile lands pay rent. He apparently wishes, like Malthus, to regard rent as a blessing, not a curse. The point is not worth arguing. See *Works*, xix. 320.

[418] *Works*, xix. 304-5.

[419] *Ibid.* xix. 370.

[420] *Ibid.* xix. 366.

[421] *Ibid.* xix. 322.

[422] *Works*, xx. 247, 296.

[423] *Ibid.* xx. 290.

[424] *Works*, xix. 380.

[425] The copy of Malthus's second edition with Coleridge's notes used by Southey is in the British Museum.

[426] See Southey's *Political.*

[427] *Thoughts occasioned by Dr. Parr's Spital Sermon.* A copy annotated by Coleridge is in the British Museum.

[428] *Thoughts*, etc., pp. 56, 61, 62.

[429] *Ibid.*

[430] Lines added to Goldsmith's *Traveller.*

[431] *Reply to the Essay on Population*, etc., 1807. The book was anonymous. The first three letters had appeared in Cobbett's *Register*. Two others with an appendix are added.

[432] Bentham's *Works*, x. 603, 604; and *Dictionary of National Biography*.

[433] See *Dictionary of National Biography*.

[434] Hazlitt's *Reply*, p. 19.

[435] *Ibid.*

[436] *Ibid.*

[437] *Reply*, p. 263.

[438] *Ibid.*

[439] *Ibid.*

[440] *Ibid.*

[441] *Reply*, p. 351.

[442] *Ibid.*

[443] *Ibid.*

[444] Ensor's *Enquiry*, p. 294.

[445] *Ibid.*

[446] *Godwin on Population*, p. 506.

[447] *Ibid.*

[448] *Ibid.*

[449] Godwin, p. 219.

[450] See account of him reprinted from Mackenzie's *History of Newcastle* and *Dictionary of National Biography*.

[451] Reprinted by Mr. Hyndman in 1822, with a preface.

[452] See *Dictionary of National Biography*. Hall's book was reprinted by J. M. Morgan in the 'Phœnix Library,' 1850. See Anton Menger's *Das Recht auf den vollen Arbeitsertrag* (second edition, 1891), for notices of Hall, Thompson, and others.

[453] *Effects of Civilisation* (1850), p. 86.

[454] *Ibid.*

[455] *Ibid.*

[456] *Autobiography,* p. 125. See Holyoake's *History of Co-operation,* i. 16, 109, 278-83, 348, for some interesting notices of Thompson. Menger (*Recht auf den vollen Arbeitsertrag,* p. 100 *n.*) holds that Thompson not only anticipated but inspired Marx: Rodbertus, he says, drew chiefly upon St. Simon and Proudhon.

[457] *An Inquiry into the Principles of the Distribution of Wealth most conducive to Human Happiness; applied to the Newly Proposed System of Voluntary Equality of Wealth.* —1824.

[458] *Distribution of Wealth,* p. 327.

[459] *Distribution of Wealth,* p. 167, etc.

[460] *Ibid.*

[461] He wrote, as J. S. Mill observes, an *Appeal* [1825] against James Mill's views on this matter—a fact which no doubt commended him to the son.

[462] *Distribution of Wealth,* pp. 425, 535, etc.

[463] *Labour Defended,* p. 16.

CHAPTER VII
PSYCHOLOGY

I. THOMAS BROWN

The politicians and economists, of whom I have spoken, took first principles for granted. The intellectual temperament, which made certain methods congenial to them, would no doubt have led them to an analogous position in philosophy. Bentham had touched upon philosophical points in a summary way, and James Mill, as we shall see, gave a more explicit statement. But such men as Ricardo and Malthus had no systematic philosophy, though a certain philosophy was congenial to their methods. Desire to reach a solid groundwork of fact, hearty aversion to mere word-juggling, and to effeminate sentimentalism, respect for science and indifference to, if not contempt for, poetry, resolution to approve no laws or institutions which could not be supported on plain grounds of utility, and to accept no theory which could not be firmly based on verifiable experience, imply moral and intellectual tendencies, in which we may perhaps say that the Utilitarians represent some of the strongest and most valuable qualities of the national character. Taking these qualities for granted, let us consider how the ultimate problems presented themselves to the school thus distinguished.

I have already observed that the Scottish philosophy, taught by Reid and Dugald Stewart, represented the only approach to a living philosophical system in these islands at the beginning of the century. It held this position for a long period. Mill, who had heard Dugald Stewart's lectures, knew nothing of German thought. He was well read in French philosophers, and in harmony with one leading sect. The so-called *idéologues*, [464] who regarded Condillac as representing the true line of intellectual progress, were in France the analogues of the English Utilitarians. Destutt de Tracy and Cabanis were their most conspicuous leaders in this generation. The philosophy of Reid and Stewart crossed the channel, and supplied the first assailants of the *idéologues* with their controversial weapons. Thus, until the German influence came to modify the whole controversy, the vital issue seemed to lie between the doctrine of Reid or 'intuitionism' on the one hand,

and the purely 'experiential' school on the other, whether, as in France, it followed Condillac, or, as in England, looked back chiefly to Hartley. Both sections traced their intellectual ancestry to Locke and Hobbes, with some reference to Bacon, and, by the French writers, to Descartes. Stewart, again, as I have said, was the accepted Whig philosopher. It is true that the Whig sat habitually in the seat of Gallio. Jeffrey, whether he fully realised the fact or not, was at bottom a sceptic in philosophy as in politics. John Allen, the prophet of Holland House, was a thorough sceptic, and says [465] that Horner, one of Stewart's personal admirers, was really a follower of Hume. The Whigs were inclined to Shaftesbury's doctrine that sensible men had all one religion, and that sensible men never said what it was. Those who had a more definite and avowable creed were content to follow Stewart's amiable philosophising. Brougham professed, let us hope, sincerely, to be an orthodox theist, and explained the argument from design in a commentary upon Paley. Sydney Smith expounded Reid and Stewart in lectures which showed at least that he was still a wit when talking 'philosophy' at the Royal Institution; and, though he hated 'enthusiasm' in dissenters, evangelicals, and tractarians, and kept religion strictly in its place—a place well outside of practical politics—managed to preach a wholesome, commonplace morality in terms of Christian theology. The difference between the Whig and the Radical temper showed itself in philosophical as in political questions. The Radical prided himself on being logical and thoroughgoing, while the Whig loved compromise, and thought that logic was very apt to be a nuisance. The systematic reticence which the Utilitarians held to be necessary prevented this contrast from showing itself distinctly on the surface. The Utilitarians, however, though they avoided such outspoken scepticism as would startle the public, indicated quite sufficiently to the initiated their essential position. It implied what they fully recognised in private conversation—a complete abandonment of theology. They left the obvious inferences to be drawn by others. In philosophy they could speak out in a well-founded confidence that few people were able to draw inferences. I will begin by considering the doctrine against which they protested; for the antagonism reveals, I think, the key to their position.

When Stewart was obliged by infirmity to retire from the active discharge of his duties, he was succeeded by Thomas Brown (1778-1820). Brown had shown early precocity, and at the age of fifteen had attracted Stewart's notice by some remarks on a psychological point. He published at twenty a criticism of Darwin's *Zoonomia,* and he became one of the *Edinburgh Review* circle. When the *Review* was started he contributed an article upon Kant. In those happy days it was so far from necessary to prepare oneself for such a task by studying a library of commentators that the young reviewer could frankly admit his whole knowledge to be derived from Villers' *Philosophie de Kant* (1801). [466] Soon afterwards he took an important share in a once famous controversy. John Leslie, just elected to the mathematical chair at Edinburgh, was accused of having written favourably of Hume's theory of causation. Whigs and Tories took this up as a party question, [467] and Brown undertook to explain in a pamphlet what Hume's theory was, and to show that it did not lead to atheism. Leslie's friends triumphed, though it does not appear how far Brown's arguments contributed to their success. The pamphlet was rewritten and enlarged, and a third edition of 1818 gives a full exposition of his theory. Brown had meanwhile become Stewart's leading disciple, and in 1810 was elected to be his colleague. Brown held the position, doing all the active duties, until his premature death in 1820. Brown, according to his biographer, wrote his lectures immediately before delivery, and completed them during his first two years of office. His theories, as well as his words, were often, according to the same authority, extemporised. Brown found that he could not improve what he had written under 'very powerful excitement.' Moreover, he had an unlucky belief that he was a poet. From 1814 till 1819 he brought out yearly what he supposed to be a poem. These productions, the *Paradise of Coquets* and the rest, are in the old-fashioned taste, and have long passed into oblivion.

The lectures, published posthumously, became a text-book for students, and reached a nineteenth edition in 1851. Their faults, considered as philosophical treatises, are palpable. They have the wordiness of hasty composition, and the discursive rhetoric intended to catch the attention of an indolent audience. Brown does not see that he is insulting his hearers when he apologises for introducing logic into lectures upon metaphysics, and indemnifies them by quotations from Akenside and the *Essay on Man*. Brown, however, showed great acuteness and originality. He made deviations, and took pains to mark his deviations, from Reid, though he spoke more guardedly of his own friend, Stewart. Stewart, who had strongly supported Brown's election, was shocked when, on the publication of the lectures, he came to discover that his colleague had been preaching heresy, and wrote with obvious annoyance of Brown's hastiness and dangerous concessions to the enemy. [468] Brown, however, impressed his contemporaries by his ability. Sydney Smith is probably reporting the current judgment of his own circle when he says [469] that in metaphysics Stewart was a 'humbug' compared with Brown. I certainly think that Stewart, whom I should be sorry to call a humbug, shows less vigour and subtlety. Brown, at any rate, impressed both the Mills, and his relation to them is significant.

Brown's essay upon Causation indicates this relation. In this, indeed, there is little, if any, divergence from Stewart, though he attacks Reid with considerable asperity. He urges that Reid, while really agreeing with Hume, affected to answer him under cover of merely verbal distinctions. [470] The main point is simple. Hume had asserted that all events seem to be 'entirely loose and separate,' or, in other words, 'conjoined but never connected.' Yet he points out that, in fact, when we have found two events to be 'conjoined,' we call one cause and the other effect, and assume a 'necessary connection' between them. He then asks, What is the origin of this belief, and what, therefore, is the logical warrant for its validity? Brown entirely accepts Hume's statement of the facts. The real meaning of our statements is evaded by appealing to the conception of 'power.' When the loadstone (in his favourite illustration) attracts the iron, we say it has a 'power' of attracting iron. But to speak thus of a power is simply to describe the same facts in other words. We assert this, and nothing more than this, that when the loadstone comes near the iron, each moves towards the other. 'Power' is a word which only covers a statement of 'invariable antecedence.' Brown traces the various confusions which have obscured the true nature of this belief. He insists especially that we can no more discover power in mental than in physical sequences. The will had been supposed to be the type of causal power; but volition, according to Brown, reveals simply another succession of desires and bodily actions. The hypothesis of 'power' has been really the source of 'illusion.' The tendency to personify leads us to convert metaphor into fact, to invent a subject of this imaginary 'power,' and thus to create a mythology of beings to carry on the processes of nature. In other words, Brown here follows Hume or even anticipates Comte. As J. S. Mill remarks, [471] this erroneous identification of 'power' with 'will' gives the 'psychological rationale of Comte's great historical generalisation'; and, so far, Brown, as a follower of Hume, is clearly on the way to positivism.

The world, then, is a vast aggregate of 'loose' phenomena. A contemplation of things reveals no reason for one order rather than another. You may look at your loadstone as long as you please, but you will find no reason for its attracting iron. You may indeed interpolate a number of minute intervening sequences, and the process often suggests a vague something more than sequence; but this is a mere illusion. [472] Could we, in fact, see all the minute changes in bodies we should actually perceive that cause means nothing but 'the immediate invariable antecedence of an event.' [473] Brown especially argues against the attempts of d'Alembert and Euler to deduce the first laws of motion from the principle of 'sufficient reason.' [474] That, as he argues in detail, is merely begging the question, by introducing the principle of causation under an alias.

What, then, is the principle? We believe, he says, [475] that 'every event must have a cause,' and that circumstances exactly 'similar must have results exactly similar.' This belief, though applicable to all events, does not give us the 'slightest aid' to determining, independently of experience, any particular event. We observe that B follows A, but, for all we can say, it might as well follow any other letter of the alphabet. Yet we are entitled to say in general that it does uniformly follow some particular letter. The metaphor which describes cause and effect as a 'bond' tying A and B together is perfectly appropriate if taken to express the bare fact of sequence; [476] but we fall into error if we fancy there is really any bond whatever beside the events themselves.

The belief, then, in causation has precisely the same import according to Hume and Brown; and both agree that it is not produced by 'reasoning.' The proposition 'B has once succeeded A,' or 'has succeeded A a thousand times,' is entirely different from the proposition 'B will for ever succeed A.' [477] No process of logical inference can extract one from the other. Shall we, then, give up a belief in causation? The belief in any case exists as a fact. Hume explains it by custom or association. Brown argues, and I think with much force, that Hume's explanation is insufficient. Association may explain (if it does more than restate) the fact that one 'idea' calls up another idea, but such association may and often does occur without suggesting any belief. The belief, too, precedes the association. We begin by believing too much, not too little, and assume a necessary connection of many phenomena which we afterwards find to be independent. The true answer is therefore different. There are three sources of belief, 'perception,' 'reasoning,' and 'intuition.' [478] Now, we cannot 'perceive' anything but a present coincidence; neither can we establish a connection by any process of 'reasoning,' and therefore the belief must be an 'intuition.' This, accordingly, is Brown's conclusion. 'There are principles,' he says, 'independent of reasoning, in the mind which save it from the occasional follies of all our ratiocinations'; [479] or rather, as he explains, which underlie all reasoning. The difference, then, between Hume and Brown (and, as Brown argues, between Hume and Reid's real doctrine) is not as to the import, but as to the origin, of the belief. It is an 'intuition' simply because it cannot be further analysed. It does not allow us to pass a single step beyond experience; it merely authorises us to interpret experience. We can discover any actual law of connection between phenomena only by observing that they occur in succession. We cannot get beyond or behind the facts—and therefore intuitionism in this sense is not opposed to empiricism, but a warrant for empirical conclusions. An 'intuition,' briefly, is an unanalysable belief. Brown asserts that a certain element of thought has not been explained, and assumes it to be therefore inexplicable or ultimate. Brown's account of causation had a great influence upon both the Mills, and especially affected the teaching of the younger Mill.

Another point is important. Reid, as I have said, had specially prided himself upon his supposed overthrow of Berkeley's idealism. He was considered to have shown, in spite of sceptics, that the common belief in an external world was reasonable. Brown in his lectures ridiculed Reid's claim. This 'mighty achievement,' the 'supposed overthrow of a great system,' was 'nothing more than the proof that certain phrases are metaphorical, which were intended by their authors to be understood *only* as metaphors.' [480] The theory was dead before Reid slew it, though the phrases were still used as a mere 'relic,' or survival of an obsolete doctrine. [481] The impossibility of constructing extension out of our sensations is the *experimentum crucis* upon which Reid was ready to stake his case. If the attempt at such a construction could succeed, he would 'lay his hand upon his mouth' and give up the argument. [482] Brown takes up the challenge thus thrown out. He holds that our knowledge of an external world is derived from a source which Reid overlooked. He modifies the Scottish psychology by introducing the muscular senses. His theory is that the infant which has learned to move discovers that on some occasions its movements are modified by a sense of 'impeded effort.' [483] The sudden interruption to a well-known series excites in its mind the notion of 'a cause which is not in itself.' This is the source of our belief in an external world. That belief is essentially the belief in some cause which we know to be other than our own mental constitution or the series of 'internal' phenomena, and of which we can know nothing else. It is enough to indicate a theory which has been elaborated by later psychologists, and plays a great part (for example) in the theories of Mill, Bain, and Mr. Herbert Spencer. It shows the real tendency of Brown's speculations. In the first place, it must be noticed that the theory itself had been already emphatically stated by Destutt de Tracy. Hamilton accuses Brown of plagiarism. [484] Whether his accusation be justifiable or not, it is certainly true that Brown had in some way reached the same principles which had been already set forth by a leading 'ideologist.' Brown, that is, though the official exponent of the Scottish philosophy, was in this philosophical tenet at one with the school which they regarded as materialistic or sceptical. The path by which he reaches his conclusions is also characteristic.

Brown has reversed the interpretation of Reid's *experimentum crucis*. I will give up my case, says Reid, if you can make the external world out of sensations. That, replies Brown, is precisely what we can do. How from sensations do we get what Berkeley called 'outness'? We get it, says Brown, from the sense of resistance or 'impeded effort.' That reveals to us the fact that there is something independent of ourselves, and the belief in such a something is precisely what we mean, and all that we mean, by the belief in an external world. Consistently with this, Brown rejects Reid's distinction between the primary and secondary qualities. The distinction corresponds no doubt to some real differences, but there is no difference of the kind suggested by Reid. 'All [the qualities] are relative and equally relative— our perception of extension and resistance as much as our perception of fragrance and bitterness.' [485] We ascribe the sensations to 'external objects,' but the objects are only known by the 'medium' of our sensations. In other words, the whole world may be regarded as a set of sensations, whether of sight, smell, touch, or resistance to muscular movement, accompanied by the belief that they are caused by something not ourselves, and of which something we can only say that it is not ourselves.

Once more, the analysis of the process by which the belief is generated is significant. From resistance, or the sensation produced when something 'resists our attempts to grasp it,' we get the 'outness.' Then perception is 'nothing more than the association of this complex notion with our other sensations—the notion of something extended and resisting, suggested by these sensations, when the suggestions themselves have previously arisen, and suggested in the same manner and on the same principle as any other associate feeling suggests any other associate feeling.' [486] The odour or colour of a rose recalls the sensation of touching and of resistance to our grasp. Thus we regard the whole group of sensations as due to the external cause which produces the sensation of resistance. Brown seems to hesitate a little as to whether he shall appeal to an 'intuition' or to 'association,' but 'as I rather think,' he says, the belief is founded 'on associations as powerful as intuition.' [487]

Whatever, then, may be the origin of the belief—'intuition' or 'association'—it is clear that it can give us no knowledge except such as is derived from sensations. Moreover, Brown is thus led, as in the doctrine of causation, to accept a really sceptical position. He declares that he is in this respect at one with both Reid and Hume. They both accept two propositions: first, that we cannot 'by mere reasoning' prove the existence of an external world; secondly, that it is 'absolutely impossible for us not to believe' in its existence. Hume, he says, pronounces the first proposition in a 'loud tone of voice' and 'whispers' the second. Reid, conversely, passes over the first rapidly and 'dwells on the second with a tone of confidence.' [488] Brown accepts both statements. He has already said that there is no argument against Berkeley's denial of matter any more than against the 'infinite divisibility of matter.' But he adds, it is 'physically impossible' for us to admit the conclusion, at least without 'an instant dissent from a momentary logical admission.' [489] This, indeed, is but a version of Hume's familiar statement that Berkeley's arguments admit of no reply and produce no conviction.

Another essential doctrine of the Mills, the 'association' theory, is treated differently by Brown. Brown, as we have seen, both in his theory of causation and in his theory of our belief in an external world, speaks of principles in the mind which somehow override 'ratiocination.' In the first case, he speaks of 'intuition,' but in the other, as I have said, he seems to prefer association. The difference is remarkable because the belief in an external world is upon his showing simply a case of causation. It means essentially the reference of our sensations as to an external cause. Now, in the argument upon causation, he has insisted upon the insufficiency of association to generate the belief; and he would have found it difficult to meet his own arguments if applied to the belief in an external world. Yet it does not seem to occur to him that there is any difficulty in explaining this belief in an external world as a case of what Mill called 'indissoluble association.' Brown, as Mill thought, was not sufficiently aware of the power of this principle, and the difference between them is marked by this divergence. Brown had a great deal to say about association, though he chose generally to substitute the word 'suggestion,' previously familiar to Reid and Berkeley. [490] He considers it, however, mainly in another relation. He proposes to trace the order in which 'trains' of ideas succeed each other in our minds. He does not dwell upon the influence of association in producing belief. His question is not primarily as to the logic, but as to the actual succession of our thoughts. He explains that he uses the word 'suggestion' in order to avoid the hypothesis that the sequence of two ideas necessarily implies a previous state of mind in which they were brought together; and endeavours to explain various cases (as, for example, association by 'contrast' as well as by 'likeness' or 'continuity') by a more 'subtle' analysis. [491] He then works out an elaborate theory of 'simple' and 'relative' suggestion. Simple 'suggestion' [492] corresponds mainly to ordinary association, as when a friend's name or his book calls up the thought of the man himself. 'Relative suggestion' arises when two or more objects are perceived and suggest various relations of likeness and so forth. [493] This provides a scheme for working out the whole doctrine of the sequences of ideas so far as the sequences depend upon the mind itself and not upon external causes. It thus leads to problems of abstraction and generalisation and to his whole theory of what he calls the 'intellectual states.' He again closely coincides with the French ideologists. He starts by examining Locke and Condillac. He of course professes to hold that Condillac's version of Locke is illegitimate, and ridicules the famous formula *penser c'est sentir*. He is, however, equally unwilling to admit Reid's 'variety of powers.' [494] In fact, his criticism of Condillac shows more affinity than contrast. Condillac erred, he says, in holding that thoughts are 'transformed sensations.' This was a false simplification into which he considers Condillac to have been led partly by the ambiguity of the word *sentir*. [495] Condillac applied to the mind the theory, true in 'the chemistry of the material chemists,' that the 'compounds are the elements themselves.' [496] He errs when he infers from the analogy that a feeling which arises out of others can be resolved into them. 'Love and hate' and other emotions are fundamentally different from the sensations by which they are occasioned, not mere 'transformations' of those sensations. We, on the other hand (that is to say, Reid and Stewart), have erred by excessive amplification. Instead of identifying different things, we have admitted a superfluous number of 'ultimate principles.'

The result is that besides the original sensations, we have to consider a number of feelings, which, while essentially different, are 'suggested' or caused by them. These are parts of the whole intellectual construction, and, though not transformed sensations, are still 'feelings' arising in consequence of the sensations. They are parts of the 'trains' or sequences of 'ideas.' It is accordingly characteristic of Brown that he habitually describes an intellectual process as a 'feeling.' The statement of a mathematical proportion, for example, is a case of 'relative suggestion.' When we consider two numbers together we have a '*feeling* of the relation of proportion.' [497] The 'profoundest reasonings' are 'nothing more than a continued analysis of our thought,' by which we resolve the 'complex *feelings* of our minds' into the simpler conceptions out of which they were constructed. [498] In other words, Brown, it would seem, really accepts the *penser c'est sentir*, only that he regards the *sentir* as including separate classes of feeling, which cannot be regarded as simple 'transformations' of sensation. They are 'states of the mind' caused by, that is, invariably following upon, the simpler states, and, of course, combining in an endless variety of different forms. Reasoning is nothing more than a series of relative 'suggestions of which the separate subjects are felt by us to be mutually related.' [499] Hence, too, arises his theory of generalisation. He is, he says, not a 'nominalist' but a 'conceptualist,' and here, for once, agrees with Reid as against Stewart. [500] The 'general term,' according to him, expresses the 'feeling or general notion of resemblance,' which arises upon a contemplation of two objects. 'In Nature,' as he observes elsewhere, [501] 'there are no classes,' but the observation of a number of particular cases and a certain feeling to which we give a name. Here, again, Brown's view coincides with that of his French contemporaries.

We may then say briefly that Brown carries out in his own fashion the conception of psychology which makes it an inductive science parallel to the physical sciences, and to be pursued by the same methods. We have to do with 'feelings' instead of atoms, and with mental instead of 'material' chemistry. Our sole method is still an analysis such as guides us in unravelling complex physical phenomena. We have, indeed, to admit certain first truths — the belief in our own identity is one of them — which are necessary to our very existence, although the assertion of such principles was carried to an extravagant and ridiculous length 'by Reid and some of his friends.' When, however, we come to ask what these principles are, it must be admitted that they are very innocent. They are not dangerous things, like 'innate ideas,' capable of leading us to a transcendental world, but simply assertions that we are warranted in trusting our sensations and applying a thoroughly inductive and empirical method. They are the cement which joins the feelings, and which, as Mill thought, could be supplanted by 'indissoluble associations.' The indefinite power thus attributed to association became, as we shall see, Mill's most characteristic doctrine. Meanwhile, I will only mention one inference which illustrates Brown's philosophical tendencies. Stewart had spoken doubtfully of the ontological argument for theology. Brown throws it over altogether. He does not even change it into an 'intuition.' He has always, he says, regarded it as 'absolutely void of force' unless it tacitly assumes the 'physical argument.' Nay, it is one proof of the force of this physical argument that it has saved us from doubts which would be rather strengthened than weakened by the 'metaphysical arguments.' [502] The 'physical argument' means the argument from design, which thus becomes the sole support of theology.

Hamilton naturally regards Brown as a mere sceptic in disguise. His theory of perception destroys his theory of personal identity. He has refused to accept our intuitive belief in one case, and cannot appeal to it in the other. He leaves no room for 'liberty of will,' and advances 'no argument in support of this condition of our moral being.' [503] Indeed, as Stewart complained, Brown, by identifying 'will' and 'desire,' has got rid of the will altogether. It is only natural that a man who is making a scientific study of the laws of human nature should find no room for an assertion that within a certain sphere there are no laws. A physiologist might as well admit that some vital processes are uncaused.

Brown thus illustrates the gravitation of the 'common-sense' philosophy to pure empiricism. He was the last in the genuine line of Scottish common-sense philosophers. When after what may be called the unphilosophical interregnum which followed Brown's death, Hamilton became professor, the Scottish tradition was blended with the very different theories derived from

Kant. Upon Brown's version, the Scottish philosophy had virtually declared itself bankrupt. The substance of his teaching was that of the very school which his predecessors had attempted to confute, carefully as the fact might be hidden by dexterous rhetoric and manipulation of technical terms. He agrees with Hume's premises, and adopts the method of Condillac. This was perceived by his most remarkable hearer. Carlyle went to Edinburgh at the end of 1809. Brown, 'an eloquent, acute little gentleman, full of enthusiasm about simple suggestions, relative, etc.,' was 'utterly unprofitable' to him, disspiriting 'as the autumn winds among withered leaves.' [504] In *Signs of the Times* (1829) Carlyle gave his view of the Scottish philosophy generally. They had, he says, started from the 'mechanical' premises suggested by Hume. 'They let loose instinct as an indiscriminatory bandog to guard them against (his) conclusions': 'they tugged lustily at the logical chain by which Hume was so coldly towing them and the world into bottomless abysses of Atheism and Fatalism. But the chain somehow snapped between them, and the issue has been that nobody now cares about either—any more than about Hartley's, Darwin's, or Priestley's contemporaneous doings in England.' [505] The judgment goes to the root of the matter. The method of Reid inevitably led to this result. Consider the philosophy as based upon, if not identical with, an inductive science of psychology, and the end is clear. You may study and analyse the phenomena as carefully as you please; and may, as the Scottish professors did, produce, if not a scientific psychology, yet a mass of acute prolegomena to a science. But the analysis can only reveal the actual combinations, chemical or mechanical, of thought. The ultimate principles which the teachers profess to discover are simply provisional; products not yet analysed, but not therefore incapable of analysis. It was very desirable to point them out: an insistence upon the insufficiency of Hume's or Condillac's theories was a most valuable service; but it was valuable precisely because every indication of such an unresolved element was a challenge to the next comer to resolve it by closer analysis. And thus, in fact, the intuitions, which had played so great a part with Reid, come in Brown's hands to be so clearly limited to the materials given by sensation or experience that any show of 'philosophy,' meaning an independent theory of the universe, was an illusory combination of fine phrases. [506]

II. JAMES MILL'S 'ANALYSIS'

James Mill's *Analysis of the Phenomena of the Human Mind* is on the one hand an exposition of the principles implied in Bentham's writings, and, on the other hand, a statement of the position from which the younger Mill started. J. S. Mill discussed the book with his father during its composition, and in 1869 he published a new edition, with elaborate notes by himself,

George Grote, Professor Bain, and Andrew Findlater. [507] The commentary is of great importance in defining the relation between the two successors to the throne of Bentham.

Mill's *Analysis*, though not widely read, made a deep impression upon Mill's own disciples. It is terse, trenchant, and uncompromising. It reminds us in point of style of the French writers, with whom he sympathised, rather than of the English predecessors, to whom much of the substance was owing. The discursive rhetoric of Brown or Stewart is replaced by good, hard, sinewy logic. The writer is plainly in earnest. If over confident, he has no petty vanity, and at least believes every word that he says. Certain limitations are at once obvious. Mill, as a publicist, a historian, and a busy official, had not had much time to spare for purely philosophic reading. He was not a professor in want of a system, but an energetic man of business, wishing to strike at the root of the superstitions to which his political opponents appealed for support. He had heard of Kant, and seen what 'the poor man would be at.' Later German systems, had he heard of them, would have been summarily rejected by him as so much transcendental moonshine. The problem of philosophy was, he held, a very simple one, if attacked in a straightforward, scientific method.

Mill, like his Scottish rivals, applies 'Baconian' principles. The inductive method, which had already been so fruitful in the physical sciences, will be equally effective in philosophy, and ever since Locke, philosophy had meant psychology. The 'philosophy of the mind' and the philosophy of the body may be treated as co-ordinate and investigated by similar methods. In the physical sciences we come ultimately to the laws of movement of their constituent atoms. In the moral sciences we come in the same way to the study of 'ideas.' The questions, How do ideas originate? and how are they combined so as to form the actual state of consciousness? are therefore the general problems to be solved. Hume had definitely proposed the problem. Hartley had worked out the theory of association of ideas which Hume had already compared [508] to the universal principle of gravitation in the physical world; and had endeavoured to show how this might be connected with physiological principles. Hartley's followers had been content to dwell upon the power of association. Abraham Tucker, Priestley, Erasmus Darwin, and Belsham represented this tendency, and were the normal antagonists of Reid and Stewart. In France the 'ideologists' mainly followed Condillac, and apparently knew nothing of Hartley. Mill, as his son testifies, had been profoundly influenced by Hartley's treatise—the 'really master-production,' as he esteemed it, 'in the philosophy of mind.' [509] Hartley's work, as the younger Mill thought, and the elder apparently agreed, was very superior to the 'merely verbal generalisation of Condillac.'

James Mill, however, admired Condillac and his successors. In his article upon education, Mill traces the association theory to Hobbes, Locke, and Hume, the last of whom, he says, was succeeded by the two 'more sober-minded' philosophers, Condillac and Hartley; while he especially praises Erasmus Darwin, Helvétius, and Cabanis. Mill, therefore, may be regarded as an independent ally of the ideologists whose influence upon Brown has been already noticed. Mill had not read Brown's *Lectures* when he began his *Analysis*, and after reading them thought Brown 'but poorly read in the doctrine of association.' [510] He had, however, read the essay upon causation, which he rather oddly describes as 'one of the most valuable contributions to science for which we are indebted to the last generation.' [511] He accepted Brown's view *minus* the 'intuition.'

The pith of Mill's book is thus determined. His aim is to give a complete analysis of mental phenomena, and therefore to resolve those phenomena into their primitive constituent atoms. Here we have at once a tacit assumption which governs his method. Philosophy, speaking roughly, is by some people supposed to start from truths, and thus to be in some way an evolution of logic. According to Mill it must start from facts, and therefore from something not given by logic. To state clearly, indeed, the relation between truth and fact may suggest very intricate problems. Mill, at any rate, must find a basis in fact, and for him the ultimate facts must be feelings. The reality at least of a feeling is undeniable. The *Penser c'est sentir*, or the doctrine that all 'ideas' are transformed sensations is his starting-point. The word 'feeling,' according to him, includes every 'phenomenon of the mind.' 'Think,' he says elsewhere, [512] does not include all our experience, but 'there is nothing to which we could not extend the term "I feel."' He proceeds to infer that our experience is either a knowledge of the feelings separately, or 'a knowledge of the order in which they follow each other; and this is all.' We may add that the knowledge is the feeling. Reid, Kant, and the Germans have indeed tried to show that there are feelings not derived from the sensations, but this, as Hartley and Condillac have shown, is a mistake. This is his first principle in a nutshell, and must give a clue to the various applications.

The next step is familiar. Hume had distinguished impressions and ideas. 'Ideas' are copies of previous 'impressions.' It is for psychology to say what are the laws by which they are related to their originals. The ultimate origin cannot be explained by psychology alone. Impressions are caused by the outward world acting in some way upon the mind; and the psychologist can only classify the various modes in which they present themselves. Mill therefore begins by the usual account of the five senses, through which comes all knowledge of the external world. He adds to Reid's list muscular sensations, and those derived from the internal organs, to which last Cabanis in particular had called attention. So far he is following the steps of his predecessors. He is, he says, simply asserting an 'indisputable' fact. [513] We have sensations and we have ideas, which are 'copies of sensations.' We may then consider how far these facts will enable us to explain the whole series of mental phenomena. 'Ideation,' which he suggests as a new word—the process by which a continuous series of thoughts goes on in our minds—is the general phenomenon to be considered. Without, as yet, pronouncing that sensations and copies of sensations will turn out to form the whole contents of our consciousness, he tries to show for what part of those contents they will account.

Here we come to the doctrine which for him and his school gave the key to all psychological problems. It was James Mill's real merit, according to his son, that he carried the principle of association of ideas further than it had been carried by Hartley or other predecessors. [514] The importance of the doctrine, indeed, is implied in the very statement of the problem. If it be true, or so far as it is true, that our consciousness reveals to us simply a series of 'sensations' and 'ideas,' the question must be how they are combined. 'Thought succeeds thought, idea follows idea incessantly,' [515] says Mill; and this phrase assumes 'thoughts' and 'ideas' to be separable atoms. How, then, do they come to coalesce into an apparently continuous stream? The mind is a stream of 'ideas.' If the stream is composed of drops, we must, of course, consider the drops as composing the stream. The question is, What laws can we assign which will determine the process of composition? The phrase 'association' admittedly expresses some general and very familiar truths. Innumerable connections may be established when there is no assignable ground of connection in the ideas themselves other than the fact of a previous contact. One idea not only calls up the other, but in some way generates a belief in an independent connection. We hear thunder, for example, and think of lightning. The two ideas are entirely distinct and separate, for they are due to different senses. Yet we not only think of lightning when we hear thunder, but we have no doubt that there is a causal connection. We believe in this connection, again, though no further explanation can be given of the fact. Thunder and lightning have occurred together, and we infer that they will, and even must, occur together. When we examine our whole structure of belief, we find such 'arbitrary' associations pervade it in every direction. Language itself is learned simply by association. There is no connection whatever between the sound of the word 'man' and the 'ideas' which the word excites, beyond the fact that the sound has been previously heard when the ideas were excited. Here, then, is a phenomenon to be explained or generalised. We have in countless cases a certain connection established for which no further reason can be assigned than the fact of its previous occurrence. On such a ground, we believe that fire burns, that bread is wholesome, that stones fall; and but for such beliefs could know nothing of the outside world. 'Contingent' truth, therefore, or truth derived from mere contact, pervades, if it does not constitute, the whole fabric of our whole knowledge. To prove that all our knowledge is derived from experience is, according to Mill, to prove that in some sense or other association of ideas lies at the base of all intellectual processes. When Locke introduced a chapter upon 'Association of Ideas' into the fourth edition of his essay, he treated it as the exceptional case. Some ideas had a connection traceable by reason; others were only connected by 'chance and custom.' Association does not explain reasoning, only the deviations from reasoning. But with Hume and Hartley the relation is inverted. The principle, instead of being an exceptional case, is simply the universal rule from which logical connection may be deduced as a special case.

The facts upon which Mill relied, and the account of them which he gave, require notice and embodiment in any sound psychology. In some shape or other they form the starting-point of all later systems. Mill's vigorous application of his principle, worked out with imperfect appreciation and with many oversights, had therefrom, at least, the merit of preparing the ground for a more scientific method. In any case, however, his conclusions, so far as sound, must be placed in a different framework of theory. It becomes necessary to dwell chiefly upon the curious defects of his theory, if taken as he wished it to be taken, for an ultimate scientific statement. The fact that there is a synthesis and an analysis is expressed by 'association.' But what more can we say? What are the 'laws' of association? Unless some rule can be given, we shall get nothing that can be called a theory. One idea is not suggested by the other through any logical process. They are still 'conjoined' but not 'connected.' The connection, therefore, must be given by something different from the ideas themselves. Now the order of the original 'sensations' depends upon the 'objects of nature,' and is therefore left to 'physical philosophy.' [516] They occur, however, either in 'synchronous' or in 'successive' order. Then 'ideas' spring up in the order of 'sensations,' and this is the 'general law of association of ideas.' [517] The synchronous sensations produce synchronous ideas and the successive sensations successive ideas. Finally, the strength of the association between the ideas depends upon 'the vividness of the associated feelings, and the frequency of the association.' [518] Hume had said that association depended upon three principles, 'contiguity in time and place,' 'causation,' and 'resemblance.' Contiguity in time corresponds to the successive, and contiguity in place to the synchronous, order. Causation, as Brown had finally proved, [519] means simply antecedence and consequence. 'Resemblance' remains and is, as Mill afterwards says, [520] a most important principle; but in an unlucky moment he is half inclined to reduce even 'resemblance' to 'contiguity.' [521] Resemblance is, he even suggests, merely 'a case of frequency,' because we generally see like things together. When we see one tree or sheep, we generally see several trees or sheep. J. S. Mill mildly remarks upon this quaint suggestion as the 'least successful simplification' in the book. He argues the point gravely. Sheep, it is clear, are not seen to be like because they often compose a flock, but are considered to be a flock because they are seen to be like. To do James Mill justice, he drops the argument as soon as he has struck it out. It is only worth notice as showing his aim. 'Likeness' seems to imply a relation dependent on the ideas themselves; not purely external and arbitrary. If we could get rid of likeness, all association would ultimately be 'contiguity.' 'The fundamental law of association,' as he says elsewhere, [522] 'is that when two things have been frequently found together, we never perceive or think of the one without thinking of the other.' The two ideas are associated as two balls are associated when they are in the same box. So far as they are themselves concerned, they might be separated without any alteration in their own properties. What, then, corresponds to the 'box'? Association depends upon relations of time and space. Things are associated by occurring in succession or together; the red colour of a rose is in the same place with the shape of the leaf; the scent is perceived at the same time with the colour. The thunder follows the lightning. What, then, he might ask, are 'time' and 'space'? Are they 'ideas' or 'sensations' or qualities of the objects? or, in any case, as supplying the ultimate principle of association, do they not require investigation? Before coming to that problem, however, we have to settle other knotty points. We must clear away illusions which seem to introduce something more than association. Elements of thought not at first sight expressible simply in terms of sensations and ideas must be analysed to show that they are only disguises for different combinations of the facts. Reasoning, according to most logicians, supposes, first, concepts, and therefore some process of classification of the objects of thought; and, secondly, some process of combining these concepts to bring out hitherto unknown truths. What, then, is the meaning of the general or abstract symbols employed in the process? Mill's provision of raw materials consists so far of sensations and ideas, which are worked up so as to form 'clusters' (the word is taken from Hartley) and 'trains.' This corresponds to synchronous and successive associations. How does the logical terminology express these 'clusters' and 'trains'? Mill answers by a theory of 'naming.' Language fulfils two purposes; it is required in order to make our ideas known to others; and in order to fix our own ideas. Ideas are fluctuating, transitory, and 'come into the mind unbidden.' We must catch and make a note of these shifting crowds of impalpable entities. We therefore put marks upon the simple sensations or upon the 'clusters.' We ticket them as a tradesman tickets bundles of goods in his warehouse, and can refer to them for our own purposes or those of others. As the number of objects to be marked is enormous, as there are countless ideas and clusters and clusters of clusters of endless variety to be arranged in various ways, one main object of naming is economy. A single word has to be used to mark a great number of individuals. This will account for such general names as are represented by noun-substantives: man, horse, dog, and so forth. Mill then proceeds, with the help of Horne Tooke, to explain the other grammatical forms. An adjective is another kind of noun marking a cross division. Verbs, again, are adjectives marking other sets of facts, and enabling us to get rid of the necessity of using a new mark for every individual or conceivable combination into clusters. J. S. Mill remarks that this omits the special function of verbs—their 'employment in predication.' [523] James Mill, however, has his own view of 'predication.' 'Man' is a mark of John, Peter, Thomas, and the rest. When I say 'John is a man,' I mean that 'man is another mark to that idea of which John is a mark.' [524] I am then able to make a statement which will apply to all the individuals, and save the trouble of repeating the assertion about each. 'Predication,' therefore, is simply a substitution of one name for another. So, for example, arithmetic is simply naming. What I call two and two, I also call four. The series of thoughts in this case is merely 'a series of names applicable to the same thing and meaning the same thing.' [525] This doctrine, as J. S. Mill remarks, is derived from Hobbes, whom Leibniz in consequence called *plus quam nominalis*. [526] My belief that two and two make four explains why I give the same name to certain numbers; but the giving the name does not explain the belief. Meanwhile, if a class name be simply the mark which is put upon a bundle of things, we have got rid of a puzzle. Mill triumphs over the unfortunate realists who held that a class meant a mysterious entity, existing somewhere apart from all the individuals in which it is embodied. There is really nothing mysterious; a name is first the mark of an individual, the individual corresponding to a 'cluster' or a set of 'simple ideas, concreted into a complex idea.' [527] Then the name and the complex idea are associated reciprocally; each 'calls up' the other. The complex idea is 'associated' with other resembling ideas. The name becomes a talisman calling up the ideas of an indefinite number of resembling individuals, and the name applied to one in the first instance becomes a mark which calls up all, or, as he says, is the 'name of the whole combination.' Classification, therefore, 'is merely a process of naming, and is all resolvable into association.' [528] The peculiarity of this theory, as his commentators again remark, is that it expressly omits any reference to abstraction. The class simply means the aggregate of resembling individuals without any selection of the common attributes which are, in J. S. Mill's phrase, 'connoted' by the class-name. Abstraction, as James Mill explains, is a subsidiary process, corresponding to the 'formation of *sub-species*.' [529]

Mill has now shown how the various forms of language correspond to ideas, formed into clusters of various orders by the principle of association. The next step will naturally be to show how these clusters are connected in the process of reasoning. Here the difficulty about predication recurs. J. S. Mill [530] remarks that his father's theory of predication consistently omits 'the element Belief.' When I say, 'John is a man,' I make an affirmation or assert a belief. I do not simply mean to call up in the mind of my hearer a certain 'cluster' or two coincident clusters of ideas, but to convey knowledge of truths. The omission of reference to belief is certainly no trifle. Mill has classified the various ideas and combinations of ideas which are used in judgment, but the process of judgment itself seems to have slipped out of account. He may have given us, or be able to give us, a reasoned catalogue of the contents of our minds, but has not explained how the mind itself acts. It is a mere passive recipient of ideas, or rather itself a cluster of ideas cohering in various ways, without energy of its own. One idea, as he tells us, calls up another 'by its own associating power.' [531] Ideas are things which somehow stick together and revive each other, without reference to the mind in which they exist or which they compose. This explains his frequent insistence upon one assertion. As we approach the question of judgment he finds it essential. 'Having a sensation and having a feeling,' he says, 'are not two things.' To 'feel an idea and be conscious of that feeling are not two things; the feeling and the consciousness are but two names for the same thing.' [532] So, again, 'to have a sensation and to believe that we have it, are not distinguishable things.' [533] Locke's reflection thus becomes nothing but simple consciousness, and having a feeling is the same as attending to it. [534] The point is essential. It amounts to saying that we can speak of a thought as though it were simply a thing.

Thus belief not only depends upon, but actually *is* association. 'It is not easy,' he says, 'to treat of memory, belief, and judgment separately.' [535] As J. S. Mill naturally asks, 'How is it possible to treat of belief without including in it memory and judgment?' Memory is a case of belief, and judgment an 'act of belief.' [536] To James Mill, however, it appears that as these different functions all involve association, they may be resolved into varying applications of that universal power. Memory involves 'an idea of my present self' and an 'idea of my past self,' and to remember is to 'run over the intervening states of consciousness called up by association.' [537]

Belief involves association at every step. The belief in external objects is, as 'all men admit' ... 'wholly resolvable into association.' [538] 'That a cause means and can mean nothing to the human mind but constant antecedence' (and therefore 'inseparable association,' as he thinks) 'is no longer a point in dispute.' [539] Association, it is true, may produce wrong as well as right beliefs; right beliefs when 'in conformity with the connections of things,' [540] and wrong beliefs when not in conformity. In both cases the belief is produced by 'custom,' though, happily, the right custom is by far the commonest. The 'strength of the association follows the frequency.' The crow flies east as well as west; but the stone always falls downwards. [541] Hence I form an 'inseparable association' corresponding to a belief in gravitation, but have no particular belief about the direction of a crow's flight.

This gives the doctrine of 'indissoluble association'—the pivot of the whole scheme—the doctrine, says J. S. Mill, which, 'if it can be proved, is the greatest of all the triumphs of the Association Philosophy.' [542] The younger Mill always insisted upon the vast importance of the principle; but he here admits a difficulty. In a long note [543] upon James Mill's chapter on 'Belief,' conspicuous for his usual candour, he confesses the inadequacy of his father's view. The comment indicates the point of divergence and yet shows curiously the ground common to both. James Mill's theory states facts in some sense undeniable. Our 'ideas' cohere and combine to form a tissue: an imagery or series of pictures which form the content and are somehow the ground of our beliefs. The process of formation clearly involves 'association.' The scent of the rose is associated with the colour: both with the visible form and so forth. But is this process the same thing as believing, or have we to explain the belief by some mental activity different from, however closely connected with, the imagination, or in his phrase the 'ideation'? Here J. S. Mill finds a difficulty. The statement, 'I believe that thunder will follow lightning,' is something more than the statement, 'the sight suggests or calls up the sound.' The mental picture considered by itself may be described as a fact, without considering what belief, or whether any belief, is implied. J. S. Mill therefore makes a distinction intended to clear up his father's confusion. There is a difference, he says, between remembering 'a real fact' and remembering a 'thought.' [544] He illustrates this by the difference between the idea of Lafayette and the idea of Falstaff. Lafayette was real, and had been seen by the rememberer. Falstaff is a figment who, having never existed, can never have been seen. Yet the idea of Falstaff may be quite as vivid as the idea of Lafayette. What, then, is the difference between the two states of mind? One, says J. S. Mill, is a belief about 'real facts'; the other about 'thoughts.' This, he observes, corresponds to James

Mill's distinction between a 'sensation' and an 'idea,' [545] a difference which he had admitted to be 'primordial.' Then, says J. S. Mill, we may as well admit that there is an 'element' in the remembrance of a real fact not implied in the remembrance of a thought and not dependent on any difference in the 'ideas' themselves. It, too, may be taken as 'primordial,' or incapable of further analysis. This doctrine becomes important in some of Mill's logical speculations, [546] and is connected with his whole theory of belief in an external world. It has an uncomfortable likeness to Reid's 'common-sense' view, and even to the hated 'intuitionism'; and Mill deserves the more credit for his candour.

Meanwhile it seems clear that the criticism implies an important confusion. The line of distinction is drawn in the wrong place. So far as the simple 'imagination' is concerned, there may be no question of belief or disbelief. The picture of Falstaff or of Lafayette, a horse or a centaur, arises equally, and is put together, let us suppose, by simple association. But as soon as I think about either I believe or disbelieve, and equally whether I judge the object to be a thought or to be a 'real fact,' whether I say that I could have seen Lafayette, or that I could not have seen Falstaff. It is not a question between reality or unreality, but between two classes of reality. A dream is a real dream, just as a man is a real man. The question is simply where or how it exists, not whether it exists. The picture is, in one case, put together by my mind; in the other, due to a stimulus from without; but it exists in both cases; and belief is equally present whether I put it in one class of reality or the other: as we form a judgment equally when we pronounce a man to be lying, and when we pronounce him to be speaking the truth. J. S. Mill seems to suppose that association can explain the imagination of a centaur or a Falstaff, but cannot explain the belief in a horse or Lafayette. The imagination or 'ideation,' he should have said, accounts in both cases for the mere contents of the thought; but in neither case can it by itself explain the judgment as to 'reality.' That is to say, James Mill may have described accurately a part of the process by which the mental picture is constructed, but has omitted to explain the action of the mind itself. Belief, we may agree, is a 'primordial' or ultimate faculty; but we must not interpret it as belief in a 'real fact' as distinguished from belief in 'a thought': that is a secondary and incidental distinction.

This confusion, as I have said, apparently prevents J. S. Mill from seeing how deeply his very frank admissions cut into the very structure of his father's system. He has, as I have said, remarked upon the singular absence of any reference to 'belief,' 'abstraction,' and so forth; but he scarcely observes how much is implied by the omission. His criticism should have gone further. James Mill has not only omitted a faculty which enables us to distinguish between 'thoughts' and 'things,' images of fancy and pictures of reality, but also the faculty which is equally present whenever we properly think instead of simply seeing images passively; and equally whether we refer an image to fact or fancy. His 'analysis of the mind' seems to get rid of the mind itself.

The omission becomes important at the next step. 'Under the modest title of an explanation of the meaning of several names,' says his son, James Mill discusses 'some of the deepest and most intricate questions in all metaphysics.' A treatise on chemistry might almost as well be 'described as an explanation of the names, air, water, potass, sulphuric acid, and so forth.' [547] Why does the chapter come in this place and in this peculiar form? Probably because James Mill was partly conscious of the inadequacy of his previous chapters. The problems which he has been considering could not be adequately treated by regarding ideas as 'things' bound together by association. What, after all, is a proposition? What is meant by 'true' or 'false,' as distinguished from real and unreal? If an association actually *is* a truth, what is the difference between right and wrong associations? Both are facts, and the very words 'right' and 'wrong,' that is, true and false, apply not to facts but to propositions. [548] The judgment is tested in some way by correspondence to the 'order of Nature,' or of our sensations and ideas. What precisely is meant by this order? So far as we have gone, it seems as if ideas might be combined in any order whatever, and the most various beliefs generated in different minds. Perhaps, however, the principle of association itself may reveal something as to the possible modes of coalescence. Mill makes contiguity an ultimate ground of association; and contiguity implies that things have certain relations expressible in terms of space and time and so forth. These primitive relations now come up for consideration, and should enable us to say more precisely what kind of order is possible. In fact, Mill now endeavours to analyse the meanings of such words as relation in general, time, space, number, likeness, personal identity and others. The effect of his analysis is that the principles, whatever they may be, which might be supposed to underlie association appear to be products of association. He begins by asking what is the meaning of 'relative terms.' Their peculiarity is that they 'always exist in pairs,' such as 'father and son,' 'high and low,' 'right and left.' 'If it is asked, Why do we give names in pairs? the general answer immediately suggests itself; it is because the things named present themselves in pairs, that is, are joined by association.' [549] J. S. Mill thinks that no part of the *Analysis* is more valuable than the 'simple explanation' which follows. There is no 'mystical bond called a relation' between two things, but 'a very simple peculiarity in the concrete fact' marked by the names. In 'ordinary names of objects, the fact connoted by a name ... concerns one object only'; in the case of relative names, 'the fact connoted concerns two objects, and cannot be understood without thinking of them both.' A 'fact concerning an object' is a curiously awkward expression; but one point is clear. If the two objects concerned are the same, whether considered apart or together, the 'relation' must be something more than the facts, and therefore requires to be specified. If they are, in fact, one thing, or parts of a continuous process, we must ask how they come to be distinguished, and what ground there is for speaking of association. James Mill, by considering the problem as a mere question of 'names,' seems to intimate that the relation is a mere figment. In fact, as J. S. Mill perceives, the 'explanations' become nugatory. They simply repeat the thing to be explained. He begins with 'resemblance.' To feel two things to be alike is, he says, the same thing as to have the two feelings. He means to say, apparently, that when there are two 'ideas' there is not also a third idea of 'likeness.' That would be what Bentham called a 'fictitious entity.' But this cannot 'explain' the likeness of the ideas. 'Their being alike,' as his son interprets, 'is nothing but their being felt to be alike—which does not help us.' [550] So 'antecedence and consequence' are 'explained' by saying that one of two feelings calls up the other; or, as the son again remarks, antecedence is explained by antecedence, and succession by succession. Antecedence and consequence, like likeness and unlikeness, must therefore, according to J. S. Mill, be 'postulated as universal conditions of Nature, inherent in all our feelings whether of external or internal consciousness.' [551] In other words, apparently, time is an ultimate form of thought. Time and space, generally, as James Mill thinks, are the 'abstract names' respectively of successive and simultaneous order, which become 'indissolubly associated with the idea of every object.' [552] Space, of course, is said to be a product of touch and muscular sensations, and the problem as to how these varying sensations and these alone give rise to apparently necessary and invariable beliefs is not taken into consideration. Mill is here dealing with the questions which Kant attempted to answer by showing how the mind imposes its forms upon sense-given materials, forms them into concepts, and combines the concepts into judgments and reasoning. Mill evades the mysterious and transcendental at the cost of omitting reason altogether. He represents the result of accepting one horn of a dilemma, which presses upon philosophies of loftier pretensions. Those who accept the other horn speak of a 'fact' as though it were a truth, and argue as though the world could be spun out of pure logic, or a tissue be made of relations without any things to be related. Mill, with scarcely a glance at such doctrines, tries systematically to speak of a truth as if it were a fact. The world for him is made up of ideas sticking together; and nothing else exists. The relation is the fact; belief is the association; consciousness and reflection, considered apart, are nothing but the sensations, ideas, clusters, and trains. The attempt to base all truth upon experience, to bring philosophy into harmony with science was, as I hold, perfectly right. Only, upon these assumptions it could not be carried out. Mill had the merit which is implied even by an unsuccessful attempt to hold by fact. He raises a number of interesting questions; and I think that it is more remarkable that so many of his observations have still an interest for psychologists than that so much is obviously wrong. Mill, it may be said, took an essay upon association for a treatise upon psychology in general. He was writing what might be one important chapter in such a treatise, and supposes that he has written the whole, and can deduce 'philosophy' from it, if, indeed, any philosophy can be said to remain. Meanwhile, I may observe, that by pushing his principles to extremes, even his 'association' doctrine is endangered. His *Analysis* seems to destroy even the elements which are needed to give the simplest laws of association. It is rather difficult to say what is meant by the 'contiguity,' 'sequence,' and 'resemblance,' which are the only conditions specified, and which he seems to explain not as the conditions but as the product of association. J. S. Mill perceived that something was wanting which he afterwards tried to supply. I will just indicate one or two points, which may show what problems the father bequeathed to the son. James Mill, at one place, discusses the odd problem 'how it happens that all trains of thought are not the same.' [553] The more obvious question is, on his hypothesis, how it happens that any two people have the same beliefs, since the beliefs are made of the most varying materials. If, again, two ideas when associated remain distinct, we have Hume's difficulty. Whatever is distinguishable, he argued, is separable. If two ideas simply lie side by side, as is apparently implied by 'contiguity,' so that each can be taken apart without change, why should we suppose that they will never exist apart, or, indeed, that they should ever again come together? The contiguity does not depend upon them, but upon some inscrutable collocation, of which we can only say that it exists now. This is the problem which greatly occupied J. S. Mill.

The 'indissoluble' or 'inseparable' association, which became the grand arcanum of the school, while intended to answer some of these difficulties, raises others. Mill seems to insist upon splitting a unit into parts in order that it may be again brought together by association. So J. S. Mill, in an admiring note, confirms his father's explanation ('one of the most important thought in the whole treatise') of the infinity of space. [554] We think space infinite because we always 'associate' position with extension. Surely space is extension; and to think of one without the other implies a contradiction. We think space infinite, because we think of a space as only limited by other space, and therefore indefinitely extensible. There is no 'association,' simply repetition. Elsewhere we have the problem, How does one association exclude another? Only, as J. S. Mill replies, when one idea includes the idea of the absence of the others. [555] We cannot combine the ideas of a plane and a convex surface. Why? Because we have never had both sets of sensations together. The 'commencement' of one set has always been 'simultaneous with the cessation of another set,' as, for instance, when we bend a flat sheet of paper. The difficulty seems to be that one fact cannot be contradictory of another, since contradiction only applies to assertions. When I say that A is above B, however, I surely assert that B is below A; and I cannot make both assertions about A and B at the same time without a contradiction. To explain this by an association of simultaneous and successive sensations seems to be a curiously roundabout way of 'explaining.' Every assertion is also a denial; and, if I am entitled to say anything, I am enabled without any help from association to deny its contradictory. On Mill's showing, the assertion and the denial of its contradiction, instead of being identical, are taken to be two beliefs accidentally associated. Finally, I need only make one remark upon the fundamental difficulty. It is hard to conceive of mere loose 'ideas' going about in the universe at large and sticking accidentally to others. After all, the human being is in true sense also an organised whole, and his constitution must be taken into account in discovering the laws of 'ideation.' This is the point of view to which Mill, in his anxiety to get rid of everything that had a savour of *a priori* knowledge about it, remains comparatively blind. It implies a remarkable omission. Mill's great teacher, Hartley, had appealed to physiology in a necessarily crude fashion. He had therefore an organism: a brain or a nervous system which could react upon the external world and modify and combine sensations. Mill's ideas would have more apparent connection if they could be made to correspond to 'vibratiuncles' or physical processes of some kind. But this part of Hartley's hypothesis had been dropped: and all reality is therefore reduced to the whirl of vagrant and accidentally cohering ideas in brains and clusters. His one main aim is to get rid of everything that can be called mystical and to trace all mental processes to 'experience,' as he understands experience—to show that we are never entitled to assert that two ideas may not be joined in any way whatever.

The general tendency of the 'Association Philosophy' is sufficiently clear. It may be best appreciated by comparing it to the method of the physical sciences, which it was intended to rival. The physicist explains the 'laws of nature' by regarding a phenomenon as due to the varying arrangements of an indefinite multitude of uniform atoms. I need not ask whether these atoms are to be regarded as realities, even the sole realities, or, on the other hand, as a kind of logical scaffolding removable when the laws are ascertained. In any case, the assumption is necessary and most fruitful in the search for accurate and quantitative formulæ. Mill virtually assumes that the same thing can be done by breaking up the stream of consciousness into the ideas which correspond to the primitive atoms. What precisely these atoms may be, how the constantly varying flow of thought can be resolved into constituent fractions, is not easy to see. The physicist at least supposes his atoms to have definite space relations, but there is nothing clearly corresponding to space in the 'ideas.' They are capable of nothing but co-existence, sequence, and likeness; but the attempt to explain the meaning of those words ends in nothing but repeating them. One result is the curious combination of the absolute and the indefinitely variable. We get absolute statements because the ultimate constituents are taken to be absolutely constant. We have indefinite variability because they may be collocated in any conceivable or inconceivable way. This becomes evident when we have to do with organisms of any kind: with characters or societies an organism varies, but varies along definite lines. But, on Mill's showing, the organic relations correspond to the indefinitely variable. Education is omnipotent; state constitutions can be manufactured at will, and produce indefinite consequences. And yet he can lay down laws of absolute validity, because he seems to be deducing them from one or two formulæ corresponding to the essential and invariable properties of the ultimate unit—whether man or ideas. From this follows, too, the tendency to speak as if human desires corresponded to some definite measurable things, such as utility in ethics, value in political economy, and self-interest in politics. This point appears in the application of Mill's theories to the moral sciences.

III. JAMES MILL'S ETHICS

James Mill in his ethical doctrine follows Bentham with little variation; but he shows very clearly what was the psychology which Bentham virtually assumed. I may pass very briefly over Mill's theory of conduct [556] in general. The 'phenomena of thought,' he says, may be divided into the 'intellectual' and the 'active' powers. Hitherto he has considered 'sensations' and 'ideas' merely as existing; he will now consider them as 'exciting to action.' [557] The phenomena consist in both cases of sensations and ideas, combined into 'clusters,' and formed into trains 'according to the sense laws.' We have now to consider the ideas as active, and 'to demonstrate the simple laws into which the phenomena of human life, so numerous and apparently so diversified, may all be easily resolved.'

A desire is an 'idea' of a pleasant sensation; an 'aversion' an idea of painful sensation. The idea and the sensation are not two things, but two names for the same thing. Desire, again, has a 'tacit reference to future time' when applied to a given case. We associate these pains and pleasures with the causes; and in the important case our own actions are the causes. Thus the association produces the motive, and the readiness to obey the motive is, as Bentham says, the 'disposition.' Then, following Hartley, Mill explains the will. Bodily actions are muscular contractions, which are slowly co-ordinated by habit—association, of course, acting at every stage of the process. Now, it is a plain fact that muscular contractions follow 'ideas.' It is easy, then, to see how the 'idea of a pleasure should excite the idea of the action which is the cause of it; and how, when the idea exists, the action should follow.' [558] An 'end' is a pleasure desired, and gives the 'motive.' When we start from the motive and get the pleasure the same association is called 'will.' 'Free-will' is of course nonsense. We have a full account of the human mechanism, and can see that it is throughout worked by association, admitting the primary fact of experience that the idea causes the muscular contraction.

This, and the ethical conclusions which follow, substantially coincide with Bentham's doctrine, or supply the first principles from which Bentham might be deduced. A fuller exposition of the ethics is given in the *Fragment on Mackintosh*. Mackintosh, in 1829, wrote a Dissertation upon 'Ethical Philosophy,' for the *Encyclopædia Britannica*. [559] The book stirred Mill's 'indignation against an evil-doer.' [560] He wrote a *Fragment on Mackintosh*, which was suppressed for a time in consequence of his antagonist's death in 1832, but published in the year of his own death, 1835. [561] According to Professor Bain, the book was softened in consequence of remonstrances from Bickersteth. It would be curious to see the previous version. Professor Bain says that there are 'thousands' of books which contain 'far worse severities of language.' I confess that I cannot remember quite 'a thousand.' It is at least difficult to imagine more unmitigated expressions of contempt and aversion. Mackintosh, says Mill, uses 'macaroni phrases,' 'tawdry talk,' 'gabble'; he gets 'beyond drivelling' into something more like 'raving'; he 'deluges' us with 'unspeakable nonsense.' 'Good God!' sums up the comment which can be made upon one sentence. [562] Sir James, he declares, 'has got into an intellectual state so thoroughly depraved that I doubt whether a parallel to it is possible to be found.' [563] There is scarcely a mention of Mackintosh without an insult. A partial explanation of Mill's wrath may be suggested by the chapter upon Bentham. Mackintosh there accused the Utilitarians generally of 'wantonly wounding the most respectable feelings of mankind'; of 'clinging to opinions because they are obnoxious'; of taking themselves to be a 'chosen few,' despising the multitude, and retorting the dislike which their arrogance has provoked by using still more exasperating language. [564] He suggested that they should do more justice to 'the Romillys and the Broughams,' who had been the real and judicious reformers; and he illustrated the errors of Bentham by especial reference to Mill's arguments upon government and education. There had long been an antipathy. Mackintosh, said Mill in 1820, 'lives but for London display; *parler et faire parler de lui* in certain circles is his heaven.' [565]

Mackintosh would have been most at home in a professorial chair. He was, indeed, professor at Haileybury from 1818 to 1824, and spoken of as a probable successor to Brown at Edinburgh. But he could never decidedly concentrate himself upon one main purpose. Habits of procrastination and carelessness about money caused embarrassment which forced him to write hastily. His love of society interfered with study, and his study was spread over an impossible range of subjects. His great abilities, wasted by these infirmities, were seconded by very wide learning. Macaulay describes the impression which he made at Holland House. [566] He passed among his friends as the profound philosopher; the man of universal knowledge of history; of ripe and most impartial judgment in politics; the oracle to whom all men might appeal with confidence, though a little too apt to find out that all sides were in the right. When he went to India he took with him some of the scholastic writers and the works of Kant and Fichte, then known to few Englishmen. One of Macaulay's experiences at Holland House was a vision of Mackintosh verifying a quotation from Aquinas. [567] It must have been delightful. The ethical 'dissertation,' however, had to be shortened by omitting all reference to German philosophy, and the account of the schoolmen is cursory. It is easy to see why the suave and amiable Mackintosh appeared to Mill to be a 'dandy' philosopher, an unctuous spinner of platitudes to impose upon the frequenters of Holland House, and hopelessly confused in the attempt to make compromises between contradictory theories. It is equally easy to see why to Mackintosh the thoroughgoing and strenuous Mill appeared to be a one-sided fanatic, blind to the merits of all systems outside the narrow limits of Benthamism, and making even philanthropy hateful. Had Mackintosh lived to read Mill's *Fragment*, he would certainly have thought it a proof that the Utilitarians were as dogmatic and acrid as he had ever asserted.

Mackintosh's position in ethics explains Mill's antagonism. Neither Aquinas nor Kant nor Fichte influenced him. His doctrine is the natural outcome of the Scottish philosophy. Hutcheson had both invented Bentham's sacred formula, and taught the 'Moral Sense' theory which Bentham attacked. To study the morality from the point of view of 'inductive psychology' is to study the moral faculty, and to reject the purely 'intellectual' system. To assign the position of the moral faculty in the psychological system is to show its utility. On the other hand, it was the very aim of the school to avoid the sceptical conclusions of Hume in philosophy, and in ethics to avoid the complete identification of morality with utility. There must be a distinction between the judgments, 'this is right,' and 'this is useful'; even 'useful to men in general.' Hence, on the one hand, morality is immediately dictated by a special sense or faculty, and yet its dictates coincide with the dictates of utility. I have spoken of this view as represented by Dugald Stewart; and Brown had, according to his custom, moved a step further by diminishing the list of original first principles, and making 'virtue' simply equivalent to 'feelings' of approval and disapproval. [568] Virtue, he said, is useful; the utility 'accompanies our moral approbation; but the perception of that utility does not constitute our moral approbation, nor is it necessarily presupposed by it.' [569] He compares the coincidence between virtue and utility to Leibniz's pre-established harmony. [570] The position is familiar. The adaptation of an organism to its conditions may be taken either as an explanation of its development or as a proof of a creative purpose.

Mackintosh takes nearly the same position. Ethical inquiries, he says, relate to 'two perfectly distinct subjects.' We have the problem of the 'criterion' (What is the distinction between right and wrong?) and the problem of the 'moral sentiments' (What are the feelings produced by the contemplation of right and wrong?). In treating of the feelings, again, we must avoid the confusion caused in the older philosophy by the reduction of 'feeling' to 'thought.' [571] Reason and sensation are distinct though inseparably combined; and hence, he argues, it is a fallacy to speak with Clarke as if reason could by itself be a motive. An argument to influence conduct must always be in the last resort an appeal to a 'feeling.' [572] It is idle to tell a man that conduct is infamous unless he *feels* infamy to be painful. We have then to ask what are the feelings which prompt to morality. So far as the criterion is concerned, Mackintosh fully agrees with Hume, whose theory that 'general utility constitutes a general ground of moral distinctions can never be impugned until some example can be produced of a virtue generally pernicious or a vice generally beneficial.' [573] Hume, however, overlooks the 'rightful supremacy of the moral faculty over every other principle of human action.' Mackintosh thought that his best service, as he told Macvey Napier, [574] had been his 'endeavour to slip in a foundation under Butler's doctrine of the supremacy of the conscience, which he left baseless.' To slip in a foundation is a very delicate operation in logical as in material architecture; and the new foundation seems here to be in danger of inverting the edifice. The 'supremacy of conscience' [575] means with him that the 'moral sentiments' form a separate class. They are the feelings with which we contemplate voluntary actions in general, and therefore those aroused by the character and conduct of the agent. Mackintosh thus takes an æsthetic view of morality. We have a 'moral taste' or perception of beauty. The same qualities which make a horse beautiful make him also swift and safe, but we perceive the beauty without thinking of the utility, or rather when we do not think of it. So we admire a hero or martyr for the beauty of his character without reference to his services to us. [576] This moral taste, though not identical with the conscience, becomes 'absorbed into it.' The conscience differs from the 'moral taste' because it acts upon the will. But its supremacy seems to be this quality which it shares with or derives from the taste—its immediate and spontaneous operation. It is, he seems to mean, a direct perception of beauty in character applied to the regulation of conduct. Virtue corresponds to an instinctive and so far ultimate appreciation of beauty of character. Mackintosh insists upon this intrinsic charm of virtue in the language which struck Mill as simply foppish affectation. The pleasure of 'benevolence' itself, says Mackintosh, is infinitely superior to the pleasures to which it may lead. Could it become 'lasting and intense,' it would convert the heart into a heaven. [577] To love virtue, you must love it 'for its own sake.' [578] The delights of being virtuous (as he interprets the phrase) are greater than any delight from the consequences of virtue. And he holds up as a model Fletcher of Saltoun, who would 'lose his life to serve his country, but would not do a base thing to save it.' [579]

How, then, is this view to be reconciled with the unreserved admission of 'utility' as the 'criterion' of right and wrong? One answer is that Mackintosh fully accepts Hartley's doctrine of association. He even criticises previous philosophers for not pushing it far enough. He says that association, instead of merely combining a 'thought' and a 'feeling,' 'forms them into a new compound, in which the properties of the component parts are no longer discoverable, and which may itself become a substantive principle of human virtue.' [580] The question of origin, therefore, is different from the question of nature. He follows Hartley in tracing the development of various desires, and in showing how the 'secondary desires' are gradually formed from the primitive by transference to different objects. [581] We must start from feelings which lie beneath any intellectual process, and thus the judgment of utility is from the first secondary. We arrive at the higher feelings which are 'as independent as if they were underived,' [582] and yet, as happiness has been involved at every stage as an end of each desire, it is no wonder that the ultimate result should be to make the general happiness the end. The coincidence, then, of the criterion with the end of the moral sentiments is 'not arbitrary,' but arises necessarily from 'the laws of human nature and the circumstances in which mankind are placed.' [583] Hence we reach the doctrine which 'has escaped Hartley as well as every other philosopher.' [584] That doctrine is that the moral faculty is one; it is compound, indeed, in its origin; but becomes an independent unit, which can no longer be resolved even in thought into its constituent elements.

The doctrine approximates, it would seem, to Mill's; but was all the more unpalatable to him on that account. The agreement implies plagiarism, and the difference hopeless stupidity. To Mill Bentham was the legitimate development of Hartley, while to Mackintosh Bentham was the plausible perverter of Hartley. Mill regarded Mackintosh as a sophist, whose aim was to mislead honest Utilitarians into the paths of orthodoxy, and who also ignored the merits of Mill himself. 'It was Mr. Mill,' he says, 'who first made known the great importance of the principle of the indissoluble association'; [585] 'Mr. Mill' who had taken up Hartley's speculations and 'prosecuted the inquiry to its end'; [586] 'Mr. Mill' who explained affections and motives and dispositions; [587] and 'Mr. Mill' who had cleared up mistakes about classification which 'had done more to perpetuate darkness on the subject of mind than any other cause, perhaps than all other causes taken together.' [588] Sir James blundered because he had not read Mill's book, as he pretended to have done. Mill does not say all this from vanity; he is simply stating an obvious matter of fact.

Mill's polemic against the Moral Sense theory, even against a moral sense produced by association, reveals the really critical points of the true Utilitarian doctrine. Mill would cut down the moral sense root and branch. The 'moral sense' means a 'particular faculty' necessary to discern right and wrong. But no particular faculty is necessary to discern 'utility.' [589] Hence the distinction between the 'criterion' and the 'moral sentiments' is absurd. The utility is not the 'criterion' of the morality but itself constitutes the morality. To say that conduct is right, according to the Utilitarians, is the same thing as to say that it produces happiness. If the moral sense orders conduct opposed to the criterion, it is so far bad. If it never orders such conduct, it is superfluous. Happiness, as with Bentham, is a definite thing—a currency of solid bullion; and 'virtue' means nothing except as calculated in this currency. Mill, again, like Bentham, regards the 'utility' principle as giving the sole 'objective' test. The complaint that it sanctions 'expediency' is a simple fallacy.

If you do not love virtue 'for its own sake,' said Mackintosh, you will break a general law wherever the law produces a balance of painful consequences. Mill replies with great vigour. [590] All general rules, it is true, imply exceptions, but only when they conflict with the supreme rule. 'There is no exception to a rule of morality,' says Mill, 'but what is made by a rule of morality.' [591] There are numerous cases in which the particular laws conflict; and one law must then be broken. The question which to break must then be decided by the same unequivocal test, 'utility.' If a rule for increasing utility diminishes utility in a given case, it must be broken in that case. Mackintosh's Fletcher of Saltoun illustrates the point. [592] What is the 'base' thing which Fletcher would not do to save his country? Would he not be the basest of men if he did not save his country at any cost? To destroy half a population and reduce the other half to misery has been thought a sacrifice not too great for such an end. Would not Mackintosh himself allow Fletcher, when intrusted with an important fortress, to sacrifice the lives and properties of innocent people in defence of his position? [593] What, then, does the love of virtue 'for its own sake' come to? If you refuse to save your country, because you think the means base, your morality is mischievous, that is, immoral. If, on the other hand, you admit that the means cease to be base, the supposed supremacy is an empty brag. The doctrine is then verbally maintained, but interpreted so as to conform to the criterion of utility. In other words, Mackintosh cannot reconcile his admission of utility as a 'criterion' with his support of a moral sense entitled to override the criterion. Mackintosh's moral sense is meant to distinguish the moral motive from 'expediency.' To this, again, Mill has a very forcible answer. A man is blameable who makes exceptions to laws in his own private interest. But if a man consistently and invariably acted for the 'greatest happiness of the greatest number,' and paid no more attention to his own happiness than to other people's, he would certainly have a very lofty and inflexible test, assuming—as we must allow Mill to assume—that we can calculate the effect of conduct upon happiness at large. Again, upon the assumption that 'moral' is equivalent to 'felicific,' we get a general rule entitled to override any individual tastes or fancies, such as Mill supposes to be meant by the 'Moral Sense.' The rule is derived from the interests of all, and gives an ultimate 'objective criterion.' J. S. Mill, describing his father's system, observes that the teaching of such a man was not likely to err on 'the side of laxity or indulgence.' [594] It certainly did not. And, in fact, his criterion, however obtained, had in his eyes the certainty of a scientific law. This or that is right as surely as this or that food is wholesome. My taste has nothing to do with it. And, moreover, the criterion certainly gives a moral ground. If I know that any conduct will produce more happiness than misery that is a moral reason for adopting it. A 'moral sense' which should be radically inconsistent with that criterion, which should order me to inflict suffering as suffering, or without some ulterior reason, would be certainly at fault. Mackintosh indeed would have agreed to this, though, if Mill was right, at the expense of consistency.

Mill, however, deduces from his criterion doctrines which involve a remarkable paradox. The mode in which he is led to them is characteristic of the whole method. Mill, like Bentham, puts morality upon the same plane with law. Conduct is influenced either by the 'community in its conjunct capacity'—that is, by law; or by 'individuals in their individual capacity'—that is, by morality. [595] The sanction of one, we may infer, is force; of the other, approval and disapproval. With this we must take another Benthamite doctrine, of which I have already spoken. [596] 'Mr. Bentham demonstrated,' says Mill, 'that the morality of an act does not depend upon the motive,' and, further, that it 'is altogether dependent on the intention.' [597] Upon this he constantly insists. Mackintosh's view that virtue depends upon motive will be 'scorned by every man who has any knowledge of the philosophy of the human mind.... The virtue does not depend upon the motive. There is no bad motive. Every motive is the desire of good; to the agent himself or to some one else.' [598] He gives an analysis of action to put the point beyond doubt. Action supposes a 'motive,' a 'volition,' and an 'external act' or muscular contraction. So far there is nothing moral. But then an act has consequences, good or bad, to human beings, which constitute its utility. To make it moral, the agent must anticipate 'beneficial consequences,' and must have no reason to anticipate a balance of evil consequences. Intention means the calculation of consequences, and without that calculation there can be no morality. [599] Hence the morality is equivalent to a 'conviction of the general utility' of the action. [600] 'All this,' he concludes, 'is settled by universal consent. It is vain, therefore, to think of disputing it.' One may, however, ask what it means. I have already observed that the view of the non-moral character of motive was a natural corollary from the purely legal point of view. I must now consider the results of applying it unreservedly in the inappropriate sphere of ethics.

In the first place, the denial of any moral quality in motive seems to be inconsistent with Mill's own principles. The Utilitarian, according to him, holds that the moral law is essentially the statement that certain conduct produces general happiness. If, then, we ask, Who is a good man? we first reply that he is a man whose conduct produces happiness. Another conclusion is obviously necessary, and is implied in Mill's statement that the 'intention' is essential to morality. The man, that is, must foresee that his conduct will produce happiness. The 'calculation' is precisely what makes an action moral as well as accidentally useful. In other words, the man is good to whom the knowledge that an act will produce happiness is the same thing as a command to perform the act. The 'intention' could not affect conduct without the corresponding motive, and Mill can at times recognise the obvious consequence. The 'physical law' (meaning the law enforced by physical coercion), he says incidentally, has 'extrinsic' sanctions; [601] the moral law is different, because it sanctions good actions for their goodness. 'Moral approval' must therefore include approval of character. A man, to be moral, must be one who does useful things simply because they are useful. He must then, it would seem, be at least benevolent. The same thing is implied by the doctrine of 'intention' or 'calculation.' An action may be useful or the reverse without being moral when the consequences are unknown to the agent. To make it moral he must know the consequences—for otherwise he is merely acting at random; and the foreseen consequences constitute the 'intention.' To this Mill adds that he must have taken into account the consequences which 'might have been foreseen.' [602] Otherwise we should have to excuse a man because he had neglected to calculate, whereas to calculate is the very essence of virtue. A man who fired a gun down a crowded street would not be excusable because he had not thought of the result. He 'ought' to have thought of it. The question of moral approval of any given action turns upon these questions. Did a man foresee evil consequences and disregard them? He is then cruel. Did he neglect to consider them? He is then culpably careless, though not actually malignant. Were the consequences altogether beyond the powers of reasonable calculation? Then he may be blameless. The whole moral question, therefore, depends upon the character indicated; that is, upon the motives which induce a man to calculate consequences and which determine his conduct when the calculation is made.

The truth is, I think, and it is characteristic of Mill's modes of analysis, that he is making an impossible abstraction. He is separating parts of a single process and treating them as independent. If actions are bad because they have bad consequences, motives are bad because they are causes of bad actions. You cannot suppress the effect without suppressing the cause, and therefore the cause of the cause. Mill relies chiefly upon one argument. The same conduct will produce the same consequences whatever the motives. That is undeniable. It is the same to me whether I am burnt because the persecutor loves my soul or because he hates me as a rebel to his authority. But when is conduct 'the same'? If we classify acts as the legislator has to classify them by 'external' or 'objective' relations, we put together the man who is honest solely from fear of the gallows and the man who is honest from hatred of stealing. So long as both act alike, the 'consequences' to their neighbours are alike. Neither is legally punishable. But if acts are classified by their motives, one is a rogue and the other virtuous; and it is only then that the question of morality properly arises. In that case, it is idle to separate the question of motive and consequences, because the character determines the motive and therefore the action. Nobody should have seen this more clearly than Mill as a good 'determinist.' Conduct and character are related as the convex and concave of the curve; conduct is simply the manifestation of character, and to separate them is absurd.

Why did he not see this? For reasons, I think, which illustrate his whole method. From a scientific point of view, the ethical problem raises the wide questions, What are the moral sentiments? and, What functions do they discharge in regard to the society or to its individual members? We might hold that morality is justified by 'utility' in the sense that the moral rules and the character which they indicate are essential to the welfare of the race or its individual constituents. But to Mill this proposition is interpreted as identical with the proposition that conduct must be estimated by its 'consequences.' We are to consider not the action itself, but its effects; and the effects are clearly independent of the motive when once the action has been done. We may therefore get a calculus of 'utility': general rules stating what actions will be useful considered abstractedly from their motives. The method, again, might be plausible if we could further assume that all men were the same and differed only in external circumstances. That is the point of view to which Mill, like Bentham, is always more or less consciously inclining. The moral and the positive law are equally enforced by 'sanctions'; by something not dependent upon the man himself, and which he is inclined to suppose will operate equally upon all men. Such language could be justifiable only of an average and uniform 'man,' a kind of constant unit, whose varying behaviour must always be explained by difference in circumstance. We have sufficiently seen the results elsewhere, and in this ethical doctrine they are especially manifest.

Mackintosh recognised the fact that morality is essentially a function of character. Mill cannot fully admit that, because he virtually assumes all character to be the same. Regarding morality as something co-ordinate with law, he does not perceive that the very possibility of law implies the moral instincts, which correspond to the constitution of character, and belong to a sphere underlying, not on the same plane with, the legislative sphere. They are the source of all order; not themselves the product of the order. It is impossible to deduce them, therefore, from the organisation which presupposes them. Now, in one direction, Mill's theory leads, as his son remarked, not to laxity but to excessive strictness. The 'criterion' is laid down absolutely. The 'moral sense' is rejected because it means an autocratic faculty, entitled to override the criterion by its own authority. To appeal to 'motives' is to allow the individual to make his own feeling the ultimate test of right and wrong. If we follow Mill in this we are not really assuming the moral neutrality of motive or the indifference, but an impossible profession of character. Men are not governed by abstract principles but by their passions and affections. The emotions, as Mackintosh rightly said, cannot be resolved into the mere logic. Utility may give the true criterion of morality, but it does not follow that the perception of utility is implied in moral conduct. The motives are good which in fact produce useful conduct, though the agent does not contemplate the abstract principle. It is impossible that men should be moved simply by a desire for the 'greatest happiness of the greatest number.' What does and always must guide men is their personal relation to the little circle which they actually influence. The good man is the man so constituted that he will spontaneously fulfil his duties. The moral law, that is, will be also the law of his character and conduct. The mother is good because she loves her child, not because she sees that care of her child is dictated by the general maxim of utility. The 'utility' of character means the fitness of the agent to be an efficient member of the social structure to which he belongs. In particular cases this may lead to such problems as that of Fletcher of Saltoun. His sense of honour and his general benevolence, though both useful, might come into collision; and the most difficult of all questions of casuistry arise from such conflicts between private and public affections. Mill is justified in holding that a sense of honour cannot give an ultimate and autocratic decision. Under some pretext or other, we shall have to ask the Utilitarian question whether on the whole it may not be causing more misery than the virtuous action is worth. But that only means that the character must be so balanced as to give due weight to each motive; not that we can abstract from character altogether, as though human beings could be mere colourless and uniform atoms, embodying abstract formulæ.

Mill is following Bentham, and only brings out more clearly the psychological assumptions. A man, he says, acts from the 'same motive' whether he steals five shillings or earns it by a day's labour. The motive, in this sense, regards only one consequence, whereas the 'intention' regards all. The 'motive,' that is, is only one of the motives or a part of the character, and this way of speaking is one of the awkward results of turning 'motives' into 'things.' The obvious answer is that which Mill himself makes to Mackintosh. Mackintosh and Butler, he thinks, personify particular 'appetites.' [603] It is not really the 'conscience' which decides, but the man. That is quite true, and similarly it is the whole man who steals or works, not the 'personified' motive; and it is accordingly from the whole character that we judge. We have to consider the relation of the love of five shillings to the other qualities of industry and honesty. The same view appears in Mill's characteristic dislike of 'sentimentalism.' Wishing to attack Mackintosh's rhetoric about the delight of virtuous feeling, he for once quotes a novel to illustrate this point. When Parson Adams defined charity as a 'generous disposition to relieve the distressed,' Peter Pounce approved; 'it is, as you say, a disposition, and does not so much consist in the act as in the disposition to do it.' [604] When, therefore, Mackintosh says that he finds it difficult to separate the virtue from the act, Mill replies that nothing is easier. The virtue is 'in the act and its consequences'; the feeling a mere removable addition. Apparently he would hold that the good Samaritan and the Pharisee had the same feeling, though it prompted one to relieve the sufferer and the other to relieve himself of the sight of the sufferer. They had, of course, a feeling in common, but a feeling which produced diametrically opposite effects, because entering into totally different combinations.

If Mill's doctrine leads to an impossible strictness in one direction, it leads to less edifying results in another. We have omitted 'motive' and come to the critical question, How, after all, is the moral code to be enforced? By overlooking this question and declaring 'motive' to be irrelevant, we get the paradox already accepted by Bentham. His definition of virtue is action for the good of others as well as of ourselves. In what way is the existence of such action to be reconciled with this doctrine? What are the motives which make men count the happiness of others to be equally valuable with their own? or, in the Utilitarian language, What is the 'sanction' of morality? After all Bentham's insistence upon the 'self-preference principle' and Mill's account of selfishness in his political theory, we are suddenly told that morality means a lofty and rigid code in which the happiness of all is the one end. Here again Mill is entangled by the characteristic difficulty of his psychology. To analyse is to divide objects into separate units. When he has to do with complex objects and relations apparently reciprocal, he is forced to represent them by a simple sequence. The two factors are not mutually dependent but distinct things somehow connected in time. One result is his account of 'ends' or 'motives' (the two, as he observes, are synonymous). [605] The end is something to be gained by the act, the 'association' of which with the act constitutes a 'desire.' This, we have seen, always refers to the future. [606] In acting, then, I am always guided by calculations of future pleasures or pains. I believe this to be one of the most unfortunate because one of the most plausible of Utilitarian fallacies. If we are determined by pains and pleasures, it is in one sense as contradictory to speak of our being determined by future pains and pleasures as to speak of our being nourished to-day by to-morrow's dinner. The 'future pleasure' does not exist; the anticipated pleasure acts by making the present action pleasant; and we then move (as it is said) along the line of least resistance. Certain conduct is intrinsically pleasurable or painful, and the future pleasure only acts through the present foretaste. When, however, we regard the pleasure as future and as somehow a separable thing, we can only express these undeniable facts by accepting a purely egoistic conclusion. We are, of course, moved by our own feelings, as we breathe with our own lungs and digest with our own stomachs. But when we accept the doctrine of 'ends' this harmless and self-evident truth is perverted into the statement that our 'end' must be our own pleasure; that we cannot be really or directly unselfish. The analysis, indeed, is so defective that it can hardly be applied intelligibly. Hume observes that no man would rest his foot indifferently upon a stool or a gouty toe. The action itself of giving pain would be painful, and cannot be plausibly resolved into an anticipation of an 'end.' This, again, is conspicuously true of all the truly social emotions. Not only the conscience, but the sense of shame or honour, or pride and vanity act powerfully and instantaneously as present motives without necessary reference to any future results. The knowledge that I am giving pain or causing future pain is intrinsically and immediately painful to the normal human being, and the supposed 'analysis' is throughout a fiction. Mill, however, like Bentham, takes it for granted, but perceives more clearly than Bentham the difficulty to which it leads. How, from a theory of pure selfishness, are we to get a morality of general benevolence? The answer is given by the universal 'association.' We are governed, he holds, by our own emotions; our end is our own pleasure, and we have to consider how this end dictates a desire for general happiness. He expounds with great vigour the process by which the love of friends, children and parents and country may be gradually developed through the association of our pleasures with the fellow-creatures who caused them. J. S. Mill regards his exposition as 'almost perfect,' [607] and says that it shows how the 'acquired sentiments'—the moral sentiments and so forth—may be gradually developed; may become 'more intense and powerful than any of the elements out of which they may have been formed, and may also in their maturity be perfectly disinterested.' James Mill declares that the analysis does not affect the reality of the sentiments analysed. Gratitude remains gratitude, and generosity generosity, just as a white ray remains white after Newton had decomposed it into rays of different colours. [608] Here once more we have the great principle of indissoluble association or mental chemistry.

Granting that the emotions so generated may be real, we may still ask whether the analysis be sufficient. James Mill's account of the way in which they are generated leaves a doubt. Morality is first impressed upon us by authority. Our parents praise and blame, reward and punish. Thus are formed associations of praise and blame with certain actions. Then, we form further associations with the causes of praise and blame and thus acquire the sentiments of 'praiseworthiness' and 'blameworthiness.' The sensibility to praise and blame generally forms the 'popular sanction,' and this, when praiseworthiness is concerned, becomes the moral sanction. [609] Here we see that morality is regarded as somehow the product of a 'sanction'; that is, of the action of praise and blame with their usual consequences upon the individual. His sensibility causes him through association to acquire the habits which generally bring praise and blame; and ultimately these qualities become attractive for their own sake. The difficulty is to see where the line is crossed which divides truly moral or altruistic conduct from mere prudence. Admitting that association may impel us to conduct which involves self-sacrifice, we may still ask whether such conduct is reasonable. Association produces belief in error as well as in truth. If I love a man because he is useful and continue to love him when he can no longer be useful, am I not misguided? If I wear a ragged coat, because it was once smart, my conduct is easily explained as a particular kind of folly. If I am good to my old mother when she can no longer nurse me, am I not guilty of a similar folly? In short, a man who inferred from Mill's principles that he would never do good without being paid for it, would be hardly inconsistent. Your associations, Mill would say, are indissoluble. He might answer, I will try— it is surely not so hard to dissolve a tie of gratitude! Granting, in short, that Mill gives an account of such virtue as may be made of enlightened self-interest, he does not succeed in making intelligible the conduct which alone deserves the name of virtuous. The theory always halts at the point where something more is required than an external sanction, and supposes a change of character as well as a wider calculation of personal interest.

The imperfection of this theory may be taken for granted. It has been exposed by innumerable critics. It is more important to observe one cause of the imperfection. Mill's argument contains an element of real worth. It may be held to represent fairly the historical development of morals. That morality is first conceived as an external law deriving its sanctity from authority; that it is directed against obviously hurtful conduct; and that it thus serves as a protection under which the more genuine moral sentiments can develop themselves, I believe to be in full accordance with sound theories of ethics. But Mill was throughout hampered by the absence of any theory of evolution. He had to represent a series of changes as taking place in the individual which can only be conceived as the product of a long and complex social change. He is forced to represent the growth of morality as an accretion of new 'ends' due to association, not as an intrinsic development of the character itself. He has to make morality out of atomic sensations and ideas collected in clusters and trains without any distinct reference to the organic constitution of the individual or of society, and as somehow or other deducible from the isolated human being, who remains a constant, though he collects into groups governed by external sanctions. He sees that morality is formed somehow or other, but he cannot show that it is either reasonable or an essential fact of human nature. Here, again, we shall see what problem was set to his son. Finally, if Mill did not explain ethical theory satisfactorily, it must be added in common justice that he was himself an excellent example of the qualities for which he tried to account. A life of devotion to public objects and a conscientious discharge of private duties is just the phenomenon for which a cluster of 'ideas' and 'associations' seems to be an inadequate account. How, it might have been asked, do you explain James Mill? His main purpose, too, was to lay down a rule of duty, almost mathematically ascertainable, and not to be disturbed by any sentimentalism, mysticism, or rhetorical foppery. If, in the attempt to free his hearers from such elements, he ran the risk of reducing morality to a lower level and made it appear as unamiable as sound morality can appear, it must be admitted that in this respect too his theories reflected his personal character.

FOOTNOTES:

[464] For an account of these writers and their relation to the pre-revolutionary schools, see *Les Idéologues* by F. Picavet (1891).

[465] Macvey Napier's *Correspondence*, p. 424.

[466] Charles François Dominique de Villers (1767-1815) was a French officer, who emigrated in 1792, and took refuge at Lübeck. He became profoundly interested in German life and literature, and endeavoured to introduce a knowledge of German speculation to his countrymen. His chief books were this exposition of Kant and an essay upon the *Reformation of Luther* (1803), which went through several editions, and was translated by James Mill in 1805. An interesting account of Villers is in the *Biographie Universelle*.

[467] See Cockburn's *Memorials* for a good notice of this.

[468] Stewart's *Works*, iv. 345.

[469] Lady Holland's *Life of Smith*, ii. 388.

[470] *Inquiry into the Relations of Cause and Effect* (third edition), pp. 178, 180, and part iv. sec. 6.

[471] *Examination of Hamilton* (fourth edition), p. 379.

[472] *Cause and Effect*, pp. 184-87.

[473] *Cause and Effect*, p. 197.

[474] *Ibid.* p. 239 *seq.*

[475] *Ibid.*

[476] *Ibid.*

[477] *Ibid.*

[478] *Cause and Effect*, p. 313.

[479] *Cause and Effect*, p. 482. Brown thinks that we can logically disprove the existence of motion by the hare and tortoise argument, and should therefore disregard logic.

[480] Brown's *Lectures*, (1851), p. 167, Lect. xxvi.

[481] Lecture xxv. This question as to whether Brown had or had not grossly misrepresented Reid and other philosophers, led to an entangled argument, in which Mill defended Brown against Hamilton. I will not ask whether Reid was a 'natural realist' or a 'cosmothetic idealist,' or what Descartes or Arnauld thought about the question.

[482] Reid's *Works*, p. 128.

[483] *Lectures*, pp. 150, 158-59.

[484] *Dissertations*, p. 98. Compare Brown's Twenty-fourth Lecture with Tracy's *Idéologie*, ch. vii., and the account of the way in which the infant learns from resistance to infer a cause, and make of the cause *un être qui n'est pas moi*. The resemblance is certainly close. Brown was familiar with French literature, and shows it by many quotations, though he does not, I think, refer to Tracy. Brown, it must be noticed, did not himself publish his lectures, and a professor is not bound to give all his sources in popular lectures. An explanation would have been due in a treatise. Picavet quotes Rhétoré's *Philosophie de Thomas Brown* (a book which I have not seen) for the statement that Brown's lectures often read like a translation of Laromiguière, with whom Brown was 'perhaps' acquainted. As, however, the *Leçons*, to which reference is apparently made, did not appear till 1815 and 1818, when Brown's lectures were already written, this seems to be impossible. The coincidence, which to me seems to be exaggerated by the statement, is explicable by a common relation to previous writers.

[485] *Lectures*, p. 166 (Lect. xxvi.).

[486] *Lectures*, p. 158 (Lect. xxv.).

[487] *Ibid.* p. 151 (Lect. xxiv.).

[488] *Lectures*, p. 177 (ch. xxviii.). Brown made the same remark to Mackintosh in 1812. (Mackintosh's *Ethical Philosophy*, 1872, 236 *n.*)

[489] *Ibid.* p. 154 (Lect. xxiv.).

[490] See Hamilton's note to Reid's *Works*, p. 111.

[491] *Lectures*, p. 255 (Lect. xl.).

[492] *Ibid.* (Lect. xxxiii. and following).

[493] *Ibid.* p. 214-15 (Lect. xxxiii.). The phrase is revived by Professor Stout in his *Analytic Psychology*.

[494] *Lectures*, p. 213 (Lect. xxxiii.).

[495] This is one of the coincidences with Laromiguière (*Leçons* (1837), i. 103).

[496] *Lectures*, p. 210.

[497] *Lectures*, p. 315 (Lect. xlviii.).

[498] *Ibid.*

[499] *Lectures*, p. 335 (Lect. li.). See Lect. xi. for a general explanation. The mind is nothing but a 'series of feelings'; and to say that 'I am conscious of feeling' is simply to say 'I feel.' The same phrase often occurs in James Mill.

[500] *Ibid.* p. 298 (Lect. xlvi.).

[501] *Ibid.* p. 498 (Lect. lxxiv.).

[502] *Lectures*, p. 622 (Lect. xciii.).

[503] *Dissertations*, p. 98.

[504] Froude's *Carlyle*, p. 25.

[505] *Miscellanies* (1858), ii. 104. See, too, *Miscellanies*, i. 60, on German Literature, where he thinks that the Germans attacked the centre instead of the outworks of Hume's citadel. Carlyle speaks with marked respect of Dugald Stewart, who, if he knew what he was about, would agree with Kant.

[506] In Caroline Fox's *Memories of Old Friends* (second edition), ii. 314, is a letter from J. S. Mill, expressing a very high opinion of Brown, whom he had just been re-reading (1840) with a view to the Logic. Brown's 'analysis in his early lectures of the amount of what we can learn of the phenomena of the world seems to me perfect, and his

mode of inquiry into the mind is strictly founded upon that analysis.'

[507] I quote from this edition. Andrew Findlater (1810-1885), a Scottish schoolmaster, and editor of Chambers's *Cyclopædia*, was a philologist (*Dictionary of National Biography*), and his notes chiefly concern Mill's adaptations of Horne Tooke.

[508] *Treatise* (bk. i. pt. i. sec. iv.).

[509] J. S. Mill's *Autobiography*, p. 68.

[510] *Fragment on Mackintosh*, p. 314.

[511] *Analysis*, ii. 42. 'Odd,' because Brown was six years younger than Mill.

[512] 'Education,' p. 6.

[513] *Analysis*, i. 52.

[514] *Analysis*, i. xvii.

[515] *Ibid.* i. 70.

[516] *Analysis*, i. 71.

[517] *Ibid.* i. 78.

[518] *Ibid.* i. 83.

[519] *Analysis*, ii. 42.

[520] *Ibid.* i. 270.

[521] *Ibid.* i. 111.

[522] *Ibid.* i. 362.

[523] *Analysis*, i. 154 *n.*

[524] *Ibid.* i. 161.

[525] *Analysis*, i. 189.

[526] *Ibid.* i. 163 *n.*

[527] *Ibid.* i. 266.

[528] *Ibid.* i. 269.

[529] *Ibid.* i. 295.

[530] *Analysis*, i. 162 *n.*, 187 *n.*

[531] *Ibid.* ii. 21.

[532] *Ibid.* i. 224-25.

[533] *Analysis*, i. 342.

[534] *e.g. Ibid.* ii. 176.

[535] *Ibid.* i. 341.

[536] *Ibid.* i. 342 *n.*

[537] *Ibid.* i. 331.

[538] *Ibid.* i. 345.

[539] *Ibid.* i. 352.

[540] *Ibid.* i. 381.

[541] *Analysis*, i. 363.

[542] *Ibid.* i. 402.

[543] *Ibid.* i. 402-23.

[544] *Analysis*, i. 423.

[545] *Ibid.* i. 413, 419.

[546] See especially his account of definition, *Logic*, bk. i. ch. viii., and the problem about the serpent and the dragon.

[547] *Analysis*, ii. 2.

[548] This point puzzles Destutt de Tracy. All error, he says, arises in judgments: 'Cependant les jugements, les perceptions de rapports, en tant que perceptions que nous avons actuellement, sont aussi certaines et aussi réelles que toutes les autres.'—*Éléments d'Idéologie* (1865), iii. 449.

[549] *Analysis*, ii. 6, 7.

[550] *Analysis*, ii. 18 *n.*

[551] *Analysis*, ii. 24 *n.*

[552] *Ibid.* ii. 132-33.

[553] *Analysis*, ii. 67-69.

[554] *Analysis*, ii. 113 *n.*

[555] *Ibid.* i. 97 *n.*

[556] Professor Bain points out that Mill is occasionally confused by his ignorance of the triple division, intellect, feelings: and will, introduced in the next generation.— *Analysis*, ii. 180 *n.*

[557] *Analysis*, ii. 181-83.

[558] *Analysis*, ii. 351.

[559] Also privately printed in 1830. Later editions, edited by Whewell, appeared in 1836, 1862, 1873. I quote the last. See M. Napier's *Correspondence*, pp. 57-59, for the composition.

[560] Mill's *Fragment* (Preface).

[561] See Bain's *James Mill*, pp. 374, 415-18.

[562] *Fragment*, pp. 190, 192, 213, 298, 307, 326.

[563] *Ibid.* p. 210.

[564] *Ethical Philosophy* (1873), pp. 188, 193.

[565] M. Napier's *Correspondence*, p. 25.

[566] *Essay on Sir J. Mackintosh.*

[567] *Essay on Lord Holland.*

[568] *Lectures*, p. 500 (Lect. lxxv.).

[569] *Ibid.* p. 519 (Lect. lxxvii.).

[570] *Ibid.* p. 522 (Lect. lxxviii.).

[571] *Ethical Philosophy* (Hobbes), pp. 62-64.

[572] *Ibid.*

[573] *Ibid.*

[574] *Ibid.*

[575] *Ibid.*

[576] *Ethical Philosophy*, pp. 14, 170.

[577] *Ibid.*

[578] *Ibid.*

[579] *Ibid.*

[580] *Ethical Philosophy* p. 242.

[581] *Ibid.*

[582] *Ibid.*

[583] *Ibid.*

[584] *Ibid.*

[585] *Fragment*, p. 173.

[586] *Ibid.*

[587] *Ibid.*

[588] *Fragment*, p. 247. Mackintosh quotes Mill's *Analysis* at p. 197. It had only just appeared.

[589] *Fragment*, p. 11.

[590] *Fragment*, p. 246, etc.

[591] *Ibid.*

[592] *Ibid.*

[593] Cf. Newman's *Apologia.* 'The Catholic Church holds it better for the sun and moon to drop from heaven, for the earth to fail, and for all the millions on it to die of starvation in extremest agony, so far as temporal affliction goes, than that one soul,—I will not say should be lost, but should commit one single venial sin, tell one wilful untruth, or should steal one poor farthing without excuse.' I should steal the farthing and assume the 'excuse.' I confess that I would not only lie, but should think lying right under the supposed circumstances.

[594] *Autobiography*, p. 51.

[595] *Fragment*, p. 251.

[596] Vol. i. p. 257.

[597] *Fragment*, p. 161.

[598] *Fragment*, pp. 315-16.

[599] *Ibid.*

[600] *Ibid.*

[601] *Fragment*, p. 102.

[602] *Ibid.*

[603] *Analysis*, p. 73.

[604] *Fragment*, p. 209.

[605] *Fragment*, p. 316.

[606] At one point, as J. S. Mill notes, he speaks of an 'unsatisfied desire' as a motive, which seems to indicate a

present feeling; but this is not his usual view.—*Analysis*, ii. 361, 377 *n.*

[607] *Analysis*, ii. 233 *n.* Mill adds that though his father explains the 'intellectual,' he does not explain the 'animal' element in the affections. This, however, is irrelevant for my purpose.

[608] *Fragment*, pp. 51-52.

[609] *Analysis*, ii. 292-300; *Fragment*, pp. 247-65. Note Mill's interpretation of this theory of 'praiseworthiness.'—*Analysis*, ii. 298 *n.*

CHAPTER VIII
RELIGION

I. PHILIP BEAUCHAMP

The application of Mill's *Analysis* to the views of orthodox theologians required, one might have supposed, as little interpretation as a slap in the face. But a respectable philosopher may lay down what premises he pleases if he does not avowedly draw his conclusions. Mill could argue in perfect safety against the foundations of theology, while Richard Carlile was being sent to gaol again and again for attacking the superstructure. The Utilitarians thought themselves justified in taking advantage of the illogicality of mankind. Whether it was that the ruling powers had no philosophical principles themselves, or that they did not see what inferences would follow, or that they thought that the average person was incapable of drawing inferences, they drew the line at this point. You may openly maintain doctrines inconsistent with all theology, but you must not point out the inconsistency. The Utilitarians contented themselves with sapping the fort instead of risking an open assault. If its defenders were blind to the obvious consequences of the procedure, so much the better. In private, there was obviously no want of plain speaking. In Bentham's mss. the Christian religion is nicknamed 'Jug' as the short for 'Juggernaut.' He and his friends were as anxious as Voltaire to crush the 'infamous,' but they would do it by indirect means. They argued resolutely for more freedom; and Samuel Bailey's essay upon the formation of opinions—a vigorous argument on behalf of the widest possible toleration—was enthusiastically praised by James Mill in the *Westminster Review*. For the present they carefully abstained from the direct avowal of obnoxious opinions, which were still legally punishable, and which would undoubtedly excite the strongest hostility. Bentham, as we have seen, had ventured, though anonymously, to assail the church catechism and to cross-examine St. Paul. One remarkable manifesto gave a fuller utterance to his opinions. A book called *The Analysis of the Influence of Natural Religion on the Temporal Happiness of Mankind*, by 'Philip Beauchamp,' appeared in 1822. The publisher was Richard Carlile, who was then 'safe in Dorchester gaol.' No legal notice was taken of 'Philip

Beauchamp.' The reason may have been that the book excited very little attention in general. Yet it is probably as forcible an attack as has often been written upon the popular theology. The name of 'Philip Beauchamp' covered a combination of Bentham and George Grote. [610] The book, therefore, represents the view of representative Utilitarians of the first and third generation, and clearly expressed the real opinions of the whole party. In his posthumous essays J. S. Mill speaks of it as the only explicit discussion known to him of the question of the utility, as distinguished from the question of the truth, of religion. Obviously, it was desirable to apply the universal test to religious belief, and this very pithy and condensed statement shows the result.

A short summary may indicate the essence of the argument. It is only necessary to observe that the phrase 'natural religion' is part of the disguise. It enables the author to avoid an explicit attack upon revelation; but it is superabundantly obvious that the word 'natural' is superfluous. Revelation is really a fiction, and all religions are 'natural.' A religion is called a 'superstition,' as 'Philip Beauchamp' remarks at starting, when its results are thought to be bad; and allowed to be a religion only when they are thought to be good. [611] That device covers the familiar fallacy of distinguishing between uses and abuses, and, upon that pretence, omitting to take bad consequences into account. We must avoid it by defining religion and then tracing all the consequences, good or bad. Religion is accordingly taken to mean the belief in the existence of 'an Almighty Being, by whom pains and pleasures will be dispensed to mankind during an infinite and future state of existence.' The definition is already characteristic. 'Religion' may be used in a far wider sense, corresponding to a philosophy of the universe, whether that philosophy does or does not include this particular doctrine. But 'Philip Beauchamp's' assumption is convenient because it gives a rational reasoning to the problem of utility. Religion is taken to be something adventitious or superimposed upon other beliefs, and we can therefore intelligibly ask whether it does good or harm. Taking this definition for granted, let us consider the results.

The first point is that we are of necessity in absolute ignorance as to a posthumous state. Now, fear is from our earliest infancy the 'never-failing companion and offspring of ignorance.' Knowledge alone can rescue us from perpetual suffering, because all security depends upon knowledge. Pain, moreover, is far more 'pungent' and distinct than pleasure. 'Want and pain are natural; satisfaction and pleasure artificial and invented.' Pain, therefore, as the strongest, will dictate our anticipations. The hope of immortality is by the orthodox described as a blessing; but the truth, deducible from these principles of human nature and verified by experience, is that natural religion, instead of soothing apprehensions, adds fresh grounds of apprehension. A revelation, as 'Philip Beauchamp' admits, might conceivably dispel our fears; but he would obviously say that the religion which is taken to be revealed gives a far more vivid picture of hell than of heaven. [612] In the next place, it is 'obvious at first sight' that natural religion can properly give 'no rule of guidance.' It refers us to a region of 'desperate and unfathomable' darkness. [613] But it nevertheless indirectly suggests a pernicious rule. It rests entirely upon conjectures as to the character of the invisible Being who apportions pain or pleasure for inscrutable reasons. Will this Being be expected to approve useful or pernicious conduct? From men's language we might suppose that he is thought to be purely benevolent. Yet from their dogmas it would seem that he is a capricious tyrant. How are we to explain the discrepancy? The discrepancy is the infallible result of the circumstances already stated. [614] The Deity has limitless power, and therefore is the natural object of our instinctive fears. The character of the Deity is absolutely incomprehensible, and incomprehensibility in human affairs is identical with caprice and insanity. [615] The ends and the means of the Deity are alike beyond our knowledge; and the extremes both of wisdom and of folly are equally unaccountable. Now, we praise or blame human beings in order to affect their conduct towards us, to attract favours or repel injuries. A tyrant possessed of unlimited power considers that by simple abstinence from injury he deserves boundless gratitude. The weak will only dare to praise, and the strong will only blame. The slave-owner never praises and the slave never blames, because one can use the lash while the other is subject to the lash. If, then, we regard the invisible Being as a capricious despot, and, moreover, as a despot who knows every word we utter, we shall never speak of him without the highest eulogy, just because we attribute to him the most arbitrary tyranny. Hence, the invisible despot will specially favour the priests whose lives are devoted to supporting his authority, and, next to priests, those who, by the practice of ceremonies painful or useless to themselves, show that their sole aim is to give him pleasure. He will specially detest the atheists, and, next to atheists, all who venture to disregard his arbitrary laws. A human judge may be benevolent, because he is responsible to the community. They give and can take away his power. But the invisible and irresponsible ruler will have no motives for benevolence, and approve conduct pernicious to men because it is the best proof of a complete subservience to himself. [616] In spite of this, it has been generally asserted that religion supplies a motive, and the only adequate motive, to moral conduct. But the decay of religion would leave the sources of pain and pleasure unchanged. To say, then, that the conduct prescribed by religion would disappear if the religious motives were removed is virtually to admit that it produces no 'temporal benefit.' Otherwise, the motives for practising such conduct would not be affected. In fact, morality is the same in all countries, though the injunctions of religion are various and contradictory. If religion ordered only what is useful, it would coincide with human laws, and be at worst superfluous. As a fact, it condemns the most harmless pleasures, such as the worst of human legislators have never sought to suppress. People have become tolerant, that is, they have refused to enforce religious observances, precisely because they have seen that such observances cannot be represented as conducive to temporal happiness.

Duty, again, may be divided into duty to God and duty to man. Our 'duty to God' is a 'deduction from the pleasures of the individual without at all benefiting the species.' It must therefore be taken as a tax paid for the efficacy supposed to be communicated to the other branch—the 'duty to man.' [617] Does religion, then, stimulate our obedience to the code of duty to man? 'Philip Beauchamp' admits for once that, in certain cases, it '*might possibly*' be useful. It might affect 'secret crimes,' that is, crimes where the offender is undiscoverable. That, however, is a trifle. These cases, he thinks, would be 'uncommonly rare' under a well-conceived system. The extent of evil in this life would therefore be trifling were superhuman inducements entirely effaced from the human bosom, and if 'human institutions were ameliorated according to the progress of philosophy.' [618] On the other hand, the imaginary punishments are singularly defective in the qualities upon which Bentham had insisted in human legislation. They are remote and uncertain, and to make up for this are represented as boundless in intensity and durability. For that reason, they precisely reverse the admitted principle that punishment should be so devised as to produce the greatest possible effect by the smallest infliction of pain. Supernatural sanctions are supposed to maximise pain with a minimum of effect. The fear of hell rarely produces any effect till a man is dying, and then inflicts great suffering, though it has been totally inefficient as a preventive at the time of temptation. The influence of supernatural penalties is therefore in 'an inverse ratio to the demand for it.' [619] In reality, the efficacy of the sanctions is due to their dependence upon public opinion. Our real motive for acting rightly is our desire for the praise of our fellows and our interest in their good conduct. We conceal this motive even from ourselves, because we wish to have the credit of serving the Deity exclusively. This is confirmed by the familiar instances of a conflict between public opinion and religious sanctions. Duelling, fornication, and perjury are forbidden by the divine law, but the prohibition is ineffectual whenever the real sentiment of mankind is opposed to it. The divine law is set aside as soon as it conflicts with the popular opinion. In exceptional cases, indeed, the credit attached to unreasonable practices leads to fanaticism, asceticism, and even insanity;

but superhuman terrors fail at once when they try to curb the action of genuine substantial motives. Hence we must admit that they are useless in the case even of 'secret crimes.' Religion, in short, prescribes mischievous practices, becomes impotent except for the production of misery, and is really, though not avowedly, dependent on the popular sanction. [620]

We can now classify the evils actually produced. Religion injures individuals by prescribing useless and painful practices: fasting, celibacy, voluntary self-torture, and so forth. It suggests vague terrors which often drive the victim to insanity, and it causes remorse for harmless enjoyments. [621] Religion injures society by creating antipathies against unbelievers, and in a less degree against heretics and nonconformists. It perverts public opinion by making innocent actions blameable; by distorting the whole science of morality and sanctioning the heterogeneous dictates of a certain blind and unaccountable impulse called the 'moral instinct or conscience.' [622] Morality becomes a 'mere catalogue of reigning sentiments,' because it has cast away the standard of utility. A special aversion to improvement is generated, because whatever changes our conceptions of the 'sequences of phenomena' is supposed to break the divine 'laws of nature.' 'Unnatural' becomes a 'self-justifying' epithet forbidding any proposed change of conduct, which will counteract the 'designs of God.' Religion necessarily injures intellectual progress. It disjoins belief from its only safe ground, experience. The very basis, the belief in an inscrutable and arbitrary power, sanctions supernatural or 'extra-experimental' beliefs of all kinds. You reject in the case of miracles all the tests applicable to ordinary instruction, and appeal to trial by ordeal instead of listening to witnesses. Instead of taking the trouble to plough and sow, you expect to get a harvest by praying to an inscrutable Being. You marry without means, because you hold that God never sends a child without sending food for it to eat. Meanwhile you suborn 'unwarranted belief' by making belief a matter of reward and penalty. It is made a duty to dwell upon the arguments upon one side without attending to those upon the other, and 'the weaker the evidence the greater the merit in believing.' [623] The temper is depraved not only by the antipathies generated, but by the 'fitful and intermittent character' of the inducements to conduct. [624]

The final result of all this is still more serious. It is that religion, besides each separate mischief, 'subsidises a standing army for the perpetuation of all the rest.' [625] The priest gains power as a 'wonder-worker,' who knows how to propitiate the invisible Being, and has a direct interest in 'depraving the intellect,' cherishing superstition, surrounding himself with mysteries, representing the will of the Deity as arbitrary and capricious, and forming an organised 'array of human force and fraud.' [626] The priesthood sets up an infallible head, imposes upon the weak and dying, stimulates antipathy, forms the mass of 'extra-experimental' beliefs into the likeness of a science, and allies itself with the state. Heresy becomes a crime. The ruler helps the priests to raise a tax for their own comfort, while they repay him by suppressing all seditious opinions. Thus is formed an unholy alliance between the authorities of 'natural religion' and the 'sinister interests of the earth.' The alliance is so complete that it is even more efficient than if it had been openly proclaimed. 'Prostration and plunder of the community is indeed the common end of both' (priests and rulers). The only chance of dissension is about the 'partition of the spoil.' [627]

The book is as characteristic of the Utilitarians in style as in spirit. It is terse, vigorous reasoning, with no mere rhetorical flourishes. The consequences of the leading principle are deduced without flinching and without reserve. Had the authors given their names, they would no doubt have excited antipathies injurious to the propaganda of Utilitarianism. They held, for that reason presumably, that they were not bound to point out the ultimate goal of their speculations. No intelligent reader of their other writings could fail to see what that goal must be; but an 'open secret' is still for many purposes a real secret. Whatever might be the suspicions of their antagonists, they could only be accused of a tendency. The book amounts to an admission that the suspicions were well founded. Utilitarianism, the Utilitarians clearly recognised, logically implied the rejection of all theology. Religion—on their understanding of the word—must, like everything else, be tested by its utility, and it was shown to be either useless or absolutely pernicious. The aim of the Utilitarians was, in brief, to be thoroughly scientific. The man of science must be opposed to the belief in an inscrutable agent of boundless power, interfering at every point with the laws of nature, and a product of the fancy instead of the reason. Such a conception, so far as accepted, makes all theory of human conduct impossible, suggests rules conflicting with the supreme rule of utility, and gives authority to every kind of delusion, imposture, and 'sinister interest.'

It would, I think, be difficult to mention a more vigorous discussion of the problem stated. As anonymous, it could be ignored instead of answered; and probably such orthodox persons as read it assumed it to be a kind of *reductio ad absurdum* of the Utilitarian creed. It might follow, they could admit, logically from the Utilitarian analysis of human nature, but it could only prove that the analysis was fundamentally wrong. Yet its real significance is precisely its thorough applicability to the contemporary state of opinion. Beauchamp's definition coincides with Paley's. The coincidence was inevitable. Utilitarians both in ethical and philosophical questions start from the same assumptions as Paley, and the Paley doctrine gave the pith of the dominant theology. I have observed that the Scottish philosophers had abandoned the *a priori* argument, and laid the whole stress of their theological doctrine upon Paley's argument from final causes. The change of base was an inevitable consequence of their whole system. They appealed to experience, to 'Baconian' methods, and to 'inductive psychology.' The theory of 'intuitions,' effective where it fell in with admitted beliefs, was idle against an atheist, who denied that he had the intuition. The 'final causes' argument, however, rested upon common ground, and supplied a possible line of defence. The existence of the Deity could perhaps be proved empirically, like the existence of the 'watchmaker.' Accordingly, this was the argument upon which reliance was really placed by the average theologian of the time. Metaphysical or ontological reasoning had been discarded for plain common-sense. The famous *Bridgewater Treatises* are the characteristic product of the period. It had occurred to the earl of Bridgewater, who died in 1829, that £8000 from his estate might be judiciously spent in proving the existence of a benevolent creator. The council of the Royal Society employed eight eminent men of science to carry out this design. [628] They wrote some interesting manuals of popular science, interspersed with proper theological applications. The arguments were sincere enough, though they now seem to overlook with singular blindness the answer which would be suggested by the 'evolutionist.' The logical result is, in any case, a purely empirical theology. The religion which emerges is not a philosophy or theory of the world in general, but corresponds to a belief in certain matters of fact (or fiction). The existence of the Deity is to be proved, like the existence of Caesar, by special evidence.

The main results are obvious. The logical base of the whole creed is 'natural theology,' and 'natural theology' is simply a branch of science, amenable to the ordinary scientific tests. It is intended to prove the existence of an agent essential to the working of the machinery, as from the movements of a planet we infer the existence of a disturbing planet. The argument from design, in this acceptation, is briefly mentioned by 'Philip Beauchamp.' It is, he argues, 'completely extra-experimental'; for experience only reveals design in living beings: it supposes a pre-existing chaos which can never be shown to have existed, and the 'omnipotent will' introduced to explain the facts is really no explanation at all, but a collection of meaningless words. [629] The argument is briefly dismissed as concerning the truth, not the utility, of religion, but one point is sufficiently indicated. The argument from 'design' is always plausible, because it applies reasoning undeniably valid when it is applied within its proper sphere. The inference from a watch to a watchmaker is clearly conclusive. We know sufficiently what is meant by the watchmaker and by 'making.' We therefore reason to a *vera causa*—an agent already known. When the inference is to the action of an inconceivable Being performing an inconceivable operation upon inconceivable materials, it really becomes illusory, or amounts to the simple assertion that the phenomenon is inexplicable. Therefore, again, it is essentially opposed to science though claiming to be scientific. The action of the creator is supposed to begin where the possibility of knowledge ends. It is just the inexplicable element which suggests the creative agency. Conversely, the satisfactory explanation of any phenomenon takes it out of the theological sphere. As soon as the process becomes 'natural' it ceases to demand the supernatural artificer. 'Making,' therefore, is contradistinguished from 'growing.' If we see how the eye has come into existence, we have no longer any reason to assume that it was put together mechanically. In other words, 'teleology' of this variety is dispelled by theories of evolution. The hypothesis of interference becomes needless when we see how things came to be by working out perfectly natural processes. As science, therefore, expands, theology recedes. This was to become more evident at a later period. For the present, the teleological argument in the Paley form, triumphantly set forth in Bridgewater Treatises and the like, rested the defence of theology on the proofs of the discontinuity of the universe and the consequent necessity for admitting supernatural interference. Science was therefore invoked to place absolute limits on its own progress.

But other vital difficulties were already felt. The argument from contrivance naturally implies limitation. The maker of a machine is strictly limited by the properties of the matter upon which he works. The inference might be verbally saved by saying that the maker was 'potentially' omnipotent; but the argument, so far as it goes, is more easily satisfied by the hypothesis of a Being of great but still limited powers. The Deity so proved, if the proof be valid, is not himself the ground of the universe, the source from which nature itself emanates, as well as the special laws of nature, but a part of the whole system; interfering, guiding, and controlling, but still only one of the powers which contribute to the formation of the whole. Hence arise questions which theologians rather evaded than attempted to answer. If with the help of Paley we can prove the existence of an invisible Being— potentially omnipotent, though always operating as though limited—there would still remain the question as to his attributes. He is skilful, we may grant, but is he benevolent or is he moral? The benevolence could of course be asserted by optimists, if facts were amenable to rhetoric. But a theory which is essentially scientific or empirical, and consistently argues from the effect to the cause, must start from an impartial view of the facts, and must make no presupposition as to the nature of the cause. The cause is known only through the effects, and our judgment of them cannot be modified by simply discovering that they are caused. If, then, contrivance is as manifest in disease as in health, in all the sufferings which afflict mankind as well as in the pleasures which solace him, we must either admit that the creator is not benevolent, or frankly admit that he is not omnipotent and fall into Manichæism. Nature, we are frequently told, is indifferent if not cruel; and though Paley and his followers choose to shut their eyes to ugly facts, it could be only by sacrificing their logic. They were bound to prove from observation that the world was so designed as to secure the 'greatest happiness' before they could logically infer a purely benevolent designer. It was of the very essence of their position that observed facts should be the ultimate basis of the whole theory; and to alter the primary data by virtue of deductions drawn from them could obviously not be logically justifiable.

Such reflections, though sufficiently obvious, might be too far from practical application to have much immediate effect. But the question of the moral bearing of theology was of more interest; and, here, the coincidence of the Utilitarianism with the accepted theology of the day is especially important. The Deity regarded as the artificer appears to be far from purely benevolent. In respect to morality, is he not simply indifferent? Does he not make men fragile and place them amidst pitfalls? Does he not constantly slay the virtuous and save the wicked? How, indeed, from the purely empirical or scientific base, do you deduce any moral attributes whatever? 'Natural theology,' as it was called, might reveal a contriver, but could it reveal a judge or a moral guide? Here the difficulty of a purely matter-of-fact theology made itself felt on many sides. The remarkable influence of Butler upon many minds was partly due to a perception of this omission. Butler avowedly appeals to the conscience, and therefore at least recognises God as directly revealed in a moral character. That seemed to supply a gap in the ordinary theology. But in the purely empirical view Butler's argument was untenable. It appealed to one of the 'intuitions' which were incompatible with its fundamental assumptions. The compunctions of conscience were facts to be explained by 'association,' not to be regarded as intimations of wrath. Butler's view might be inverted. The 'conscience' does, in truth, suggest the divine wrath; but that only means that it suggests the quack remedies upon which 'wonder-working' priests establish their power. Instead of proving the truth of the religion, it explains the origin of superstition. To James Mill, as we have seen, Butler's argument would logically prove not a righteous governor but a cruel creator. Theologians, again, of the Paley school, were bound in consistency to the empirical or Utilitarian view of morality. Paley accepted the consequences unreservedly; and if such philosophers as Brown and Mackintosh persisted in regarding the coincidence between morality and happiness as indicative of a pre-established harmony, not of an identification of morality with the pursuit of general happiness, they still admitted that 'utility' was the 'criterion' of morality. The moral law, that is, coincides in its substance with the law, 'maximise happiness,' and happiness means, as 'Philip Beauchamp' calls it, 'temporal' happiness—the happiness of actual men living in this world and knowing nothing of any external world. How, then, is the moral law related to theology? To know what is moral, we must appeal to experience and 'utility.' We must discover what makes for happiness, just as in medicine we must discover what makes for health or pleasure, by the ordinary methods of observation. What place is left for any supernatural intervention? The ostensible answer was that though the moral code could be deduced from its utility, the motives by which it was to be enforced required some supernatural agency. The natural man might see what was right, but need not therefore do what was right. Here 'Philip Beauchamp' comes to a direct issue with the theologians. He denies that the supernatural motive will be on the side of morality. When J. S. Mill remarked that there had been few discussions of the 'utility' as distinguished from the truth of religion, he scarcely recognises one conspicuous fact. The great argument of divines had always been the absolute necessity of religion to morality; and if morality be understood to mean utility, this is simply an argument from utility. The point, indeed, was often taken for granted; but it certainly represents one of the strongest persuasives, if not one of the strongest reasons. The divines, in fact, asserted that religion was of the highest utility as supplying the motive for moral conduct. What motives, then, can be derived from such knowledge of the Deity as is attainable from the 'Natural theology' argument? How can we prove from it that he who puts the world together is more favourable to the virtues than to the vices which are its results; or, if more favourable, that he shows any other favour than can be inferred from experience? He has, it is agreed, put men, as Bentham had said, under the command of two sovereign masters, Pleasure and Pain; and has enabled them to calculate consequences, and therefore to seek future pleasure and avoid future pain. That only proves that we can increase our happiness by prudence; but it suggests no additional reasons either for seeking happiness or for altering our estimate of happiness. As 'Philip Beauchamp' argues, we cannot from the purely empirical ground get any motive for taking into account anything beyond our 'temporal' or secular interests. This, again, was in fact admitted by Paley. His mode of escape from the dilemma is familiar. The existence of a supreme artificer is inferred from the interventions in the general order of nature. The existence of a moral ruler, or the fact that the ruler approves morality, is inferred from his interference by the particular manifestations of power which we call miraculous. We know that actions will have other consequences than those which can be inferred from our own experience, because some two thousand years ago a Being appeared who could raise the dead and heal the sick. If sufficient evidence of the fact be forthcoming, we are entitled to say upon his authority that the wicked will be damned and the virtuous go to heaven. Obedience to the law enforced by these sanctions is obviously prudent, and constitutes the true *differentia* of moral conduct. Virtue, according to the famous definition, is doing good 'for the sake of everlasting happiness.' The downright bluntness with which Paley announced these conclusions startled contemporaries, and yet it must be admitted that they were a natural outcome of his position.

In short, the theological position of the Paley school and the Utilitarian position of 'Philip Beauchamp' start from the common ground of experience. Religion means the knowledge of certain facts, which are to be inferred from appropriate evidence. It does not modify the whole system of thought, but simply adds certain corollaries; and the whole question is whether the corollaries are or are not proved by legitimate reasoning. Can we discover heaven and hell as we discovered America? Can observation of nature reveal to us a supernatural world?' The first difficulty is that the argument for natural theology has to rest upon interference, not upon order, and therefore comes into conflict with the first principles of scientific procedure. The Deity is revealed not by the rational but by the arbitrary; and the more the world is explained, the less the proof that he exists, because the narrower the sphere of his action. Then, as such a Deity, even if proved, is not proved to be benevolent or moral, we have to rely for the moral element upon the evidence of 'miracles,' that is, again, of certain interruptions of order. The scientific tendency more or less embodied in Protestantism, so far as it appealed to reason or to 'private judgment,' had, moreover, made it necessary to relegate miracles to a remote period, while denying them at the present. To prove at once that there are no miracles now, and that there were a few miracles two thousand years ago, was really hopeless. In fact, the argument had come to be stated in an artificial form which had no real relation to the facts. If the apostles had been a jury convinced by a careful legal examination of the evidence; if they had pronounced their verdict, in spite of the knowledge that they would be put to death for finding it, there would have been some force in Paley's argument. But then they had not. To assume such an origin for any religion implied a total misconception of the facts. Paley assumed that the apostles resembled twelve respectable deans of Carlisle solemnly declaring, in spite of the most appalling threats, that John Wesley had been proved to have risen from the dead. Paley might plausibly urge that such an event would require a miracle. But, meanwhile, his argument appeared to rest the whole case for morality and religion upon this narrow and perilous base. We can only know that it is our interest to be moral if we know of heaven and hell; and we only know of heaven and hell if we accept the evidence of miracles, and infer that the worker of miracles had supernatural sources of information. The moral difficulty which emerges is obvious. The Paley conception of the Deity is, in fact, coincident with Bentham's conception of the sovereign. He is simply an invisible sovereign, operating by tremendous sanctions. The sanctions are 'external,' that is to say, pains and pleasures, annexed to conduct by the volition of the sovereign, not intrinsic consequences of the conduct itself. Such a conception, thoroughly carried through, makes the relation between religion and morality essentially arbitrary. Moreover, if with 'Philip Beauchamp' we regard the miracle argument as obviously insufficient, and consider what are the attributes really attributed to the sovereign, we must admit that they suggest such a system as he describes rather than the revelation of an all-wise and benevolent ruler. It is true, as 'Philip Beauchamp' argues, that the system has all the faults of the worst human legislation; that the punishment is made atrociously—indeed infinitely—severe to compensate for its uncertainty and remoteness; and that (as he would clearly add), to prevent it from shocking and stunning the intellect, it is regarded as remissible in consideration of vicarious suffering. If, then, the religion is really what its dogmas declare, it is easier to assume that it represents the cunning of a priesthood operating upon the blind fears and wild imaginations of an inaccessible world; and the ostensible proofs of a divine origin resting upon miraculous proofs are not worth consideration. It professes to be a sanction to all morality, but is forced to construct a mythology which outrages all moral considerations. Taken as a serious statement of fact, the anthropomorphism of the vulgar belief was open to the objections which Socrates brought against the Pagan mythology. The supreme ruler was virtually represented as arbitrary, cruel, and despotic.

If we ask the question, whether in point of fact the religion attacked by 'Philip Beauchamp' fairly represented the religion of the day, we should have, of course, to admit that it was in one sense a gross caricature. If, that is, we asked what were the real roots of the religious zeal of Wilberforce and the Evangelicals, or of the philanthropists with whom even James Mill managed to associate on friendly terms, it would be the height of injustice to assume that they tried to do good simply from fear of hell and hope of heaven, or that their belief in Christianity was due to a study of Paley's *Evidences*. Their real motives were far nobler: genuine hatred of injustice and sympathy for suffering, joined to the conviction that the sects to which they belonged were working on the side of justice and happiness; while the creeds which they accepted were somehow congenial to their best feelings, and enabled them to give utterance to their deepest emotions. But when they had to give a ground for that belief they could make no adequate defence. They were better than their ostensible creed, because the connection of their creed with their morality was really arbitrary and traditional. We must always distinguish between the causes of strong convictions and the reasons officially assigned for them. The religious creed, as distinguished from the religious sentiment, was really traditional, and rested upon the simple fact that it was congenial to the general frame of mind. Its philosophy meanwhile had become hopelessly incoherent. It wished to be sensible, and admitted in principle the right of 'private judgment' or rationalism so far as consistent with Protestantism. The effect had been that in substance it had become Utilitarian and empirical; while it had yet insisted upon holding on to the essentially irrational element.

The religious tradition was becoming untenable in this sense at the same time as the political tradition. If radicalism in both were to be effectually resisted, some better foundation must be found for conservatism. I should be tempted to say that a critical period was approaching, did I not admit that every period can always be described as critical. In fact, however, thoughtful people, perceiving on the one hand that the foundations of their creed were shaking, and yet holding it to be essential to their happiness, began to take a new position. The 'Oxford movement,' started soon afterwards, implied a conviction that the old Protestant position was as untenable as the radical asserted. Its adherents attempted to find a living and visible body whose supernatural authority might maintain the old dogmatic system. Liberal thinkers endeavoured to spiritualise the creed and prove its essential truths by philosophy, independently of the particular historical evidence. The popular tendency was to admit in substance that the dogmas most assailed were in fact immoral: but to put them into the background, or, if necessary, to explain them away. The stress was to be laid not upon miracles, but upon the moral elevation of Christianity or the beauty of character of its founder. The 'unsectarian' religion, represented in the most characteristic writings of the next generation, in Tennyson and Browning, Thackeray and Dickens, reflects this view. Such men detested the coarse and brutalising dogmas which might be expounded as the true 'scheme of salvation' by ignorant preachers seeking to rouse sluggish natures to excitement; but they held to religious conceptions which, as they thought, really underlay these disturbing images, and which, indeed, could hardly be expressed in any more definite form than that of a hope or a general attitude of the whole character. The problem seemed to be whether we shall support a dogmatic system by recognising a living spiritual authority, or frankly accept reason as the sole authority, and, while explaining away the repulsive dogmas, try to retain the real essence of religious belief.

II. CONTEMPORARY THOUGHT

If I were writing a general history of opinion, it would be necessary to discuss the views of Mill's English contemporaries; to note their attitude in regard to the Utilitarian position, and point out how they prepared the way for the later developments of thought. The Utilitarians were opposed to a vague sentiment rather than to any definite system. They were a small and a very unpopular sect. They excited antipathy on all sides. As advocating republicanism, they were hardly more disliked by the Tories, who directly opposed them, than by the Whigs, who might be suspected of complicity. As enthusiastic political economists, they were equally detested by sentimental Radicals, Socialists, and by all who desired a strong government, whether for the suppression of social evils or the maintenance of social abuses. And now, as suspected of atheism, they were hated by theologians. But though the Utilitarians were on all sides condemned and denounced, they were met by no definite and coherent scheme of philosophy. The philosophy of Stewart and Brown had at least a strong drift in their direction. Though 'political economy' was denounced in general terms, all who spoke with authority accepted Adam Smith. Their political opponents generally did not so much oppose their theories as object to theory in general. The Utilitarian system might be both imperfect and dogmatic; but it had scarcely to contend with any clear and assignable rival. The dislike of Englishmen to any systematic philosophy, whether founded upon the national character or chiefly due to special conditions, was still conspicuous outside of the small Utilitarian camp.

To discover, therefore, the true position of contemporary opinion, we should have to look elsewhere. Instead of seeking for the philosophers who did not exist, we should have to examine the men of letters who expressed the general tendencies. In Germany, philosophical theories may be held to represent the true drift of the national mind, and a historian of German thought would inquire into the various systems elaborated by professors of philosophy. He would at least be in no want of materials for definite logical statements. In England, there was no such intellectual movement. There we should have to consider poetry and literature; to read Wordsworth and Coleridge, Scott and Byron and Shelley, if we would know what men were really thinking and feeling. The difficulty is, of course, that none of these men, unless Coleridge be an exception, had any conscious or systematic philosophy. We can only ask, therefore, what they would have said if they had been requested to justify their views by abstract reasoning; and that is a rather conjectural and indefinite enterprise. It lies, fortunately, outside of my field; and it will be enough if I try to suggest one or two sufficiently vague hints. In the first place, the contrast between the Utilitarians and their opponents may almost be identified with the contrast between the prosaic and the poetical aspects of the world in general. Bentham frankly objected to poetry in general. It proved nothing. The true Utilitarian was the man who held on to fact, and to nothing but the barest, most naked and unadorned fact. Poetry in general came within the sweep of his denunciations of 'sentimentalism' and 'vague generalities.' It was the 'production of a rude age'; the silly jingling which might be suitable to savages, but was needless for the grown-up man, and was destined to disappear along with the whole rubbish of mythology and superstition in whose service it had been enlisted. There is indeed a natural sympathy between any serious view of life and a distrust of the æsthetic tendencies. Theologians of many different types have condemned men for dallying with the merely pleasurable, when they ought to be preoccupied with the great ethical problems or the safety of their souls. James Mill had enough of the old Puritan in him to sympathise with Carlyle's aspiration, 'May the devil fly away with the fine arts!' To such men it was difficult to distinguish between fiction and lying; and if some concession might be made to human weakness, poets and novelists might supply the relaxations and serve to fill up the intervals of life, but must be sternly excluded if they tried to intrude into serious studies. Somehow love of the beautiful only interfered with the scientific investigation of hard facts.

Poets, indeed, may take the side of reform, or may perhaps be naturally expected to take that side. The idealist and the dreamer should be attracted most powerfully by the visions of a better world and the restoration of the golden age. Shelley was among the most enthusiastic prophets of the coming era. His words, he hoped, were to be 'the trumpet of a prophecy' to 'unawakened earth.' Shelley had sat at the feet of Godwin, and represented that vague metaphysical dreaming to which the Utilitarians were radically hostile. To the literary critic, Shelley's power is the more remarkable because from a flimsy philosophy he span an imaginative tissue of such magical and marvellous beauty. But Shelley dwelt in an ethereal region, where ordinary beings found breathing difficult. There facts seemed to dissolve into thin air instead of supplying a solid and substantial base. His idealism meant unreality. His 'trumpet' did not in fact stimulate the mass of mankind, and his fame at this period was confined to a few young gentlemen of literary refinement. The man who had really stirred the world was Byron; and if the decline of Byron's fame has resulted partly from real defects, it is partly due also to the fact that his poetry was so admirably adapted to his contemporaries. Byron at least could see facts as clearly as any Utilitarian, though fact coloured by intense passion. He, like the Utilitarians, hated solemn platitudes and hypocritical conventions. I have noticed the point at which he came into contact with Bentham's disciples. His pathetic death shortly afterwards excited a singularly strong movement of sympathy. 'The news of his death,' said Carlyle at the time, 'came upon my heart like a mass of lead; and yet the thought of it sends a painful twinge through all my being, as if I had lost a brother.' At a later time he defines Byron as 'a dandy of sorrows and acquainted with grief.' [630] That hits off one aspect of Byronism. Byron was the Mirabeau of English literature, in so far as he was at once a thorough aristocrat and a strong revolutionist. He had the qualification of a true satirist. His fate was at discord with his character. He was proud of his order, and yet despised its actual leaders. He was ready alternately to boast of his vices and to be conscious that they were degrading. He shocked the respectable world by mocking 'Satanically,' as they held, at moral conventions, and yet rather denounced the hypocrisy and the heartlessness of precisians than insulted the real affections. He covered sympathy with human suffering under a mask of misanthropy, and attacked war and oppression in the character of a reckless outlaw. Full of the affectation of a 'dandy,' he was yet rousing all Europe by a cry of pure sentimentalism. It would be absurd to attribute any definite doctrine to Byron. His scepticism in religious matters was merely part of a general revolt against respectability. What he illustrates is the vague but profound revolutionary sentiment which indicated a belief that the world seemed to be out of joint, and a vehement protest against the selfish and stolid conservatism which fancied that the old order could be preserved in all its fossil institutions and corresponding dogmas.

What was the philosophy congenial to Conservatism? There is, of course, the simple answer, None. Toryism was a 'reaction' due to the great struggle of the war and the excesses of the revolution. A 'reaction' is a very convenient phrase. We are like our fathers; then the resemblance is only natural. We differ; then the phrase 'reaction' makes the alteration explain itself. No doubt, however, there was in some sense a reaction. Many people changed their minds as the revolutionary movement failed to fulfil their hopes. I need not argue now that such men were not necessarily corrupt renegades. I can only try to indicate the process by which they were led towards certain philosophical doctrines. Scott, Wordsworth, and Coleridge represent it enough for my purpose. When Mill was reproaching Englishmen for their want of interest in history, he pointed out that Thierry, 'the earliest of the three great French historians' (Guizot and Michelet are the two others), ascribed his interest in his subject to *Ivanhoe*. [631] Englishmen read *Ivanhoe* simply for amusement. Frenchmen could see that it threw a light upon history, or at least suggested a great historical problem. Scott, it is often said, was the first person to teach us that our ancestors were once as much alive as ourselves. Scott, indeed, the one English writer whose fame upon the Continent could be compared to Byron's, had clearly no interest in, or capacity for, abstract speculations. An imaginative power, just falling short of the higher poetical gift, and a masculine common-sense were his most conspicuous faculties. The two qualities were occasionally at issue; his judgment struggled with his prejudices, and he sympathised too keenly with the active leaders and concrete causes to care much for any abstract theory. Yet his influence upon thought, though indirect, was remarkable. The vividness of his historical painting—inaccurate, no doubt, and delightfully reckless of dates and facts—stimulated the growing interest in historical inquiries even in England. His influence in one direction is recognised by Newman, who was perhaps thinking chiefly of his mediævalism. [632] But the historical novels are only one side of Scott. Patriotic to the core, he lived at a time when patriotic feeling was stimulated to the utmost, and when Scotland in particular was still a province, and yet in many ways the most vigorous and progressive part of a great empire. He represents patriotism stimulated by contact with cosmopolitan movements. Loving every local peculiarity, painting every class from the noble to the peasant, loving the old traditions, and yet sharing the great impulses of the day, Scott was able to interest the world at large. While the most faithful portrayer of the special national type, he has too much sense not to be well aware that picturesque cattle-stealers and Jacobite chiefs were things of the past; but he loves with his whole heart the institutions rooted in the past and rich in historical associations. He transferred to poetry and fiction the political doctrine of Burke. To him, the revolutionary movement was simply a solvent, corroding all the old ties because it sapped the old traditions, and tended to substitute a mob for a nation. The continuity of national life seemed to him the essential condition; and a nation was not a mere aggregate of separate individuals, but an ancient organism, developing on an orderly system—where every man had his rightful place, and the beggar, as he observes in the *Antiquary*, was as ready as the noble to rise against foreign invasion. To him, the kings or priests who, to the revolutionist, represented simple despotism, represented part of a rough but manly order, in which many virtues were conspicuous and the governing classes were discharging great functions. Though he did not use the phrase, the revolutionary or radical view was hateful to him on account of its 'individualism.' It meant the summary destruction of all that he cherished most warmly in order to carry out theories altogether revolting to his common-sense. The very roots of a sound social order depend upon the traditions and accepted beliefs which bind together clans or families, and assign to every man a satisfactory function in life. The vivid realisation of history goes naturally with a love—excessive or reasonable—of the old order; and Scott, though writing carelessly to amuse idle readers, was stimulating the historical conceptions, which, for whatever reason, were most uncongenial to the Utilitarian as to all the revolutionists.

The more conscious philosophical application is illustrated by Wordsworth and Coleridge. Both of them had shared the truly revolutionary enthusiasm, and both came in time to be classed with the Tories. Both, as will be seen, had a marked influence upon J. S. Mill. Wordsworth has written in the *Prelude* one of the most remarkable of intellectual autobiographies. He was to be, though he never quite succeeded in being, a great philosophical poet. He never succeeded, because, in truth, he was not a great philosopher. But no one has more clearly indicated the history of his mental evolution. His sympathy with the revolution was perfectly genuine, but involved a vast misconception. A sturdy, independent youth, thoroughly imbued with the instincts of his northern dalesmen, he had early leaned to a republican sentiment. His dislike of the effete conventionalism of the literary creed blended with his aversion to the political rule of the time. He caught the contagion of revolutionary enthusiasm in France, and was converted by the sight of the 'hunger-bitten' peasant girl—the victim of aristocratic oppression. 'It is against that,' said his friend, 'that we are fighting,' and so far Wordsworth was a convert. The revolution, therefore, meant to him the restoration of an idyllic state, in which the homely virtues of the independent peasant should no longer be crushed and deprived of reward by the instruments of selfish despotism. The outbreak of war put his principles at issue with his patriotism. He suffered keenly when called upon to triumph over the calamities of his countrymen. But gradually he came to think that his sympathies were misplaced. The revolution had not altered human nature. The atrocities disturbed him, but for a time he could regard them as a mere accident. As the war went on, he began to perceive that the new power could be as tyrannical and selfish as the old. Instead of reconstructing a simple social ideal, it was forming a military despotism. When the French armies put down the simple Swiss peasantry, to whom he had been drawn by his home-bred sympathies, he finally gave up the revolutionary cause. He had gone through a mental agony, and his distracted sympathies ultimately determined a change which corresponded to the adoption of a new philosophy. Wordsworth, indeed, had little taste for abstract logic. He had imbibed Godwin's doctrine, but when acceptance of Godwin's conclusions involved a conflict with his strongest affections— the sacrifice not only of his patriotism but of the sympathies which bound him to his fellows—he revolted. Godwin represents the extreme of 'individualism,' the absolute dissolution of all social and political bonds. Wordsworth escaped, not by discovering a logical defect in the argument, but by yielding to the protest of his emotions. The system, he thought, was fatal to all the affections which had made life dear to him; to the vague 'intimations' which, whatever else they might be, had yet power to give harmony to our existence.

By degrees he adopted a new diagnosis of the great political evils. On one side, he sympathised with Scott's sense of the fatal effects upon the whole social organism. Among his noblest poems are the 'Brothers' and 'Michael,' to which he specially called the attention of Fox. They were intended, he explained, to show the surpassing value of the domestic affections conspicuous among the shepherds and 'statesmen' of the northern dales. He had now come to hold that the principles of Godwin and his like were destructive to the most important elements of human welfare. The revolutionists were not simply breaking the fetters of the simple peasant, but destroying the most sacred ties to which the peasant owed whatever dignity or happiness he possessed. Revolution, in short, meant anarchy. It meant, therefore, the destruction of all that gives real value to life. It was, as he held, one product of the worship of the 'idol proudly named the "wealth of nations,"' [633] selfishness and greed replacing the old motives to 'plain living and high thinking.' Wordsworth, in short, saw the ugly side of the industrial revolution, the injury done to domestic life by the factory system, or the substitution of a proletariate for a peasantry, and the replacement of the lowest social order by a vast inorganic mob. The contemporary process, which was leading to pauperism and to the evils of the factory system, profoundly affected Wordsworth, as well as the impulsive Southey; and their frequent denunciations gave colour to the imputations that they were opposed to all progress. Certainly they were even morbidly alive to the evil aspects of the political economy of Malthus and Ricardo, which to them seemed to prescribe insensibility and indifference to most serious and rapidly accumulating evils.

Meanwhile, Wordsworth was also impressed by the underlying philosophical difficulties. The effect of the revolutionary principles was to destroy the religious sentiment, not simply by disproving this or that historical statement, but by making the whole world prosaic and matter-of-fact. His occasional outbursts against the man of science—the 'fingering slave' who would 'peep and botanise upon his mother's grave'—are one version of his feeling. The whole scientific method tended to materialism and atomism; to a breaking up of the world into disconnected atoms, and losing the life in dissecting the machinery. His protest is embodied in the pantheism of the noble lines on Tintern Abbey, and his method of answering might be divined from the ode on the 'Intimations of Immortality.' Somehow or other the world represents a spiritual and rational unity, not a mere chaos of disconnected atoms and fragments. We 'see into the heart of things' when we trust to our emotions and hold by the instincts, clearly manifested in childhood, but clouded and overwhelmed in our later struggles with the world. The essential thing is the cultivation of our 'moral being,' the careful preservation and assimilation of the stern sense of duty, which alone makes life bearable and gives a meaning to the universe.

Wordsworth, it is plain, was at the very opposite pole from the Utilitarians. He came to consider that their whole method meant the dissolution of all that was most vitally sacred, and to hold that the revolution had attracted his sympathies on false pretences. Yet it is obvious that, however great the stimulus which he exerted, and however lofty his highest flights of poetry, he had no distinct theory to offer. His doctrine undoubtedly was congenial to certain philosophical views, but was not itself an articulate philosophy. He appeals to instincts and emotions, not to any definite theory. In a remarkable letter, Coleridge told Wordsworth why he was disappointed with the *Excursion*. [634] He had hoped that it would be the 'first and only true philosophical poem in existence.' Wordsworth was to have started by exposing the 'sandy sophisms of Locke,' and after exploding Pope's *Essay on Man*, and showing the vanity of (Erasmus) Darwin's belief in an 'ourang-outang state,' and explaining the fall of man and the 'scheme of redemption,' to have concluded by 'a grand didactic swell on the identity of a true philosophy with true religion.' He would show how life and intelligence were to be substituted for the 'philosophy of mechanism.' Facts would be elevated into theory, theory into laws, and laws into living and intelligent powers—true idealism necessarily perfecting itself in realism, and realism refining itself into idealism.'

The programme was a large one. If it represents what Coleridge seriously expected from Wordsworth, it also suggests that he was unconsciously wandering into an exposition of one of the gigantic but constantly shifting schemes of a comprehensive philosophy, which he was always proposing to execute. To try to speak of Coleridge adequately would be hopeless and out of place. I must briefly mention him, because he was undoubtedly the most conspicuous representative of the tendencies opposed to Utilitarianism. The young men who found Bentham exasperating imbibed draughts of mingled poetry and philosophy from Coleridge's monologues at Hampstead. Carlyle has told us, in a famous chapter of his *Life of Sterling*, what they went out to see: at once a reed shaken by the wind and a great expounder of transcendental truth. The fact that Coleridge exerted a very great influence is undeniable. To define precisely what that influence was is impossible. His writings are a heap of fragments. He contemplated innumerable schemes for great works, and never got within measurable distance of writing any. He poured himself out indefinitely upon the margins of other men's books; and the piety of disciples has collected a mass of these scattered and incoherent jottings, which announce conclusions without giving the premises, or suggest difficulties without attempting to solve them. He seems to have been almost as industrious as Bentham in writing; but whereas Bentham's fragments could be put together as wholes, Coleridge's are essentially distracted hints of views never really elaborated. He was always thinking, but seems always to be making a fresh start at any point that strikes him for the moment. Besides all this, there is the painful question of plagiarism. His most coherent exposition (in the *Biographia Literaria*) is simply appropriated from Schelling, though he ascribes the identity to a 'genial coincidence' of thought. I need make no attempt to make out what Coleridge really thought for himself, and then to try to put his thoughts together,—and indeed hold the attempt to be impossible. The most remarkable thing is the apparent disproportion between Coleridge's definite services to philosophy and the effect which he certainly produced upon some of his ablest contemporaries. That seems to prove that he was really aiming at some important aspect of truth, incapable as he may have been of definitively reaching it. I can only try to give a hint or two as to its general nature. Coleridge, in the first place, was essentially a poet, and, moreover, his poetry was of the type most completely divorced from philosophy. Nobody could say more emphatically that poetry should not be rhymed logic; and his most impressive poems are simply waking dreams. They are spontaneous incarnations of sensuous imagery, which has no need of morals or definite logical schemes. Although he expected Wordsworth to transmute philosophy into poetry, he admitted that the achievement would be unprecedented. Even in Lucretius, he said, what was poetry was not philosophy, and what was philosophy was not poetry. Yet Coleridge's philosophy was essentially the philosophy of a poet. He had, indeed, great dialectical ingenuity—a faculty which may certainly be allied with the highest imagination, though it may involve certain temptations. A poet who has also a mastery of dialectics becomes a mystic in philosophy. Coleridge had, it seems, been attracted by Plotinus in his schooldays. At a later period he had been attracted by Hartley, Berkeley, and Priestley. To a brilliant youth, anxious to be in the van of intellectual progress, they represented the most advanced theories. But there could never be a full sympathy between Coleridge and the forefathers of English empiricism; and he went to Germany partly to study the new philosophy which was beginning to shine—though very feebly and intermittingly—in England. When he had returned he began to read Kant and Schelling, or rather to mix excursions into their books with the miscellaneous inquiries to which his versatile intellect attracted him.

Now, it is abundantly clear that Coleridge never studied any philosophy systematically. He never acquired a precise acquaintance with the technical language of various schemes, or cared for their precise logical relations to each other. The 'genial coincidence' with Schelling, though an unlucky phrase, represents a real fact. He dipped into Plotinus or Behmen or Kant or Schelling, or any one who interested him, and did not know whether they were simply embodying ideas already in his own mind, or suggesting new ideas; or, what was probably more accurate, expressing opinions which, in a general way, were congenial to his own way of contemplating the world. His power of stimulating other minds proves sufficiently that he frequently hit upon impressive and suggestive thoughts. He struck out illuminating sparks, but he never diffused any distinct or steady daylight. His favourite position, for example, of the distinction between the Reason and the Understanding is always coming up and being enforced with the strongest asseverations of its importance. That he had adopted it more or less from Kant is obvious, though I imagine it to be also obvious that he did not clearly understand his authority. [635] To what, precisely, it amounts is also unintelligible to me. Somehow or other, it implies that the mind can rise into transcendental regions, and, leaving grovelling Utilitarians and the like to the conduct of the understanding in matters of practical expediency, can perceive that the universe is in some way evolved from the pure reason, and the mind capable of ideas which correspond to stages of the evolution. How this leads to the conclusions that the Christian doctrines of the Logos and the Trinity are embodiments of pure philosophy is a problem upon which I need not touch. When we have called Coleridge a mystic, with flashes of keen insight into the weakness of the opposite theory, I do not see how we are to get much further, or attribute to him any articulate and definite scheme.

Hopelessly unsystematic as Coleridge may have been, his significance in regard to the Utilitarians is noteworthy. It is indicated in a famous article which J. S. Mill contributed to the *Westminster Review* in March 1840. [636] Mill's concessions to Coleridge rather scandalised the faithful; and it is enough to observe here that it marks the apogee of Mill's Benthamism. Influences, of which I shall have to speak, had led him to regard his old creed as imperfect, and to assent to great part of Coleridge's doctrine. Mill does not discuss the metaphysical or theological views of the opposite school, though he briefly intimates his dissent. But it is interesting to observe how Coleridge impressed a disciple of Bentham. The 'Germano-Coleridgian doctrine,' says Mill, was a reaction against the philosophy of the eighteenth century: 'ontological,' 'conservative,' 'religious,' 'concrete and historical,' and finally 'poetical,' because the other was 'experimental,' 'innovative,' 'infidel,' 'abstract and metaphysical,' and 'matter-of-fact and prosaic.' Yet the two approximate, and each helps to restore the balance and comes a little nearer to a final equilibrium. The error of the French philosophers had been their negative and purely critical tendency. They had thought that it was enough to sweep away superstition, priestcraft, and despotism, and that no constructive process was necessary. They had not perceived the necessity of social discipline, of loyalty to rulers, or of patriotic feeling among the subjects. They had, therefore, entirely failed to recognise the historical value of old creeds and institutions, and had tried to remodel society 'without the binding forces which hold society together.' [637] Hence, too, the *philosophes* came to despise history; and D'Alembert is said to have wished that all record of past events could be blotted out. Their theory, in its popular version at least, came to be that states and churches had been got up 'for the sole purpose of picking people's pockets.' [638] This had become incredible to any intelligent reasoner, and any Tory could prove that there was something good in the past. The peculiarity of the 'Germano-Coleridgian' school was that they saw beyond the immediate controversy. They were the first to inquire with any power into 'the inductive laws of the existence and growth of human society'; the first to recognise the importance of the great constructive principles; and the first to produce not a piece of party advocacy, but 'a philosophy of society in the only form in which it is yet possible, that of a philosophy of history.' Hence arose that 'series of great writers and thinkers, from Herder to Michelet,' who have given to past history an intelligible place in the gradual evolution of humanity. [639] This very forcible passage is interesting in regard to Mill, and shows a very clear perception of some defects in his own philosophy. It also raises an important question.

Accepting Mill's view, it is remarkable that the great error of his own school, which professed to be based upon experience, was the rejection of history; and the great merit of the *a priori* and 'intuitionist' school was precisely their insistence upon history. To this I shall have to return hereafter. Meanwhile, Mill proceeds to show how Coleridge, by arguing from the 'idea' of church and state, had at least recognised the necessity of showing that political and social institutions must have a sufficient reason, and be justified by something more than mere obstinate prejudice. Men like Pitt and Sir Robert Peel, if they accepted Coleridge's support, would have to alter their whole position. Coleridge's defence of his ideal church was at once the severest satire upon the existing body and a proof, as against Bentham and Adam Smith, of the advantages of an endowed class for the cultivation and diffusion of learning. Coleridge, moreover, though he objected to the Reform Bill, showed himself a better reformer than Lord John Russell. He admitted what the Whigs refused to see, the necessity of diminishing the weight of the landowner interest. Landowners were not to be ultimate sources of power, but to represent one factor in a reasoned system. In short, by admitting that all social arrangements in some sense were embodiments of reason, he admitted that they must also be made to conform to reason.

Coleridge and Bentham, then, are not really enemies but allies, and they wield powers which are 'opposite poles of one great force of progression.' [640] The question, however, remains, how the philosophy of each leader is really connected with his practical conclusions. Mill's view would apparently be that Coleridge somehow managed to correct the errors or fill the gaps of the Utilitarian system—a very necessary task, as Mill admits— while Coleridge would have held that those errors were the inevitable fruit of the whole empirical system of thought. The Reason must be restored to its rightful supremacy over the Understanding, which had been working its wicked will since the days of Locke and eighteenth century. The problem is a wide one. I must be content to remark the inevitable antithesis. Whether enemies or allies, the Utilitarians and their antagonists were separated by a gulf which could not be bridged for the time. The men of common-sense, who had no philosophy at all, were shocked by the immediate practical applications of Utilitarianism, its hostility to the old order which they loved, its apparent helplessness in social questions, its relegation of all progress to the conflict of selfish interests, its indifference to all the virtues associated with patriotism and local ties. By more reflective minds, it was condemned as robbing the world of its poetry, stifling the religious emotions, and even quenching sentiment in general. The few who wished for a philosophy found the root of its errors in the assumptions which reduced the world to a chaos of atoms, outwardly connected and combined into mere dead mechanism. The world, for the poet and the philosopher alike, must be not a congeries of separate things, but in some sense a product of reason. Thought, not fact, must be the ultimate reality. Unfortunately or otherwise, the poetical sentiment could never get itself translated into philosophical theory. Coleridge's random and discursive hints remained mere hints—a suggestion at best for future thought. Mill's criticism shows how far they could be assimilated by a singularly candid Utilitarian. To him, we see, they represented mainly the truth that his own party, following the general tendency of the eighteenth century, had been led to neglect the vital importance of the constructive elements of society; that they had sacrificed order to progress, and therefore confounded progress with destruction, and failed to perceive the real importance in past times even of the institutions which had become obsolete. Social atomism or individualism, therefore, implied a total misconception of what Mill calls the 'evolution of humanity.' This marks a critical point. The 'Germano-Coleridgians' had a theory of evolution. By evolution, indeed, was meant a dialectical evolution; the evolution of 'ideas' or reason, in which each stage of history represents a moment of some vast and transcendental process of thought. Evolution, so understood, seemed rightly or wrongly to be mere mysticism or intellectual juggling. It took leave of fact, or managed by some illegitimate process to give to a crude generalisation from experience the appearance of a purely logical deduction. In this shape, therefore, it was really opposed to science, although the time was to come in which evolution would present itself in a scientific form. [641] Meanwhile, the concessions made by J. S. Mill were not approved by his fellows, and would have been regarded as little short of treason by the older Utilitarians. The two schools, if Coleridge's followers could be called a school, regarded each other's doctrines as simply contradictory. In appealing to experience and experience alone, the Utilitarians, as their opponents held, had reduced the world to a dead mechanism, destroyed every element of cohesion, made society a struggle of selfish interests, and struck at the very roots of all order, patriotism, poetry, and religion. They retorted that their critics were blind adherents of antiquated prejudice, and sought to cover superstition and despotism either by unprovable dogmatic assertions, or by taking refuge in a cloudy mystical jargon, which really meant nothing.

They did not love each other.

FOOTNOTES:

[610] See *Dictionary of National Biography*, under 'George Grote.' Bentham's ms. is in the British Museum, and shows, I think, that Grote's share in the work was a good deal more than mere editing. I quote from a reprint by Truelove (1875). It was also privately reprinted by Grote himself in 1866.

[611] Cf. Hobbes's definition: 'Fear of power invisible feigned by the mind, or imagined from tales publicly allowed, [is] Religion: not allowed, Superstition. And when the power imagined is truly such as we imagine, True Religion.'—*Works* (Molesworth), iii. 45.

[612] 'Philip Beauchamp,' ch. ii. pp.

11-15.[613] *Ibid.*

[614] 'Philip Beauchamp,' p. 21.

[615] *Ibid.* pp. 22 and 104.

[616] 'Philip Beauchamp,' ch. iii.

[617] 'Philip Beauchamp,' ch. iv.

[618] *Ibid.* p. 45, ch. v.

[619] *Ibid.* p. 52, ch. vi.

[620] 'Philip Beauchamp,' ch. viii.

[621] *Ibid.* part ii. ch. i.

[622] *Ibid.* p. 80, part ii. ch. ii.

[623] 'Philip Beauchamp,' pp. 97, 99.

[624] *Ibid.*

[625] *Ibid.*

[626] 'Philip Beauchamp,' p. 163.

[627] *Ibid.*

[628] The writers were Chalmers, Kidd, Whewell, Sir Charles Bell, Roget, Buckland, Kirby, and Prout. The essays appeared from 1833 to 1835. The versatile Brougham shortly afterwards edited Paley's *Natural Theology*.

[629] 'Philip Beauchamp,' p. 88.

[630] Froude's *Carlyle*, i. 215; ii. 93.

[631] Mill's *Dissertations*, i. 235; ii. 130.

[632] George Borrow's vehement dislike of Scott as the inventor of Puseyism and modern Jesuitism of all kinds is characteristic.

[633] *Prelude*, bk. xiii.

[634] Coleridge's *Letters* (1890), pp. 643-49.

[635] Mr. Hutchison Stirling insists upon this in the *Fortnightly Review* for July 1867. He proves, I think, that Coleridge's knowledge of the various schemes of German philosophy and of the precise relation of Kant, Fichte, and Schelling was altogether desultory and confused. How far this is important depends upon whether we attach much or little importance to precise combinations of words used by these philosophers.

[636] *Dissertations*, i. 392-474.

[637] *Ibid.* i. 424.

[638] *Dissertations*, i. 437.

[639] *Ibid.* i. 425-27.

[640] *Dissertations*, i. 437.

[641] Coleridge's *Hints towards the Formation of a more Comprehensive Theory of Life*, edited by S. B. Watson, in 1848, is a curious attempt to apply his evolution doctrine to natural science. Lewes, in his *Letters on Comte's Philosophy of the Sciences*, says that it is a 'shameless plagiarism' from Schelling's *Erster Entwurf*, etc. It seems, as far as I can judge, that Coleridge's doctrines about magnetism, reproduction, irritability, sensibility, etc., are, in fact, adapted from Schelling. The book was intended, as Mr. E. H. Coleridge tells me, for a chapter in a work on Scrophula, projected by Gillman. As Coleridge died long before the publication, he cannot be directly responsible for not acknowledging obligations to Schelling. Unfortunately he cannot claim the benefit of a good character in such matters. Anyhow, Coleridge's occasional excursions into science can only represent a vague acceptance of the transcendental method represented, as I understand, by Oken.